WOMEN'S LIVES
AND
PUBLIC POLICY

WOMEN'S LIVES AND PUBLIC POLICY

The International Experience

Edited by Meredeth Turshen
and Briavel Holcomb

Foreword by Charlotte Bunch

Westport, Connecticut
London

Library of Congress Cataloging-in-Publication Data

Women's lives and public policy : the international experience /
   edited by Meredeth Turshen and Briavel Holcomb : foreword by
   Charlotte Bunch.
       p.   cm.
   Includes bibliographical references and index.
   ISBN 0–275–94523–5 (alk. paper)
       1. Women—Government policy.   2. Sex role.   3. Women in
   development.   4. Women—Economic conditions.   5. Women—Social
   conditions.   I. Turshen, Meredeth.   II. Holcomb, Briavel.
   HQ1236.W6518   1993
   305.42—dc20   92–33331

British Library Cataloguing in Publication Data is available.

A hardcover edition of *Women's Lives and Public Policy* is
available from the Greenwood Press imprint of Greenwood
Publishing Group, Inc. (Contributions in Women's Studies,
Number 132; ISBN 0–313–27354–5).

Library of Congress Catalog Card Number: 92–33331
ISBN: 0–275–94523–5

First published in 1993

Praeger Publishers, 88 Post Road West, Westport, CT 06881
An imprint of Greenwood Publishing Group, Inc.

Printed in the United States of America

The paper used in this book complies with the
Permanent Paper Standard issued by the National
Information Standards Organization (Z39.48–1984).

10 9 8 7 6 5 4 3 2 1

Contents

Foreword

Over the past two decades, there has been enormous growth in women's consciousness and organizing, touching people's lives in remote villages as well as urban centers in almost every part of the world. Millions of women globally are involved in this process, redefining their own reality and society's problems from the perspective of their experiences. Yet, public policy makers rarely engage in gender analysis or show much awareness of these developments or of how their policies affect women's lives. This book helps to redress this omission by examining several important issues in which the intersection between feminism and public policy is critical to women's future.

Women must address many aspects of public policy, including virtual exclusion from its formulators' innermost circles. This process often begins with defining new areas that affect women, which were not previously seen as political, such as reproductive rights, equal pay, childcare policies, or violence against women. Usually these are labeled "women's issues," a classification that unfortunately denies their importance to men's lives (and power), as well as assigns them to a separate and secondary sphere of public concern. Thus, although feminism has brought many problems onto the public agenda and out of the silence of the private sphere, the women's issues approach has not resulted in women being at the center of public policy discourse.

Another way of looking at women and public policy is to seek the integration of women into existing policies in major areas, such as development or democracy. This approach is particularly popular in Asia, Africa, and Latin America, where political discussion is dominated by questions of national liberation and/ or development. However, women are finding that the issue is not simply one of integration into existing processes—be they revolutionary or mainstream. Rather, women must participate in developing policies at every stage and in shaping both the questions asked and the policies formulated so that they include diverse women as well as men.

Acting out of both these approaches, women are redefining existing concepts and seeking to shape the terms of debate to include female lives and perspectives as a distinct gendered part of the overall picture—a part that too often is missing. In the discussion of women and development, this redefinition means a shift away from simply integrating women and toward feminist analysis of what are the goals and methods of development and how development policies work against women. In this effort, women are taking leadership in the global discussion of transforming the development process to make it more inclusive and more effective. For example, how can the definition of work and of the gross national product exclude the reproductive labor of maintaining life? How can it exclude the informal sector in which the vast majority of Third World women and often the poor of both sexes labor for long hours?

Women are examining other major concepts, such as democracy, peace, and human rights, in terms of what these mean to women's lives. A slogan coined in the Chilean struggle against dictatorship, *"democracia en el pais y en la casa"* (democracy in the country and in the home), exemplifies women's determination throughout Latin America and elsewhere to see democracy move beyond the ballot box. In looking at the barriers to women's full participation as citizens in public life, women have begun to ask what is democracy if women do not have self-determination at home.

Similarly, women ask if this world can be called peaceful when over half the female population is beaten regularly (and too often killed) by their families and when almost all women shape some part of their daily lives in response to the fear of violence in the home, on the job, or in public spaces. Such a massive denial of human rights to half the population has serious policy implications not only for "women's issues" but in such diverse areas as housing, transportation, immigration, and criminal justice.

This volume should be read within the broad context of a global effort to see how gender affects public policy. By taking up specific case illustrations of how economic and social policies affect women in varied areas from the urban household, to migration, to the sexual entertainment industry, we clearly see the need for more gender analysis within public policy considerations. Often, the lens one looks through shapes the view one gets of reality. Yet, little effort has been made to bring women's views into the policy arena. Only when the full range of human diversity is reflected in the policy-making process—taking into account not only gender but also race, class, sexual orientation, age, culture, religion—will we be able to shape more just and more effective policies.

For this task, women must exert leadership in defining those aspects of public policy that are of greatest importance to women's lives. Women's many and varied experiences must be brought out of the shadows of a separate sphere—whether in the home or in isolated projects—and exposed to the light and debates of public policy discourse. This process will challenge those women and men who are not used to listening to women seriously in public matters. Just as there is not only one men's view on issues, no single women's view will emerge from this process—nor should there be only one—nor will women's views always differ from men's. Rather, the meaning of the process is that diverse and conflicting women's voices must be heard in order to expand the parameters in which public policy is shaped. Meredeth Turshen and Briavel Holcomb's collection helps to advance this process by showing what a gender analysis reveals in certain specific policy areas. This is a model of the work that needs to be done in every city and nation around every area of public policy if we are to bring gender bias to consciousness and involve women fully in the policy-making process.

Charlotte Bunch

Preface

Feminist discussions of how public policies affect women's lives, especially in the countries of Africa, Asia, and Latin America, are a post–World War II phenomenon. They are an outgrowth of more general debates about the nature and goal of economic and social development, which have preoccupied economists in academia and at the United Nations for several decades. Historically, these debates and discussions are framed by the bilateral experience of postwar assistance to Europe and by multilateral movements to aid the formerly colonized nations of the Third World.

Two approaches have dominated development assistance since World War II: emergency relief and aid to economic growth. Emergency relief traces its origins to religious obligations of charity and later secular arrangements, pioneered by the Elizabethan Poor Laws at the end of the sixteenth century, which institutionalized society's duty to care for the disabled and destitute. The moral baggage of welfare and its association with women and children living in poverty still permeate the relief efforts of governmental and nongovernmental organizations today. People support emergency relief because it assuages the conscience and because, as Tinker (1991, 37) observes, it poses no threat to the status quo.

Development aid policy makers proceeded on the theory that infusions of capital in the former colonial economies would stimulate growth, and they based programs and projects on the successful model of the Marshall Plan of U.S. aid to postwar Europe. They directed their efforts to men and did not acknowledge that the development process affects men and women differently, nor did they collect the sex-specific data that would enable them to monitor differential impacts. The failure of the first UN development decade to alleviate poverty led to a reconsideration of development assistance. Ester Boserup's publication of *Woman's Role in Economic Development* in 1970 showed that most benefits of economic growth (for example, industrial production and communications infrastructure to support heavy industry) accrue to men, that (contrary to opinion) women are productive and so contribute to economic efficiency, and that development can have negative consequences for many women and children as well as increase inequalities between women and men.

International Women's Year (1975) inaugurated a decade of challenges to sex-stereotyped aid: welfare for women, development for men. Women from the Third World found a voice at the three conferences organized around the women's decade. They demanded the allocation of significant financial resources to projects for women and the implementation of activities oriented toward production. Underlying the demand was a shift from family-centered definitions of women's place in society, which focused on women's roles as mothers and on the mother-child dyad, to a women-centered definition, which promoted recognition of women's productive roles (Buvinić 1986, 659).

Not content to be passive recipients of aid, women stepped forward to formulate policies that emphasized action to alleviate women's poverty and persistent inequalities between women and men. Although women in grass-roots organizations are sometimes suspicious of their academic sisters, women in universities, women's research institutes, women's divisions of international agencies, and women's bureaus in national governments have carried out much of the research upon which these policies are based. Women studied women, often in participatory research projects; they catalogued and measured women's work, argued about productive and unproductive activities, and assessed needs.

Two theoretical approaches dominate these studies: women in development and global feminism. The first approach advocates more attention to women's work and its role in economic development (Tinker 1991). This analysis is gender-based, but it rests on liberal economic theories of dualism and the political science concept of modernization, which posit a modern, industrial, developed economic sector that men dominate and a traditional, stagnant, undeveloped sector in which women participate. The goal is to bring women into the waged labor force, in other words to modernize them. The second approach, global feminism, is based on an analysis of the intersection of gender, race, and class; it considers social as well as economic and political dimensions of development, and it values the paid and unpaid work that women do (Benería 1981). In the formulation of Bunch and Carrillo (1991), global feminism advocates the inclusion of political issues such as gender inequality and violence against women in economic analyses of development.

Most of the literature in this field examines the impact of national rural development policies on women (see, for example, Hemmings-Gapihan 1982; ILO 1980; Lewis 1984; Loutfi 1980; Rogers 1980). A few studies pay attention to urban and rural international development policy (see, for example, Boserup 1970; Michel, Fatoumata-Diarra, and Agbessi-Dos Santos 1981; Papanek 1979; Sen and Grown 1987). Recently, agencies and individual researchers have begun to explore the impact of structural adjustment policies on women (see, for example, Commonwealth Secretariat 1989). The contribution of Victoria Daines and David Seddon to this volume is the first to report the responses of the women who bear the hardships engendered by these policies.

GENDER, THE STATE, AND POLITICS

Women's legal status is perhaps the first women's issue that the United Nations addressed, based on the work of the longstanding Commission on the Status of Women (Columbia Human Rights Law Review 1977). A number of subsequent studies explore various dimensions of the law—marriage and divorce, property, customary and criminal law (Armstrong 1987; Hay and Wright 1982; Schuler 1986). The legal status of women is a concern whenever adult women are considered legal minors. This inferior position is often codified in marriage laws and family policies (McIntosh 1978). The rights of women to land and other property, including the marital home, may not be recognized or they may not be enforced (Loutfi 1987, 118). Although the UN Commission on the Status of Women has recorded progress since it began its work in 1946, recent reversals are matters of grave concern. With the accession of fundamentalist religious parties to power, several governments have moved toward institutionalizing gender discrimination in civil law as well as in directives concerning professional working women.

Traditional human rights programs do not address violations of women's human rights. In human rights law, first generation civil and political rights are the prohibition of slavery, freedom of thought and religion, the right of every accused person to a fair trial, and the rights to life, liberty, and citizenship (Zalaquett 1981). Second generation rights include economic, social, and cultural rights, such as employment and fair working conditions, a standard of living that ensures health and well-being, social security, special rights of motherhood and childhood, and participation in the cultural life of the community. Women first dramatized violations of their human rights at the International Tribunal on Crimes against Women held in Brussels in 1976 (Russell and Van de Ven 1976; see also Barry, Bunch, and Castley 1984). They expanded the definition to include forced motherhood, compulsory nonmotherhood, persecution of virgins and unmarried mothers, medical brutality toward women giving birth, compulsory heterosexuality, economic crimes, and all forms of violence against women—rape, woman battering, forced incarceration in mental institutions, genital mutilation, torture of women political prisoners, and sexual slavery. Roxanna Carrillo's review of gender violence in chapter 6 introduces one of the main themes of this collection and frames the case studies of prostitution, dowry deaths, and arranged marriage in the four chapters that follow.

Women's political participation at the local and national levels can make it easier to change policies so that they are more responsive to women's needs. Most countries have set up some kind of national machinery to promote women's advancement—government ministry, department, commission, or bureau; a section of a political party or a women's league; or a nongovernmental council or national women's organization (Loutfi 1987, 119). Still, political rights such as the right of women to organize themselves in free and autonomous associations including trade unions are not everywhere ensured (Davies 1983).

GENDER, URBAN SERVICES, AND EMPLOYMENT

The postwar urban explosion in the Third World created 150 cities with populations over 1 million. Most of these urban agglomerations are in Latin America, the Middle East, and Asia (Africa boasts only four large cities—Addis Ababa, Kinshasa, Lagos, and Nairobi). Characterized by inner-city slums and peripheral shantytowns, these cities are poor; as many as one-fourth to one-half of their populations live in intense deprivation and denial of their basic needs (Austin 1980, 3). Squatters often choose marginal lands, such as flood plains, wetlands, and the sides of ravines for their settlements, and these undesirable physical characteristics compound the problems of life in the shantytowns.

Yet a prevalent assumption is that urban women are better off than their rural sisters because urban areas are better off than rural areas. This assumption ignores issues of social class and the physical dangers that the urban environment holds for women. The World Bank estimates that 20 percent of the world's 800 million absolute poor live in urban areas and that average income is three to five times higher in the cities than in the countryside. But it is unlikely that the urban poor benefit from higher city incomes, and it is questionable whether they have access to the more numerous services available in urban areas.

Women migrating to urban areas find that they must purchase necessities such as food and shelter, which they formerly produced themselves, and that all utilities—water, firewood, charcoal, kerosene, gas, and electricity—must be paid for in cash. In squatter settlements, women may be unable to procure basic services at any price. Shantytowns are frequently beyond the reach of public water services, electricity, and sewerage lines; at night, women must navigate dark paths pitted with pools of stagnant water, vulnerable to assault. Along with the daily use of public transport, in which women are subject to harassment, childcare also becomes an item to budget in the city. Working mothers are common in low-income urban areas; more than half the mothers in Bangkok slums work, and the proportion is similar in Rio de Janeiro (Austin 1980, 28).

The rapid growth of the service sector has been noted in countries such as Indonesia, Thailand, Malaysia, Brazil, Nigeria, and Cameroon (Lele 1986, 201). When the state is unwilling or unable to provide needed services, nongovernmental organizations (NGOs) may attempt to meet basic social and economic needs. But when relief agencies and nongovernmental organizations view women in their domestic roles only, as dependents with children or as pregnant or lactating mothers, they reinforce sex stereotypes. Foreign NGOs pride themselves on their sensitivity to local cultures and their ability to work successfully at the community level. "They do not want to be accused of cultural imperialism by tampering with sex roles, roles that are enforced by family and community and thus are the most resistant to change" (Yudelman 1987, 181).

In addition to their sensitivity to patriarchal norms, NGOs teach stereotypical skills such as sewing and canning because the projects are cheap, and they use volunteers as teachers. They generally enhance women's domestic roles and reinforce women's dependent status as homemakers rather than turn them into income earners (Buvinić 1986). In Latin America, income-generating projects tend to be grafted onto projects providing health or welfare services, according to Yudelman (1987, 180–183). NGOs also popularize crafts, which are time consuming, provide little income, and present major problems of quality control and marketing.

Employment policies are critical to ending women's dependency and subordination. Policies such as import substitution and export-led industrialization do not create many new jobs, and free-trade zones provide low-paying, insecure work (Pessar 1988, 203–204; see Lim 1991 for a more positive assessment). Male planners are frequently reluctant to implement projects for women that have an economic base and some are overtly hostile to such projects (Buvinić 1986, 653). This observation challenges the assumption that governments are benevolent and relatively efficient actors with an unlimited capacity to direct public intervention to benefit those with limited assets and access to factors of production (Lele 1986, 199). The sad conclusion drawn by contemporary feminist observers is that many policies designed to promote development have the effect of marginalizing women.

Women are poorly represented in the public service sector despite the large number of Third World families headed by women. In parts of Africa, for example, women hold jobs mainly in the health and education sectors in which specialized personnel represent more than half the labor force. According to Rose Francine Rogombe (1985, 17), secretary of state for Women's Advancement in Gabon, one reason is that women have limited access to training. In Pakistan, women working for a salary accounted for 2.4 percent of the urban population in 1981; this percentage is increasing, and the proportion of women in professional occupations—again, overwhelmingly in health and education—doubled between 1960 and mid-1970 (Korson and Maskiell 1985, 609).

Scientific knowledge also eludes the majority. Although women have primary responsibility for the health of their families, few are engaged in biological research. Women doctors, dentists, and pharmacists are increasing in number, as a direct result of government policies. In some countries, for example, Pakistan, female health personnel work in a gender segregated environment: Women doctors specialize in obstetrics and gynecology, not surgery or urology, and rarely attain top-level government jobs in the ministry of health (Korson and Maskiell 1985, 609).

The low level of urban employment presents a striking contrast with African women's traditional position in agriculture: Women farmers usually have land-use rights and keep the proceeds from the sale of their produce. In the urban setting, with no space for more more than a kitchen garden, if that, women's lack of employment presumably renders them economically dependent and erodes their autonomy. For example, Swahili women in the coastal region of Tanzania are independent farmers in the countryside but become veiled, home-bound, dependent wives in Dar es Salaam.

Similarly, Hale (1987, 120) describes the urban transition of another Muslim group: "Nubian women were among the most emancipated and autonomous in Sudan in their roles as central producers and reproducers, forming an impressive community of women. Then, after relocation, in both the resettlement area and in Greater Khartoum (a large urban area), women were relegated chiefly to the romantic, symbolic, private roles of 'keepers of the culture.' " In the countryside, keeping the culture involved the supervision of ritual and ceremony, the choice of marriage partners for children, and retention of the unwritten, non-Arabic language Nubiyyin. In the city, "women took the place of the 'homeland' with all its mysticism and romance; they became the physical focus"—to which men returned (ibid., 122). Men exalted women for their cultural "purity" while also blaming them for their "backwardness."

FAMILY AND CULTURE IN THE CITY

In many rural societies, women are the guardians of culture. By education and by example they perpetuate and transmit the culture that has been passed on to them. When they migrate, some women face a clash with urban, often foreign cultures and experience the loss of customs and rituals as tantamount to the loss of cultural identity. Other women welcome the liberation from patriarchal constraints and paint an unromantic tableau of village life. In an epilogue to this volume, Carole Boyce Davies presents these conflicting reactions to the urban experience as expressed by African women novelists.

Cast in the role of cultural guardians, older women and housewives whose status and authority derive from existing family structure become opponents of women's rights and government reforms of family policy. Reformers face a dilemma in trying simultaneously to enhance the principles of merit, equality of life chances, and the autonomy of the family. Commitment to any two of these goals precludes the third. The sanctity of the family is especially difficult to sacrifice, yet the privacy or liberty of the family is not always equal to the privacy or liberty of family members (McGlen 1985, 1305). For example, most government officials are reluctant to prosecute cases of physical or sexual abuse of wives and children. Family sanctity is interpreted as the liberty of the husband in the patriarchal family.

Sen and Grown (1987, 74) identify a crisis of culture in attempts to return women to their "proper" subordinate position in the patriarchal family. They interpret the upsurge of fundamentalist religious movements as one such attempt; another is the direct involvement of the state in efforts to subjugate women and suppress dissent or, conversely, to use improvements in women's civil status as a wedge against "traditional" power blocs in society. "The creation of an ideological climate against women working outside the home makes it easier for the government to cut back child care or health services, and for employers to justify paying even lower wages to women or to ignore statutory benefits such as maternity pay" (ibid., 75). The implications they draw from this analysis are positive: "the richness of traditional cultural forms (music, theatre, dance) have to be harnessed for the struggle to raise the consciousness of both women and men" (ibid., 76).

Organized cultural troupes performing traditional dances, music, and drama are a common feature in African countries. In Tanzania, these groups mushroomed in the 1970s at a tremendous pace especially in the urban areas. Their existence and development are part of the struggle for rulers to retain power. According to Lihamba (1986, 5), politicians constantly call for artists to align their creative efforts with the dominant political ideology—in effect to service the state by becoming vehicles for the dissemination of progovernment propaganda; "the goal is to make the audience accept the ways things are at present and not challenge the authority which perpetuates existing social institutions."

Olayinka Burney Nicol of Sierra Leone spoke of her experience as a creative artist at a 1980 seminar on creative women in changing societies sponsored by UNITAR, the UN Institute for Training and Research (Stokland, Vajrathon, and Nicol 1982, 129). Her statement is a fitting summation to this preface.

In African societies creative women are bound by opposing forces: traditional versus transitional, and colonial versus independent. In the transitional world they lose the privileges accorded them in the communal traditional society, where they are given their rightful place to serve when their gifts are recognized by the community.

In the independent world, they at first lose more than they did in the colonial period . . . the arts are neglected while the new states try to catch up. In Sierra Leone the visual arts were never understood. It was thought that those who could paint or sculpt were given that gift by God as a compensation for their lesser brain power.

The artist's relationship with the West, where her works are more easily understood, is no more rewarding. The problems of color and sex pervade. In addition, there is the Western attitude that the black mind must always be guided and guarded.

The Westerner is willing to promote, but you must register in his approved schools, and you must be "primitive" or "naive." If she says she is no puppet, then she starves until she behaves. If she cannot survive starvation, she must allow her style to be dictated to her by her promoters, who make a goldmine out of her while she receives alms.

Thus the fight is on. To win is to endure. To win is mind over matter, decolonizing the spirit, and acquiring a new born independence from slavery—mental and spiritual slavery.

WOMEN'S LIVES AND PUBLIC POLICY

This book about the impact of public policy on women's lives and the responses of women to those policies summarizes some of the major issues related to gender and international development policy. The issues are grouped into two parts. Issues relating to macroeconomic policy and women's responses form Part I, "Economic Policies and Migration." Part II, "Sex and Marriage, Violence and Control" embraces issues relating to women's interpersonal relationships. An epilogue addresses urban culture.

At all levels of government, from the international to the local, public policies are formulated mainly by men but their impacts are felt, sometimes differently, by women, men, and children. The chapters of this book explore how public policies affect various facets of women's lives, including sex and birth, marriage and death, and work and child rearing. The authors have lived on five continents and have had varied life experiences and disciplinary training. Their diverse perspectives illuminate the problems of molding policies that are responsive to the needs of multiple publics.

The five chapters of Part I examine how economic and demographic policies at various levels affect women and the ways in which women respond to those effects. Beginning at the international level and on a global scale, Victoria Daines and David Seddon show how the World Bank and the International Monetary Fund impose austerity measures such as with structural adjustment programs. These measures consistently make women's lives in debtor countries more difficult. The authors argue that in many places women do not passively accept these policies but protest and resist them. Joseph L. Scarpaci's study provides one such detailed case of how Chilean women sought empowerment during the economic and political crises of the Pinochet dictatorship; the women acted through grass-roots organizations communally to provide basic food and literacy education.

Most states have policies that affect the integration of households into the cash economy and stimulate export industries and national self-sufficiency. By affecting the conditions of work within and outside the household, these policies reverberate in women's lives. The chapter by Briavel Holcomb and Tamar Y. Rothenberg reviews changing patterns of women's work and women's contributions to household economies as urbanization and modernization proceed. Changes in household composition create new work opportunities and responsibilities for women both inside and outside the home.

Women's productive work is often constrained by reproductive responsibilities. Betsy Hartmann argues that population policies in Bangladesh focus largely on reducing birth rates through contraception and sterilization rather than through more indirect but ultimately effective strategies of improving living standards. The result is involuntarily lowered fertility. Hartmann indicates that policies emanating from such international organizations as the U.S. Agency for International Development (USAID) and the World Bank do little to improve women's health status or child health services in Bangladesh.

The rate of migration in the twentieth century has not slowed, despite increasing governmental regulation, and public policies continue to stimulate much movement. Long distance migration necessarily disrupts lives and requires adjustments. Although much has been written about the migration of male workers, the literature on women is thin. In a case study based on interviews, Meredeth Turshen, Hélène Bretin, and Annie Thébaud-Mony explore the ways in which French immigration policy shapes the lives of African women who have relocated in Paris.

The unifying theme of Part II is that of women's roles and relationships as wives, lovers, and sex providers and the impacts of government policy, legislation, and programs on these roles. At the global level, Roxanna Carrillo describes how violence against women acts as an obstacle to economic development and imposes heavy costs on society. Although the violence often occurs in their private lives, women experience the reality and threats of physical abuse as silencing them and inhibiting their public participation. Violence limits women's contributions to development and controls their resistance to some development policies.

The chapters on prostitution focus on specific forms of this violence. Heisoo Shin reports on her study of women in industrial prostitution in South Korea. She shows how uneven economic development and gender divisions of labor have lead to a flourishing "entertainment industry," which recruits women with the promise of an alternative livelihood and independence. Catherine Hill reviews policy issues surrounding the sex tourist industry in Thailand. She demonstrates how the need for foreign exchange has maintained covert government support for sex tourism, which began with the U.S. military presence in Southeast Asia.

Some effects of colonialism and postcolonial change on marriage in India are examined in the next two chapters. Veena Talwar Oldenburg shows that colonial land tenure and taxation policies were more to blame than the institution of dowry in her analysis of the current rash of murders of Indian brides. Uma Narayan challenges conventional wisdom and feminist attitudes toward arranged marriage. She argues that this institution was supportive of women in the past but that in urbanized Indian society today, the pragmatic advantages are diminished. Both of these chapters suggest a possible reappraisal of two institutions—dowry and arranged marriage—that feminists have traditionally rejected.

The epilogue, by Carole Boyce Davies, allows the fictional, but evocative voices of African women experiencing the radical transformations of rural life and urban spaces to encapsulate the contradictions in society's expectations of women.

These chapters form a focus for some continuing themes and questions related to gender and development. The literature in this field is large, burgeoning, sometimes repetitive, and sometimes obscure. This book makes no claim to be comprehensive.

Meredeth Turshen

Acknowledgments

We would like to thank the Rutgers University President's Coordinating Council of International Programs for the grant that sponsored this study. We are grateful to Salah El Shakhs and Helmut Anheier for their work on the grant. Thanks also to Deborah Popper and to several graduate students who assisted us—Ulupi Jhala, Don Mitchell, Greg Remaud, and Manijeh Saba.

Part I

Economic Policies and Migration

Confronting Austerity: Women's Responses to Economic Reform

Victoria Daines and David Seddon

INTERNATIONAL DEVELOPMENT POLICY AND THE RECESSION

The Women's Decade and the Decade of Adjustment

Between the late 1970s and the mid-1980s the world economy, and particularly the less developed economies, experienced the most severe and prolonged recession since the 1930s. The economic difficulties of the decade led many governments of developing countries to accept, more or less reluctantly, stabilization and adjustment policies along the lines recommended by the International Monetary Fund (IMF) and the World Bank. These agencies emphasize the need to cut public expenditure on unproductive areas such as welfare and food subsidies and to encourage the liberalization of the economy. Thus, in the International Decade of Women (1976–85), international development policy and practice were dominated by the ideology and interventions of the IMF and the World Bank, with their commitment to stabilization and structural adjustment as the basis for economic recovery from recession and for long-term economic growth.

In general, stabilization and adjustment programs concentrate on improving the balance of payments, managing debt, containing inflation, and introducing macroeconomic reforms, rather than on protecting the vulnerable and impoverished (see Jiggins 1989, 954). As Taylor (1983, 200) observes, "Usually income

We would like to thank Meredeth Turshen and Ruth Pearson for their comments on the first draft of this chapter, which appeared as a discussion paper in the School of Development Studies, University of East Anglia, Norwich.

(re)distribution against labour and the poor is implicit in stabilisation attempts." Pinstrup-Andersen (1987, 2) comments,

Until recently, and with a few notable exceptions, short term effects on the poor have usually been ignored or given low priority in the design of adjustment programmes unless they were perceived to threaten political stability. Yet because adjustments frequently include changes of particular concern to the poor (e.g., increasing food prices, reduced real wages, and declining government expenditure on social programmes), those effects can be severe.

As the decade progressed, the real costs of adjustment became increasingly visible and the benefits subject to more critical evaluation. Evidence began to mount that those who were the most disadvantaged and vulnerable were suffering disproportionately from what the Bank tended to refer to easily as "the social costs of transition." Pinstrup-Andersen (1987, 13) argues that the evidence from eleven countries in Latin and Central America, Africa, and Asia indicates strongly that the nutritional situation deteriorated during the first half of the 1980s in a number of countries in which macroeconomic adjustments were made. He suggests that the key factors that establish the link between macroeconomic adjustment and nutrition are the real incomes of the poor, the price of food and other necessities, and access to government services and transfers. He refers to "massive evidence of falling real wages, rapidly increasing food prices, reductions in transfer programmes to the poor, and reduced government expenditures on primary health care and education" (ibid., 29) in countries in which adjustment programs were implemented. In his review of the effects of adjustment policies between 1980 and 1985, Cornia (1987a, 66) concludes that "overall, prevailing adjustment programmes tend to increase aggregate poverty, or in other words the number of people—and of children—living below the poverty line." In addition to the overall effect on poverty, he draws attention to the fact that an adjustment package tends to have a direct and unambiguous negative impact on particular vulnerable social groups and categories. Marshall (1990, 30) argues that for Mozambique, "the human costs of the structural adjustment programme are rapidly becoming apparent. Studies have begun to reveal the impact on the most vulnerable groups—women, children and the poor."

Adjustment with a Human Face

By the middle of the 1980s, even international agencies not renowned for their radicalism, but with a commitment to the welfare of the disadvantaged, began to express concern regarding the prevailing wisdom and current international development theory and practice (see Cornia, Jolly, and Stewart 1987). In the name of "adjustment with a human face," UNICEF and like-minded commentators noted that adjustment had come to involve "a reaction too far"

(Killick 1990). All too often they took it for granted that adjustment of the kind advocated by the international financial institutions was necessary and inevitable, but they argued that the social costs of adjustment should be a matter of concern. Toward the end of the 1980s, there was also some evidence that the Bank and the IMF recognized the social, economic, and, perhaps above all, the political implications of the harsh austerity measures usually adopted as part of the package of policies recommended for adjustment. These agencies began urging more caution in the implementation of adjustment and the adoption of compensatory programs of various kinds (see Commonwealth Secretariat 1989, 88–92). Only at the end of the 1980s, however, was systematic attention beginning to be paid to more radical alternative approaches to adjustment and to more constructive and participatory programs for economic and social transformation (for example, Onimode 1989; Commonwealth Secretariat 1989; the Economic Commission for Africa report referred to in Parfitt 1990). Even the few and belated programs adopted by the World Bank and other agencies to alleviate the poverty and inequality can be shown to be inadequate and partial (for example, PAMSCAD in Ghana, see Alexander 1990, 9).

Women as Victims

Women and children in low-income groups are among those identified as suffering from the austerity package so frequently implemented as the basis of adjustment (Commonwealth Secretariat 1989). The UNICEF report *The Impact of World Recession on Children* (Jolly and Cornia 1984), which is based on materials from a dozen country case studies, shows that, with few exceptions, children and women of poorer families are the hardest hit by recession. Many other commentators also emphasize that "crises and stabilization/adjustment efforts (whether or not the Fund and Bank are involved) are likely to bear most heavily on the poor and vulnerable and among them most heavily on infants, young children and women" (Green 1989, 36). It still remains the case that "so far, there has been no large-scale systematic, internationally comparative study which disaggregates the impact of structural adjustment within households and focuses specifically on women" and that "at the moment we are forced to rely mainly on inferences from non-gender specific data . . . and on studies of the impact of structural adjustment on 'vulnerable groups' such as low-income households, children and the elderly" (Elson 1989, 65). Even with data that are not gender specific, "little is known on the mechanisms and strategies allowing poor people to survive under conditions of extreme deprivation. Even less is known on the adaptations made in recent years in those countries where the army of the poor has been swollen by the ranks of those forced out of the formal sector by dramatic falls in production and employment" (Cornia 1987a, 94).

Increasing attention is now being paid to the effects of adjustment on women in particular. Recent efforts are more systematic in considering the consequences of austerity and adjustment for women and in making proposals specifically concerned with protecting the position of women and incorporating women's concerns into the process of adjustment (for example, Commonwealth Secretariat 1989). What remains relatively rare is an appreciation of the ways in which women have not simply suffered passively and silently but have struggled to survive in the face of new adversities, have resisted the increasing pressures on their lives, and have protested against these further assaults on their living conditions and those of their families and communities. These struggles to survive, protest, and resist are poorly documented as yet, and their wider significance is only now beginning to be appreciated. The argument for adjustment with a human face has tended in practice to "focus attention mainly on women as victims, thus deteriorating into paternalism. It also tends to focus only on women in low-income households, and mainly on the detrimental impact of adjustment on women, and not on the contribution that women can make to effective adjustment" (Elson 1989, 71). Even the more recent studies with a specific concern for women in adjustment (for example, Commonwealth Secretariat 1989) tend to focus on what development agencies can do for women rather than on how women may be supported in their own struggles. Although they recognize women's groups and women as community organizers, they tend to see them as significant only in so far as they "have been particularly active in trying to protect poor and vulnerable women and harness their productive potential" (Commonwealth Secretariat 94). As for women's role in political action, the studies simply suggest that "women should become an integral part of the decision-making process—in governments, international institutions and the private sector, as well as in the house" (ibid., 107).

That alternative feminist conceptions exist is not in doubt (see Mies 1986, 219–233; Ramazanoglu 1989, 174–192), but they remain to be articulated in a systematic fashion with reference to women's struggles in Africa, Asia, and Latin America. The role of women in economic and social transformation has always been underestimated, and nowhere more strikingly than in discussions of development in the Third World. There is, however, accumulating evidence of widespread and growing involvement by women in protest and resistance to exploitation and oppression, and of their contribution to social and political transformation, particularly over the last decade or so. Women's struggles in response to austerity and adjustment are an important part of the process of transformation. In a very real sense, the decade of austerity and adjustment has also been the decade of women.

Third World Women in Protest

This chapter is a first attempt to examine with a global perspective and on a comparative basis the ways in which women in developing countries struggle, protest, and resist deteriorating economic and social conditions and, in particular, the austerity programs implemented in the name of adjustment and development.

Although the focus is primarily on urban women's responses to adjustment (notably in Latin America, Africa, and the Middle East), we are also concerned with their struggles against economic and social pressures in situations in which adjustment has been of less dramatic significance (as in many parts of Asia).

We consider first the various forms of struggle in which women are involved, pointing out that several different forms may coexist and complement each other. We argue that everyday forms of resistance and protest are as important as the more overt and organized forms of cooperative and collective struggle. We then discuss individual and household strategies for survival and resistance that characterize the decade of adjustment and austerity, pointing out that the notion of "household" is problematic and that, given the predominance of patriarchal structures within the household as well as the pervasive nature of gender inequality, such strategies may increase women's oppression and exploitation. They may also, however, constitute an effective basis from which to develop more extensive, cooperative forms of struggle and collaboration with other women outside the home. We look at some examples of cooperative activities, such as mothers' clubs and popular canteens in Latin America, before examining women's involvement in collective forms of protest and resistance. In this last section, we focus on women's resistance and protest in Latin America, where collective action is relatively well documented and where the relationship between women's protest and resistance to austerity and adjustment is clearly linked to the broader women's movement and democratic politics; in Asia, where gender politics and resistance to the exploitation and oppression of women are also associated with protest against more general threats to the economic and social condition of the poor; and in the Middle East, where one might expect women to be relatively inactive and invisible, given the strength of conservative views of women's position in society. We examine those dramatic expressions of resistance and protest that are referred to as "bread riots" and consider the role of women in such mass demonstrations. Finally, we emphasize the need to explore the connections between these and other forms of direct action by women as part of a broader political struggle.

The struggles by women concerned to defend, secure, and improve their livelihoods and their lives are undoubtedly part of the broader development throughout the world of women's protest against and resistance to intensified exploitation and oppression in a period of recession and retrenchment. We focus on the responses of women in the urban areas of the Third World, where arguably the consequences of stabilization and structural adjustment are most deeply felt. We do not explicitly consider women in rural areas, nor is it our intention to attempt a general review or evaluation of the development of women's movements and organizations in Africa, Asia, and Latin America over the International Women's Decade, although there is a growing need to do so and to recognize the increasing importance of such movements and organizations (for some recent attempts to begin such a task, see Jaquette 1989; Jayawardena 1986;

Omvedt 1986). Although our concern is more limited, it will be apparent from our discussion that we do not consider it possible to separate more specific struggles from the broader political movements of which they are a part.

FORMS OF STRUGGLE

Lives of Struggle

According to Carroll (1989, 3), women's struggle or direct action

has a more extensive history and has been more influential in the history of political action for social change than is generally recognised. The historical record is obscured by the suppression of documentary evidence and historical notice that besets all aspects of women's history, perhaps especially those aspects that would provide us with knowledge of women's resistance to patriarchy in its multiplicity of forms.

Carroll (ibid., 21) also stresses the importance of considering not only "the most spectacular or heroic examples," but also "the widely dispersed local actions, unnumbered and innumerable, of small groups of women at the grass roots."

In fact, women everywhere, and particularly in the Third World, live lives of struggle. They struggle to survive and to prevail against various forms of oppression and exploitation; they struggle to support their families; and they struggle to extend their room for maneuver through individual, cooperative, and sometimes collective forms of action. For urban women, particularly poor urban women, these struggles involve everyday forms of resistance and protest. They are directed toward concrete and often immediate objectives. As Piven and Cloward (1977, 20) remark, "People experience deprivation and oppression within a concrete setting, not as the end product of large and abstract processes, and it is the concrete experience that molds their discontent into specific grievances against specific targets." Even when the forms of resistance and protest develop beyond the individual to the cooperative and collective, this concern with tangible results and gains remains crucial, although the potential for a more comprehensive vision of the sources of exploitation and oppression, and the feasibility of seeking wider and longer-term objectives, are often greater in collective struggle.

The Coexistence of Different Forms of Struggle

The daily struggle is generally associated with everyday forms of resistance and hidden forms of protest through which women resist in an essentially ad hoc and unorganized fashion the forces that oppress and exploit them. The struggle may also take a more open, organized, and clearly identifiable form, generally in collaboration with others. The distinction between covert and overt, between unorganized and organized struggle, protest, and resistance, is rarely clear-cut. The struggle takes place in the home and outside of it, at work and in the neighborhood, in private and in public. The different forms that struggle, protest, and resistance take should be seen not as representing distinct, separate activities but as elements and dimensions of a broader struggle involving a variety of forms of direct action. Also, it should not be assumed that apparently unorganized and incoherent forms of struggle necessarily imply a different or lower form of consciousness from that associated with more overt and organized struggles. It may simply be that the objective constraints on overt and organized activities are too great to permit more visible struggles.

The idea of a quasi-evolutionary progression—from individual to collective direct action, associated with the development from less conscious to more conscious—is implicit in much of the analytical literature (including Cohen 1982; Scott 1985). Although the structure of our discussion indicates broad sympathy with the idea that cooperative and collective forms of struggle and direct action have greater political impact than do individual forms of struggle, we have serious reservations about the underlying assumptions. First, the idea tends to distinguish private from public forms of consciousness and resistance and to privilege the latter as somehow higher (more significant or more advanced). This distinction is not only highly problematic but politically loaded theoretically and practically. Second, this idea tends to privilege certain forms of political organization (namely, the hierarchical, in which a leadership amplifies and galvanizes the consciousness and actions of those imprisoned within a lower form of consciousness) as against others (namely, the egalitarian, in which cooperation and collective forms of action stem from a clear awareness of disadvantage and oppression). A different approach emphasizes the normality of the coexistence of different forms of consciousness and different forms of action. It stresses the pervasiveness of those structures of exploitation and oppression that permeate women's lives and permit only limited room for maneuver and for the more overt conventional forms of struggle. This approach also emphasizes that the personal is political and that easy distinctions between private and public politics may be a form of oppression rendering literally invisible and therefore implicitly insignificant the less conventional forms of struggle. As Tripp (1989, 2) argues, "Redefining political struggle to include non-organised and non-self-conscious action adds new dimensions to the meaning of politics and the processes of political change." That everyday forms of resistance and dissidence can create the foundation for a sudden eruption of open forms of conventionally recognizable politics has been demonstrated frequently throughout history, and never more clearly than over the last decade throughout Africa, Asia, and Latin America, and in Eastern Europe. The same is true, we submit, of women's struggles.

Everyday Forms of Resistance and Protest

Scott (1985) used the phrase *everyday forms of resistance* to describe peasant struggles in Malaysia and elsewhere. He suggests that "most of the forms this (pro-

saic but constant) struggle takes stop well short of collective outright defiance,"
and he goes on to argue that they have certain features in common: "They require
little or no coordination or planning; they often represent a form of individual self-
help; and they typically avoid any direct symbolic confrontation with authority or
with elite norms" (ibid., 29). Such forms of struggle have much in common with
the various forms of so-called passive resistance characteristic of many situations of
oppression, in which open protest, resistance, or defiance would be suicidal (see Harper 1968, on lower-caste resistance in India; Cohen 1982, on the political constraints
on African workers; and Mason 1981, on workers' opposition in Nazi Germany).

It is interesting that Scott (1985, 33) explicitly draws attention to some of the
feminist literature on peasant society and suggests that informal and covert resistance often makes possible certain immediate de facto gains for those under-
taking it. By doing so, he creates parallels between his discussion of everyday
forms of resistance among peasants and everyday forms of resistance among
women in peasant societies. But he fails to develop this observation further;
indeed, his study, though rich in insights regarding forms of everyday resistance,
does not explicitly consider women's resistance. Others, such as O'Hanlon (1988,
223), concerned with forms of struggle and resistance among subaltern groups
in Third World societies, are explicit in their rejection of the idea that resistance
by disadvantaged and oppressed groups should "necessarily take the virile form
of a deliberate and violent onslaught," arguing that among subaltern classes "we
should look for resistances of a different kind. . . . These then would be forms
of resistance more 'feminine' than masculine." Unfortunately, he never elab-
orates the full implications of this suggestion, although the notion that everyday
and hidden forms of struggle are in some way typically feminine is both challenging and troublesome.

The concept of forms of everyday resistance is valuable for women. Some
studies of other disadvantaged groups emphasize that "it is important to focus
attention on the struggles of the most deprived and desperate" (see Blaikie,
Cameron, and Seddon 1979, 56 on Nepalese untouchables). This emphasis
reveals more clearly that the life of the urban and rural poor is not mechanistically
determined by economic forces or formal institutional politics. It underlines the
fact that men and women make history (through everyday as well as more
exceptional forms of struggle), albeit not under conditions of their own choosing.
Thus interpretation stresses the active rather than the passive nature of relations
of exploitation and oppression, and the potential for challenging these relations
by constructing alternative relations of support and solidarity and by developing
some form of countervailing power.

Whether everyday forms of resistance are seen as the product of the difficult
circumstances within which struggle is undertaken or as more appropriate forms
of resistance, many commentators do identify these forms of action as distinctive
in some way. Often they are seen less as forms of struggle, resistance, and protest
than as survival strategies.

Many observers consider survival or coping strategies to be primary responses to adversity and to austerity; they tend to see them as essentially defensive strategies, providing little potential for changing the circumstances within which individuals or households struggle. Elson (1989, 69), for example, remarks that "there is a difference between survival strategies and activities that can form the basis for sustained growth and development both on a personal and a national level." Others argue that survival is women's primary concern and that "when basic survival is assured, additional assets are acquired to increase security, by diversifying portfolios . . . to spread risks and increase management flexibility" (Jiggins 1989, 956). This may be the case, but we suggest that all struggle involves an active engagement with the immediate environment and always has the potential for the development of more effective, more sustained, and more collaborative forms of struggle, even when taking place at the most basic individual level, with the most limited and immediate of objectives.

Although the concept of survival strategy is useful in that it emphasizes the active struggle of individuals and households, it does have shortcomings, primarily because "there is a danger of dismissing the radical element in the struggles by the deprived which seek to change the present political and socio-economic framework in which they are enmeshed" (Blaikie, Cameron, and Seddon 1979, 56). We urge a recognition that even defensive struggles can, in the right circumstances, develop into more extensive forms of struggle with a greater capacity for expanding the room for maneuver and for changing the conditions within which struggle takes place. We also suggest that all successful political struggles and movements focus on concrete and shorter term objectives as well as on broader and longer term objectives. We recognize that economic recession, structural adjustment, and austerity programs often weaken pre-existing cooperative structures and the room for maneuver, making it increasingly difficult to secure basic livelihoods. Existing patterns of subsistence among poor households and the popular classes are threatened. In the Caribbean, for example, "women's attempts to ensure and maintain an adequate livelihood for themselves and those in their care have been undermined during the 1980s. Deteriorating economic conditions, high levels of open unemployment, and the increasingly urgent need for cash to buy basic necessities, impact on women's efforts to earn a livelihood" (Massiah 1989, 969).

WOMEN AND HOUSEHOLD RESPONSES AND STRATEGIES

Survival Strategies

In a study for UNICEF, Cornia (1987a, 90) argues that "for the majority of low-income households . . . adjustment entails a variety of adaptations—known as survival strategies—in the creation and use of resources." He divides survival strategies into three: strategies for the creation of resources, strategies for conserving and improving the use of existing resources, and extended family and migration strategies. Under the first, he identifies increasing one's own production, increasing sale of labor, and sale of assets as strategies of individuals and individual households; increasing production through voluntary labor exchange and cooperative work or through sharing nonproductive activities (such as child-care) to allow greater involvement in production and sale of labor; and transferring income, usually within extended family or kinship groups, to aid poorer relatives as strategies involving cooperation between households. Women's activities are central to these household strategies.

Raczynski and Serrano (1985) identify increasing one's own production through the cultivation of small gardens as a strategy for increasing household resources in Santiago; Rios (1984) does the same in São Paulo; and Jiggins (1989) sees the same pattern in many African towns. Women are very involved in such urban gardening. Although the intensification of household production may effectively increase food availability, it may also significantly increase women's work loads.

Several studies reveal significantly increased labor force participation rates for women during the first part of the 1980s in many Latin American countries—Brazil (PREALC 1985a), Chile (Raczynski and Serrano 1985), Uruguay (Leslie, Lycette, and Buvinić 1986), and Costa Rica (PREALC 1985b)—as well as in the Philippines (Cornia, Jolly, and Stewart 1987, vol. 2). The growing involvement of women in the labor force as wage employees may exert additional downward pressure on wages (see Cornia 1987c, 22). It seems that, although greater involvement in the labor market is a widespread response of urban women to declining real household incomes, "on the whole, the incomes and job opportunities available to women in urban areas have probably deteriorated, though more detailed information on this is required" (Elson 1989, 66).

Certainly the situation in the formal sector has worsened. In Ghana, a recent report found that although women represent only 25 percent of total trade union membership, the areas of work in which they predominate are those worst hit by retrenchment, and given their historically weak location in formal sector employment, women figure prominently among the retrenched (Alexander 1990, 8). Increased labor force participation by women also tends to involve casual and part-time employment or various forms of part-time and unstable commercial activities. The move into precarious and degrading forms of economic activity as a means of increasing household income is well documented in countries as different as India (Mies 1984), Peru (Karp-Toledo 1983), and several African countries (Hay and Stichter 1984).

Raczynski (1989, 82) observes of Chile that "the women, many of whom stopped working outside the house when they got married, intensify their efforts to obtain some sort of supplementary income, generally through part-time activities which are unstable (sewing, knitting, washing laundry, or selling cigarettes or ice-cream, etc.). The income obtained is low." Massiah (1989, 965), writing about women's lives and livelihoods in the Caribbean, argues that it is hard for poor women to find a steady, reliable source of income and to supply food, clothing, and shelter for their households. One effect of the economic crises of the 1970s and 1980s is the curtailment of opportunities in paid employment and the opening up of more self-employment activities, especially street vending, petty commodity production, personal services, and small-scale transportation. But the self-employed sector is crowded, returns are often minimal, and there is no security. Even for the generally better off women working in the public sector, adjustment means wage freezes and redundancies. In Jamaica, for example, nurses and teachers have been leaving the public sector because of the low levels of pay, and "professional women remaining in the public service have been driven to doing extra jobs at night in the informal sector, such as running snack shops" (Elson 1989, 66).

Pryer (1987, 140) studied the ways in which women cope with severe economic deprivation in an urban slum in Bangladesh; she considers expedients that are "struggles for survival rather than solutions to the problem [of malnutrition]." She analyzed intensively 7 households, which were the most malnourished in a sample of 220 households; their only productive asset was labor. Pryer observed that during the lean months of the monsoon, the number of households in which women contributed income increased from three to five, and in two of these households, the women were major earners; the women in the two other households were unable to work as a result of severe illness or pregnancy. The kinds of economic activity in which the women were involved tended to be precarious and often illegal.

Not all of the activities women undertake outside the home to improve the welfare and security of their families are negative. Massiah (1989, 970) refers, in the case of the Caribbean, to "those activities (such as maintaining ties with kin, friends and neighbours through gift exchanges, participation in ceremonies, entertainment, and sharing of information, goods and services; and with the wider community through membership in organizations, voluntary social work and so on) through which women maintain and enhance the social standing of their families." Apart from wage-earning, purely individual strategies are actually surprisingly rare, and what are often referred to as individual or household survival strategies almost always involve developing or drawing upon extra-household ties and relations.

Survival Strategies and Women's Oppression

Many survival strategies carry with them the possibility of increased exploitation and oppression of women, who may be required to increase their labor inputs and their range of activities in order to provide for the family and household, or else reduce their own consumption levels. Apparently poor Chilean women experience more than commensurate deficiencies in food intake during periods of declining food availability (Raczynski and Serrano 1985). Also, the increase in women's involvement in market production and in the labor force as a response to the deterioration of living conditions associated with austerity measures intensifies the demand on their time, which increases economic, social, and physical pressures on them. As Jiggins (1989, 953–954) remarks, for poor women in sub-Saharan Africa, "with only meagre resources and with weak access to mainstream services, expanded economic activity has almost always meant increasing the length of their working day" and "data from official sources suggest that, for an increasing number of. . . households in sub-Saharan Africa, the stress on female labour time has become insupportable." Other commentators also draw attention to survival strategies that may actually increase exploitation and oppression and increase the burden upon women already under extreme pressure (see Pryer 1987). Cleary (1989, 48) cites an OXFAM report that records a Zambian woman's observations on the financial problems facing her and her family in the daily struggle for enough to eat. Bolles (1983, 152) reports that, in Jamaica, as a result of the IMF anti-inflationary program, the cost of living rose approximately 30 percent between May 1978 and March 1979: "This situation presented an incredible problem for mothers raising children, and much juggling and hustling was necessary just to survive." The Commonwealth Secretariat (1989, 71–72) report on women and structural adjustment points out that

as poor women's responsibilities increase, they work longer outside the home while continuing to engage in home activities. Often they forego recreation, with fewer hours for sleep and leisure. In the Philippines it was found that increases in a mother's time on paid work did not result in decreases in time spent on household tasks. In Buenos Aires, housewives with outside employment spent over ten hours a day on domestic work, while those in paid employment still spent eight hours on similar work, making a working day of at least 13 hours.

As Elson (1989, 58) notes, "Women's unpaid labour is not infinitely elastic—a breaking point may be reached, and women's capacity to reproduce and maintain human resources may collapse." The increasing pressure may reduce their ability to provide adequate health and other care for their families; when extended family or other cooperative arrangements are not available, this could have an adverse effect on the welfare of children. Cornia (1987c, 40) suggests that "increasing claims on the mother's time, coupled with declining incomes and cuts in government expenditure on education, tend also to produce negative effects on child abandonment, child labour, and school drop-out rates, particularly among girls." A study of low-income women in Indo-Guayas, Ecuador, found that only 30 percent of the women were coping with their changed circumstances; 55 percent were just hanging on, using up future resources in order to survive today, sending their sons out to work or keeping their daughters at home to take over domestic responsibilities; the remaining 15 percent were no longer coping, with their young children roaming the streets (Moser 1988). Alexander (1990, 8) reports that

research in Ghana shows women have adapted to the severe economic crises [associated with the Economic Recovery Programme] by employing a variety of means: growing their own food; reducing their consumption of protein meals including meat, fish and eggs;

having one main meal every one or two days; relying on salary advances; dealing in the black market more. Declining nutritional and health standards in children is the inevitable outcome.

Others argue that "women's full-time wage work away from the home can give rise to nutritional and childcare problems if there is no substitute home help, or if the market cannot supply reliable, cheap food-stuffs to replace foregone production" (Jiggins 1989, 957). In contrast, Leslie (1988) suggests that there is little evidence of a negative effect of maternal employment on child nutrition and therefore no justification for limiting women's labor force participation on the grounds of promoting child welfare. Even Cornia (1984) notes that some studies suggest a positive effect on child nutrition of mothers' working through the increased income coming into the household. It is generally the case that a relatively high proportion of women's cash income is devoted to household welfare (Carloni 1984, cited in Jiggins 1989). Nonetheless, "UNICEF studies reveal a widespread deterioration in the nutritional status of children and pregnant and lactating mothers in both rural and urban areas in countries with IMF stabilisation and World Bank SAPs. Mothers are unable to buy enough food of the right type to feed the whole family, and in many cases priority in feeding is given to adult males" (Elson 1989, 68).

The Struggle Against Patriarchy

Most women also struggle against patriarchal structures and forms of oppression that ensure unequal control and distribution of resources between men and women in the household. Research shows that neither joint decision making nor equal sharing of resources is at all common. Although women's control over and access to resources is generally less than that of men and is often constrained by the men, women are generally expected to be responsible for household management. All too often, women are obliged to meet their families' needs by stretching the husbands' contribution by good housekeeping, by earning extra themselves, by producing food or clothing themselves, or by engaging in petty commerce or other activities. Ultimately, "it is women who must cope and devise survival strategies when household incomes fall and prices rise" (Elson 1989, 65). It is clear that in most circumstances, women are more likely than men to spend their incomes on meeting their family's food requirements (see Jiggins 1989 for sub-Saharan Africa). Thus, women become responsible for household strategies and are obliged to manage those household resources under their control to ensure the survival and well-being of other household members.

But the structure of control over resources within the household constrains the extent to which income can be reallocated in response to increases in food prices. A recent study of one hundred households in low-income areas of Lusaka, Zambia, found that in only a tiny minority of cases was money management a joint responsibility of husband and wife. Although the women were responsible for daily meals, they had little say in the total allocation of household expenditure. They could determine only how their housekeeping allowance was spent (Muntemba 1989). "When prices rise, this requires a high degree of ingenuity in making ends meet, involving extra stress and time. Increases in the housekeeping allowance and reductions in the husbands' personal expenditure require conjugal negotiations which are often fraught with tension" (Elson 1989, 68). Massiah (1989, 972) reports how studies in the Caribbean found that women received only limited support when they tried to combine their household responsibilities with earning an income:

The prevailing gender division of labour assigns to women the responsibilities of housework, child care, care of the aged and disabled, and domestic services to male partners. Although males recognised the need for their female partners to contribute financially to the household and encouraged them to do so, few women reported help from their partners with household and other domestic chores.

The Lusaka study (Muntemba 1989, 121–123) also shows how different are husbands and wives in their preferred strategies for responding to increasing costs of living, and how different are the strategies actually adopted by male and female heads of household. In general, women chose to reduce consumption, particularly on expensive items, and men chose to borrow money or obtain a salary advance or else to grow food at home (with the wife actually doing the garden work). There is a limit, however, to the amount of time women can take from human resource production and maintenance and devote to crop production. Even if they do have some spare capacity, women may be reluctant to increase their workload because they are unlikely to enjoy the proceeds of extra work. This happens when production is under the management of men, who then control the earnings. For example, women may refuse to spend extra time working in their husbands' fields or gardens.

Household survival strategies too often appear to be mechanisms for coping that increase still further the exploitation and oppression of women; even so they are often associated with a heightened level of struggle, within and outside the household. They frequently involve drawing on informal networks and activating forms of cooperation and collaboration. As Raczynski (1989, 82) says of women's survival strategies under deteriorating conditions in Chile, "These circumstances require the maximum use of domestic resources and activation of solidarity networks." For women there is no necessary clear distinction between individual and cooperative forms of struggle.

COOPERATIVE FORMS OF STRUGGLE

Networks and Associations

Cooperative forms of activity may overcome some of the weakness of individual action and actually strengthen women's capacity to go beyond survival to improve their welfare and that of their families. Cooperation may also help develop the basis for more sustained collective forms of struggle and direct action. As Raczynski (1989, 82) observes of Chile,

Households are not isolated, they are rooted in social networks and have links of support and solidarity. The support network includes exchange of goods and services, information, moral support, loans, and child-care, as well as the extended family. In the woman's case this is formed mainly by neighbours. . . . The woman's network deals mainly with daily domestic chores: loans of food and small amounts of money, utensils, child care, washing laundry, information, advice, etc.

Elsewhere, strategies involving cooperation between households include private income transfers, usually within an extended family or kinship group. Voluntary labor exchange is another form of cooperative strategy and one reported from as far apart as Peru (Karp-Toledo 1983) and India (Cousins and Goydre 1979). In Jamaica, the operation of domestic networks of exchange by women was a major strategy adopted in response to the 1978 IMF economic reform program (Bolles 1983, 150–152). In the rural areas of sub-Saharan Africa, it appears that "women's networks are emerging in areas in which male out migration has been particularly severe, and the percentage of households headed by women is as high as 60 or 70 percent" (Jiggins 1989, 958). When women in households do cooperate, extreme poverty may be avoided: "Individually, each appears to be marginalised, but together they can spread costs, pool savings, and diversify enterprises without the risks and uncertainties of dependence on menfolk" (ibid.). In urban as well as rural areas, many women choose group organization and management of their activities to protect themselves against male interference and manipulation.

In Latin America, various mothers' clubs (*clubes de madres*) set up simple childcare centers managed by the mothers, alternating in weekly shifts to enable the freeing of labor for productive activities (Cornia, Jolly, and Stewart 1987, 1:96). Several commentators report on the experience of the popular canteens (*comedores populares*) that developed in Lima after 1980 as a response to a seriously deteriorating economic situation (Huaman n.d.; Lafosse 1984; UNICEF-Peru 1985; Van der Linde 1984). In this scheme, groups of fifteen to fifty households jointly carried out bulk purchase and preparation of food. The food preparation was done by the women of participating households on the basis of daily shifts every four or five days, with each household paying according to the number of meals required. Extremely poor households were either temporarily exempted from payment or given the meals on credit, so that the *comedores populares* became instruments of redistribution in favor of the poor. Communal food preparation also freed women on a regular basis for other productive and income-generating or supportive activities (for example, childcare).

Raczynski (1989, 93) identified various cooperative forms of association in Chile, "aimed at collectively facing the survival problem and the satisfaction of basic needs . . . called popular economic organizations (*organicaciones econom-icas populares*—OEPs)." Such forms of association are not new (they existed under Allende), but they apparently proliferated during the late 1970s and early 1980s. Some OEPs were locality-based, others based on shared religious or political beliefs or having worked for the same employer. The more common associations were basic consumption organizations, such as community kitchens, purchase and supply associations, and self-help groups; productive workshops—small units with three to fifteen people producing and selling goods and services such as bread, clothing, knitting, laundry, and carpentry; organizations for the unemployed; organizations related to housing problems, such as housing committees, water, electricity, and mortgage committees, and committees for the homeless; and diverse organizations aimed at health, education, and entertainment needs (Raczynski 1989, 83). Although the proportion of the urban poor involved in these organizations is relatively small (3 percent in Santiago), these activities, which substantially involve women, have great potential for assisting the poor in crisis and for raising morale and consciousness of the possibilities of concerted action, going well beyond the usual notion of survival strategy (see Joseph L. Scarpaci, chapter 2, this volume).

Beyond Networks and Associations

Carroll (1989, 19) points out that

preoccupation with the numerical under-representation of women in most unions, union-led strikes, and political parties has obscured the true dimensions of women's collective action, which often arises out of female community networks that are outside of these organisations but may constitute the essential foundations of support for them, and often goes beyond the narrower demands of labor unions to include a wide range of economic, social and political issues.

Forms of cooperative struggle, which can be seen as associated with survival strategies, may also provide the basis for more conventionally recognizable forms of collective direct action. As Ghai and de Alcantara (1990, 24) remark,

The challenges posed by recession and adjustment lend momentum to other kinds of family and neighbourhood cooperation which go beyond simple "survival strategies" and create centres of dialogue and mutual assistance within an inchoate civil society. Some, like neighbourhood soup kitchens in urban areas, draw families together in cooperative efforts to reduce the costs of subsistence; others grow out of broader urban grass-roots organizations in which the neighbourhood not only presents collective demands to local authorities but may be further integrated into a hierarchy of federations or confederations with the capacity to make itself heard at the national or international level.

Ghai and de Alcantara (1990) suggest that neighborhood associations tend above all to be concerned with questions of consumption, whether collective or individual; they argue that members are drawn together to protest unacceptable living conditions, the elimination of subsidies on such public goods as utilities or transport, the lack of credit for housing, the sudden rise in food prices or environmental problems. Their demands are not generally framed around issues of employment and remuneration, that is, around conditions of production. They argue that women are particularly likely to be involved in such associations "for the obvious reason that women are most likely to be concerned with difficulties arising in the sphere of consumption" (ibid., 24).

Others also suggest an intimate relationship between women's struggles and specific consumer-oriented neighborhood associations and movements. In her discussion of gender-based resistance, Eckstein (1989a, 25) argues that women's isolation within the home and their economic marginality allegedly contribute to quiescence on their part, but she observes that in Latin America their economic marginalization from the public process of production has meant that they have often been in a position to sustain struggles at home—in the squatter settlements, for example, against eviction—and in response to increased prices. She points out that "in Mexico City, for example, women in the city's largest shanty town have protected their community against land developers attempting to evict families and against police who attempted to arrest participants in a local organization that used militant tactics, including physical violence, to defend local interests" (ibid.; see also Velez-Ibanez 1983, 119–122). In São Paulo, women in charge of household consumption were the main force behind the Cost of Living movement and efforts to form communal shopping groups in the late 1970s" (Singer 1982 quoted in Eckstein 1989a, 25). Eckstein (ibid., 26) has even argued that

from an analytical perspective, the women's mobilizations in defence of housing and other consumer claims, as well as in defence of the disappeared [in Argentina], call for another important revision of orthodox Marxist thinking. [For] women's non-involvement in the production process has made it easier for them to defy the established order.

Eckstein's argument is problematic, however, not least because of her apparent acceptance of the idea that women are economically marginalized and not involved in the production process. This idea is amply contradicted by numerous studies (many of which we have cited). She also assumes that women's struggles are essentially around everyday forms of resistance associated with domestic and community issues because they tend to "remain in their neighbourhoods during the day while their men work elsewhere" (1989a, 25).

Her view is shared by others, including Ghai and de Alcantara (1990, 24), who suggest that

particularly in Latin America, where women have traditionally been far more restricted to the sphere of the home than in Africa, neighbourhood organizations are drawing women out of isolation and into organizations which must deal with the state, not necessarily because women have been originally concerned with politics but because they have been preoccupied with guaranteeing the future of their families.

The implied sharp distinction between struggles around consumption and struggles around production; between cooperative, civic, or neighborhood movements and collective, political, or workplace movements; and between struggles emerging out of domestic or private concerns and struggles emerging out of public concerns—which appears to coincide in large part with a distinction between women's and men's struggles and movements—seems to us problematic and to require further consideration. Clearly, the forms of economic activity in which women are involved may differ systematically from those of men, but what is required is less a programmatic statement that women's base is in domestic labor and in the home than a detailed analysis of the complex interrelationship between various forms of production and women's involvement in them. Equally, the complex relationship between different forms of struggle in which women are involved requires more detailed analysis. The diversity of forms of women's protest and resistance is great and the interrelationship between them complex. As Vargas (1990) argues in the case of the women's social movement in Peru, it is possible to identify three different elements—liberal women, feminists, and poor women in squatter settlements; each element of the movement has its own structures and forms of organization but they all interact and overlap. Furthermore, although women's protest and resistance often take forms quite distinct and separate from those associated with pre-existing recognized structures of opposition (for example, trades unions and political parties), they are also frequently associated with, and emerge from within such structures, as when women workers strike (see Zghal 1989) or participate in rallies and demonstrations organized by opposition political parties.

COLLECTIVE FORMS OF PROTEST AND RESISTANCE

The Diversity of Forms of Resistance and Protest

In the sections that follow, we review information on the character and extent of women's involvement in collective forms of protest and resistance against austerity and adjustment. The evidence is fragmentary. Although women are active in collective resistance throughout the world, their involvement is rarely documented, still less examined and analyzed. If our review serves to draw attention to this activity, it will have achieved something worthwhile. We recognize that our research is incomplete and that more careful and extended investigation is likely to produce further evidence of women's widespread involvement. It will also become apparent that the character and form of women's protest is extraordinarily diverse, and that involvement in such overt forms of protest as street demonstrations, strikes, and so on is but one aspect of women's protest, which is inextricably linked to other less obvious forms of struggle.

Collective forms of action generally move beyond individual survival strategies and cooperative efforts to increase the room for maneuver available to individuals and individual households. In exceptional circumstances, collective action is the product of extreme threat to a whole community or social group, and it may then be seen as a form of survival strategy. Indeed, some authors argue that many contemporary social movements should be seen as essentially defensive responses of the powerless. Fuentes and Frank (1989, 183) argue that

most of these social movements are defensive of livelihood and/or identity . . . [and] seem to respond to this crisis-generated deprivation and powerlessness, which they mostly seek defensively to stem or redress. These movements are only marginally offensive in pursuit of betterment, like the women's movement, which seeks to improve women's position in society, albeit at a time when the economic crisis is undermining women's economic opportunities.

They further argue that "most social movements leave few permanent and cumulative marks on history" (ibid., 184). We dispute this.

We agree that "the undervaluation of women has led to the underestimation of their participation in all forms of collective protest and resistance to exploitation and oppression" (Fox-Genovese 1982, 28). The same may be said for women's involvement in more organized and collective political activity in the contemporary Third World: Although extensive and sometimes of critical importance, it has tended to remain invisible, at least to social scientists and historians. In a brief introductory comment in the recent collection on *Urban Crises and Social Movements in the Middle East*, Liauzu (1989) observes that the role of women in social and political movements is little studied and merits specific research. Similarly, de Groot (1989, 229) argues that "our analysis of popular movements needs to examine not just activity and ideas about women, but also activity and ideas by women." The special issue of *Women's Studies International Forum* on women's direct action makes much the same point and begins to offer some empirical material to support the argument that "women's non-violent direct action has a more extensive history and has been more influential in the history of political action for social change than is generally recognised" (Carroll 1989, 3).

Much still remains to be done in this regard. As Jayawardena (1986, 3) remarks, "Only recently, with the rise of feminist movements all over the world, has attention been directed to early feminists and feminism in the Third World," and Jaquette (1989, 1) observes that "U.S. feminists are increasingly aware of the work of Canadian and European feminists, particularly French and British writers, but they still tend to view women in the Third World as victims of oppression rather than as creators of feminist theory or as agents of change." The recent publication in English of several works on popular protest and the women's movement in Latin America (Eckstein 1989a, b; Jaquette 1989; Jelin 1990) mark a new stage in the recognition of the importance of women's struggle in the Third World.

Forms of Popular Protest

Walton (1989, 316) identifies three major types of protest against austerity and adjustment measures: food riots, political demonstrations, and general strikes. He points out that "protest forms are highly mutable. They change with regimes and the likelihood of repression, but they also change with the circumstances of unfolding collective action." Other authors find it difficult to separate, either analytically or empirically, the different forms that collective protest may take. We argue that such separations or distinctions are premature, given the relative paucity of information relating to the dynamics of popular protest and the lack of theoretical discussion of the issues involved.

We are particularly concerned at the tendency to regard popular struggles as quite distinct from working-class struggles (for example, Chikhi 1990, 44), although some valuable preliminary attempts to consider the relationship between the two kinds of struggle do exist. Von Freyhold (1987, 29), for example, discusses labor movements and popular struggles in Africa, pointing out that "where trade unions have been able to maintain a certain degree of independence they continue to pose in overt or covert ways political challenges to the state and they often interact with a wider social movement, the latest IMF riots being an illustration of this." She emphasizes that the long process of covert and overt struggles and resistance "had had, most of the time, a populist rather than a proletarian character and that the working class has sought, and sometimes achieved, the support of other underprivileged sections of the population"; she argues that "populism from below is not at all a sign of the immaturity of the working class but rather of maturity and of an offensive. It is nothing less than a challenge to the economic, political and cultural hegemony of the ruling class."

Popular struggles are seen as both broader than and different from working-class struggles, but "where the working class speaks and acts on behalf of the people rather than just its own narrowly defined proletarian interest, it usually also begins to come closer to notions of an utopia of a free and self-organising society" (von Freyhold 1987, 30). Shivji (1984, cited by von Freyhold 1987) argues that the economic crisis has taught popular movements in Africa a lesson, and that the quest for democracy, participation and self-determination informs many of the new popular movements in Africa today." With regard to India, Kothari (1985) proves that ecology groups, women's groups, the women's movement, and minority groups are beginning to struggle in various ways to reassert democratic, civil, and human rights. The intimate relationship between various forms of everyday resistance, cooperative struggles, human rights movements, and political organization is demonstrated in the recent history of women's protest in Latin America (see Jaquette 1989).

Community-Based Struggles and Politics in Latin America

Jaquette (1989) points out that women's political mobilization has a long history in Latin America.[1] From the wars of independence against Spain in the early nineteenth century to the guerrilla wars of the 1960s and 1970s, women have been active in wider political movements. Women organized strikes, participated in urban street demonstrations, and joined political parties, even before they had the right to vote. Women have also been involved in community politics and community action of various kinds, including mothers' clubs and cost of living associations (ibid., 3). This historical tradition of political activism is relevant to an appreciation of more recent responses to austerity. Jaquette argues that the specific mobilization of poor urban women during the deep recession of the 1980s provided a grass-roots base for the emerging women's movement in Latin America. In response to the economic decline, urban poor women were forced to rely on their own resources to ensure the survival of their families. Although women's involvement in neighborhood organizations is not new, the degree of coordination among local groups, the formation of federations of groups with similar interests, and the linking of neighborhood groups to other strands of the women's movement give the various elements of community organization a new and more powerful influence. Also, the coincidence of broader political transitions to democracy and the growth of community organizations among urban poor women give these organizations a new context in which to work, more ambitious goals, new political resources, and a taste of national power (ibid., 6).

Although Brazil is not a classic instance of responses to structural adjustment, it does provide an excellent example of the complex relationship between everyday forms of resistance and the more overt and visible forms of political struggle. Though originally created as women's auxiliaries to Christian Base Communities (*Sociedades de Amigos de Bairro*) during the late 1960s and early 1970s, Brazilian women's community organizations soon took on a political dynamic of their own. Poor and working-class women began organizing around their immediate survival needs, which were sometimes neglected by mixed neighborhood groups. Working-class women were among the first to protest the authoritarian regime's regressive social and economic policies. They organized against the rising cost of living; demanded adequate local schools and day-care centers, running water, sewers, electrification, and other urban infrastructural necessities; and clamored for their right to feed their families adequately, school their children, and provide a decent life. Community-based mothers' clubs provided the organizational base for several political movements that expanded into citywide and even nationwide political campaigns (see Alvarez 1989, 21). The Feminine Amnesty movement, the Cost of Living movement, and the Day-Care movement were three such women's campaigns that drew strength as protest movements from the grass-roots clubs and associations at the local neighborhood level.

Alvarez (1989, 22–25) emphasizes the importance of political liberalization as changing "the objective possibilities for political protest in the latter part of the 1970s," but she also stresses the relevance of the state's response to protest by women. She points out, for example, that the military gave women's associations greater political leeway than was granted to other groupings (the militant left, students, and labor organizations), which were seen as more threatening to national security. Thus, the 1975 celebrations of International Women's Day were among the first public assemblies permitted since the mass mobilizations of 1967–68.

Although many Brazilian feminists later saw the period from 1975 to 1978 as a time of elementary undefined feminism, significant developments took place over the next five years. The 1978 International Women's Day celebration provided the basis for an emerging women's political platform. "Along with the gamut of issues concerning the feminine side of the Brazilian class struggle . . . the women's movement began calling attention to the politics of the private sphere, the politics of the family, and of reproduction" (Alvarez 1989, 33–34). After 1978, many neighborhood women's groups began focusing on what Alvarez refers to as gender-specific issues, such as day care and domestic labor rather than on gender-related issues such as running water and sewage. In 1979, the First Paulista Women's Congress, which drew nearly 1,000 participants, highlighted issues of women's day-to-day lives: domestic labor, discrimination in the workplace and occupational training for women, fertility control, sexuality, lack of day-care centers, and women's political participation. The congress proclaimed that power relations in daily life and not just in political society must be democratized; it also stimulated the creation of numerous other women's organizations including neighborhood women's associations. Though the Cost of Living and Amnesty movements were absorbed by the political opposition after the 1978 elections, the Struggle for Day-Care movement continued to grow during 1980 and popular women's organizations proliferated throughout urban Brazil (ibid., 38–45).

In other parts of the world, collective action in response to austerity and adjustment, rising prices, and a deterioration in economic and social conditions is also clearly associated with other forms of struggle by women and is intimately linked to broader struggles for political democracy. In Jamaica, for example, considerable political activity by women of all political persuasions characterized the period immediately following the Manley government's implementation of an IMF economic reform program. In early 1979, poor women, organized by a faction of the conservatives, marched in Kingston and elsewhere under a banner denouncing the Manley government for the rising cost of living. Meanwhile, another group of pro-Manley and anticonservative women held a counterdemonstration, calling for greater self-reliance. A third group of women, led by the progressive forces, demonstrated for an end to U.S. imperialism and decried the IMF (Bolles 1983, 156).

Women's Struggles Against Exploitation and Oppression in Asia

In countries such as India, there is a long history of women's involvement in mass demonstrations. The nationalist movement in India brought women into the streets and into mass demonstrations, even into nonviolent protests and jails. Communists and Socialists have been organizing women since the 1940s, within the All India Women's Conference (AIWC) and in independent organizations. The AIWC was largely inactive through the 1950s and 1960s, and the Communist-led National Federation of Indian Women (NFIW) remained a predominantly middle-class organization. The ten years between the mid–1960s and mid–1970s were marked by rural protest and revolt, including that of the Naxalites. Tribal populations were increasingly drawn into resistance, the classic example being the Chipko movement that began in 1973 and involved low-caste Himalayan peasants in an organized attempt to stop tree-felling. All of these movements were notable for the participation and aggressive involvement of women.

In the mid–1970s, urban women's movements became of major significance in India. The Commission on the Status of Women published a report in 1974 that thoroughly and devastatingly documented the low and even declining status of women in India. In the same year, the Progressive Organisation of Women (POW) was formed in Hyderabad; it was composed of students connected with Naxalite student groups, but its members organized on their own without party direction. The POW worked against dowry and male harassment of women and also mobilized slum women in marches against price rises. In Maharashtra the participation of rural women in antifamine agitation in 1971–73 was followed by a strong urban women's antiprice rise movement based on middle-class and working-class housewives mobilized by a coalition of Socialist and Communist women leaders (see Omvedt 1986). From the mid–1970s onward, "there has been the growth of a self-consciously feminist trend, stressing autonomy of organization, asserting itself on cultural as well as economic issues and demanding change in the personal and family life of male activists as well as public organization of women" (ibid., 18). Efforts to link issues of production and reproduction, of economy and social relations, developed "partly from the growth of feminist trends among certain sections of educated women and partly due to the involvement of wider sections of low-caste, tribal working class and rural poor women who made it very clear that economic exploitation, sexual violence and oppression (both within the family and from class enemies) were part of their lives and struggle" (ibid., 19–20).

In Thailand, as in India, the participation explosion of the mid–1970s has its roots in a combination of economic and political tensions.

Growing economic crisis, inflation, and the increasingly evident blows against U.S. imperialism in southeast Asia led to snowballing mass demonstrations in 1973, which brought down the government and inaugurated a new democratic period. As one foreign observer recalled: "there were marches, demonstrations, protests, something happening all the time. . . . " Women's participation was (apparently) active on all these fronts, but little remarked upon, for no specific women's issues were raised. Women's student groups were formed in every university, but were mainly part of the general movement (Omvedt 1986, 46).

Women were militant participants in peasants' and workers' agitations (and were among those killed by the police), but leadership remained in the hands of men. Nor were social scientists analyzing these movements of protest and resistance capable of identifying the specific role of women in these movements; as Omvedt (ibid., 47) notes, "For the middle class intellectuals (including social scientists), peasant men continued to be peasants and peasant women were simply women or wives." She cites Morell and Chai-anan (1981) in this regard, but one could also point to more recent work, including the otherwise excellent collection on *History and Peasant Consciousness in Southeast Asia* (Turton and Tanabe 1984), which fails to consider the role of women in protest and resistance and in the construction of peasant consciousness, despite Turton's explicit concern "to articulate and give priority to the suppressed discourse of the rural poor in Thailand—a discourse on livelihood, social power, and dignity—and to identify and assess some of the constraints within which that struggle has to struggle to be heard" (Turton and Tanabe 1984, 23).

The military coup of 1976 undoubtedly inhibited any further overt development of the new movements of the oppressed, including those of women. But significant new activity on women's issues and organizing of women began to develop in the 1980s. Besides government and nongovernment sponsored initiatives for women, there began to emerge new women's groups and organizations. Friends of Women, founded in 1980, is the most active of the new women's groups. Largely middle class in membership, it takes a cautiously feminist stance and links itself to broader movements for social change; it has experimented with a women's cafe and takes part in providing legal aid for working-class women and in some cases of forced prostitution.

The emerging women's movement links economic issues to issues of sexual oppression, and Omvedt (1986) reports on the formation of special organizations dealing with the problem of prostitution. As Catherine Hill (chapter 8, this volume) describes it, prostitution is part of the international sex tourism industry and is a major issue in Thailand, with some 500,000 to 700,000 women reportedly working as prostitutes in 1980 (see also CGRS 1981; Phongpaichit 1980; Thitsa 1980). The organizations range from the Thailand Night Girls' Right Guard (formed in 1984 as a phone-in center for service girls and supported by a Thammasat University women's group) to the Women's Information Center (established to provide information to women traveling abroad in search of work in prostitution). Sexual exploitation and oppression provides a major focus for women's groups and organized protest (Hantrakul 1983; Sereewat 1985). Omvedt (1986, 49) reports how, during the first half of the 1980s, "public meetings and, occasionally, protests (over sex tours, over the use of Depo-Provera and other injectable contraceptives) were held; and participants at university meetings on the issue of prostitution were reportedly struck by the outspokenness and articulateness of the massage parlour representatives invited to speak."

During the early 1980s, women also protested at the tradition of excluding women from the Buddhist *bhikku* order, of particular significance in a society where women may be mother or mistress but never a monk (see Keyes 1984). Turton (1984, 47) observes that "it is widely the case in Thai society that participation in discourse of any kind is restricted according to age, gender, social rank and status"; he adds that "in village meetings women tend to form distinct groups, and to speak up less." He suggests, however, that "increasingly it is the poor, regardless of age or sex, who have no voice . . . when a young peasant goes to town, and is told he/she is an unskilled worker, and probably an unemployable one at that, or when an armed district officer insinuates he/she is a communist for complaining about it, the discourse is felt as a material force indeed, below the belt" (ibid., 48).

The use of violence against those who protest against exploitation and oppression has been common over the last decade, and Turton draws attention to the existence or perception of a new climate of fear. He suggests that "it is arguable that the scale of violence of a political and class nature has increased in the past decade or so" (Turton 1984, 59). Nevertheless, he believes that "what also emerges is that in new material conditions, and in the processes of emergence of a range of debates and critiques of actually existing Thai democracy—for so it is called—some of the bases for a new 'popular' counter hegemony are discernible. One might say that the 'popular' movement is ahead of any specifically class movement" (ibid., 67).

Bread Riots

The most dramatic form of collective popular protest against austerity measures are those street demonstrations that all too often turn into violent confrontations with the forces of law and order and are usually referred to by the authorities as "riots." The central concern of the demonstrators with the cost of living and with the rising price of basic goods, such as bread, led to these demonstrations being referred to as "bread riots." In some cases, reference to the role of the IMF and other foreign agencies in the austerity programs was explicit in written or shouted slogans, hence, the use of the phrase *IMF riots* in some of the literature and in the media. Some organized strikes turned into demonstrations and even riots, and in other cases, what started out as more or less spontaneous demonstrations evolved into more organized and sustained forms of protest, such as marches and strikes and even political movements to overthrow the government. Although these most overt and dramatic forms of struggle appear to burst out in a more or less spontaneous fashion in response to some trigger event, they are embedded in less obvious and more pervasive forms of struggle. In a real sense, they are the tip of an iceberg that all too often remains invisible.

In modern times, certain forms of organized collective protest such as strikes have become more common in advanced capitalist countries, while street protests over rising prices are rare. In Africa, the Middle East, Asia, and Latin America, however, popular protests remain common, particularly in this period of transition, which is associated with deteriorating living standards and a sense of injustice on the part of those adversely affected and has generated outrage and resentment (see Walton 1989, 317–318). The wave of bread riots that characterized urban protest during the period 1975–86 and that continues in some parts of the Third World resembles the wave of urban protest that broke out in Europe in the late eighteenth and early nineteenth centuries in response to significant economic and social change associated with the widespread perception of industrial capitalist development as a threat to "the moral economy of the English crowd" (see Thompson 1971). Few commentators explicitly recognize the parallels between the late eighteenth-century period of transition and that of the 1970s and 1980s. Of the many historians of riots and other forms of direct action in Europe, only Bohstedt (1983, 98) suggests, in his discussion of women's role in protest movements in eighteenth-century England, a comparison with "riots over government bread policies in Egypt, Poland, East Germany, the Sudan and elsewhere in more recent times"; but he fails to develop the suggestion. This is clearly a subject for future research.

Contemporary austerity protests may have begun in Peru in 1976, although Egypt witnessed the first bread riot directly linked to austerity measures in January 1977. In an attempt at review and synthesis, Walton (1987) examined the rising tide of protest across the Third World through the late 1970s into the first half of the 1980s. His study of twenty-two instances of popular protest against austerity measures—ranging from Latin and Central America, through Africa and the Middle East, to include Poland in 1980–81—takes the historical evidence up to 1986. Analysis of these cases reveals that such unrest was most frequent in the more heavily indebted Latin and Central American countries, with several in north and sub-Saharan Africa, and one country in Europe, the Middle East, and southeast Asia, respectively. The protests were predominantly but not exclusively urban affairs. The classical bread riot launched about one-third of the actions, but in countries with strong traditions of trade unionism, such as those of Latin America, general strikes rallied various disaffected social classes together. In almost all cases, the riots generated significant political changes; in some (for example, Sudan), the protests led to a change of regime or at least a major shift in government policy. Since Walton's review, there have been numerous further instances of popular protest against austerity and adjustment in Latin America, Asia, the Middle East, and Africa.

The Invisibility of Women in the Crowd

Examination of the social base of these instances of popular protest reveals the central involvement of the working class and particularly the urban poor who are most seriously and adversely affected by rising costs of living and growing unemployment. Other social categories, notably students, are also frequently involved. According to Walton (1987, 20), "Workers and the urban poor contribute the largest number of participants, but public employees, students, churches, unions, and small businesses are frequently represented and sometimes the vanguard." Walton's discussion is silent on the gender composition of the crowds that launched and sustained these movements of popular protest.

Women are invisible in most descriptions of bread riots, although frequent reference is made to the social composition of the crowd. Little mention is made of women, even though it is known that in many cases they participated actively in support of street demonstrations (see Clement 1986; Nelson 1985; Seddon 1990; Walton 1987). There is nothing new in this invisibility of women, but it is in striking contrast with the importance generally assigned by historians over the last thirty years to women's involvement in riots in eighteenth- and nineteenth-century Europe.

It may be that those who have considered the phenomenon of popular protest in the contemporary period, even those writing in the 1970s and 1980s about popular responses to austerity and adjustment, have neglected women's participation in these forms of struggle because they hold preconceived ideas about the docility of women in the Third World.[2] Surely the rapidly growing literature on women's struggles and women's movements in Africa, Asia, and Latin America challenges such preconceptions. Yet, with a few notable exceptions, women have remained virtually invisible in most contemporary accounts, and the number of such accounts remains relatively small considering the enormous political significance of this international wave of popular struggle.

Women in Bread Riots in the Middle East

Even in the Middle East, where women might be expected to avoid involvement in public demonstrations and street protest, there is evidence of their active presence, but reference to their participation is rare and analysis of their role still rarer. One of the earliest instances of organized protest took place in Egypt in 1977. Subsequent broadly similar protest movements can be identified in Iran (1979), Turkey (1970), Tunisia (1978, 1984), Morocco (1978, 1979, 1981, 1984, 1990), Sudan (1979, 1985), Algeria (1988), and Jordan (1989).

The political protest movement that led to the overthrow of the Shah's regime and culminated in the Iranian Revolution was perhaps the most dramatic in the region. In her analysis of popular political movements in Iran, de Groot (1989) points out that women were actively involved in the demonstrations against the Shah as well as in less overt forms of political activity. She observes that "the protest which challenged the Shah's regime . . . drew on the experience of an urban population pressured by underemployment, inflation, state interference and the complex tensions between the *bazaar* economy, other internal economic forces and Iran's ties . . . to the international economy" (ibid., 219). She argues that "the hardships of life in the 1970s could well be especially sharp to women with their responsibility for household provision and welfare" (ibid., 229). She draws attention to the long history of women's involvement in active politics in Iran, referring to the fact that even at the beginning of the century, "the popular politics of the constitutional movement also had its women participants. They appeared on the streets of Iranian towns to give loyal backing to particular *mullahs* under attack, to protest over food supplies and prices, and to lend support to constitutionalists in the *majles* (national assembly) facing royal and foreign pressures" (ibid.). Abrahamian (1968, 198–199) also refers to the involvement of women in bread riots during the constitutional revolution and the far-reaching political consequences:

A peaceful procession of women presenting a petition to the president of the municipality asking for cheaper bread, turned into a riot when they were given "an obscene answer." They chased him through the streets and eventually killed him, sacked the government offices, and opened the city prison. By the time the governor ordered the troops to fire, the bread riot had turned into a political movement led by the reactionary clergy.

In Turkey, the growing economic crisis of the late 1970s precipitated a political crisis in which open violence between contending political movements and factions grew more common, until martial law was declared, and in September 1980, a military coup brought a decade of parliamentary politics to an end. In the general strike and demonstrations of 1970, women had been actively involved in street demonstrations and protests. When in Istanbul more than 100,000 workers and unemployed went out onto the streets, many were women, and when clashes with the security forces led to the deaths of several demonstrators, women were active in the reprisals that followed. Guzel (1989, 173) refers to the lynching of a policeman by a group of women demonstrators. Women were actively involved also in the struggles that took place over government policies of austerity and adjustment in the late 1970s, and many were arrested and jailed for their role in popular protest.

In Tunisia, when a wave of demonstrations broke out across the country in January 1984, in response to price increases in basic commodities, women in the southern towns where the demonstrations originated were reported to have supported the demonstrators by shouting and screaming from their houses. In one small southern town, Al-Mabrouka, women factory workers, the majority of them young, marched from the textile factory to Al-Mabrouka chanting slogans against the decision to double the price of bread. They were joined by men as they passed a cafe near the first poor neighborhood and then by students as they marched to the high school. Subsequently they were joined by a few neighborhood people and eventually men, women, and children stormed the police station, as well as the delegation headquarters of the local Destour party, the town hall, and the local headquarters of the National Guard. During these demonstrations, the security forces fired at the crowd and several people were killed. Many others, including women, were injured (see Zghal 1989). The demonstrations spread throughout the country and took a particularly dramatic turn in Tunis; "when police tried to intervene, thousands of demonstrators gave battle. Barricades went up everywhere. Again and again, troops opened fire on the crowds with automatic weapons. Tanks and armoured personnel carriers rumbled through the streets, often firing on anything that moved. Many protesters were killed and many more wounded, including women and children" (Paul 1984, 4).

In the case of Morocco, evidence shows that many of the protestors in the bread riots of 1984 were women. Clement (1985) refers, in passing, to women students in his analysis of the judicial proceedings involving demonstrators after the events; unfortunately, his discussion fails to examine the social composition of those brought to trial. Elsewhere he refers to the involvement of high school girls in the demonstrations, with a small number on the street and others on strike or shouting in support from their schools (Clement 1986). In Fes, lawyers' wives, and in Rabat, a woman doctor, were arrested for their part in the demonstrations; in the northeast women supported the demonstrations with shouting and crying, and some even joined their menfolk in the streets (Seddon 1990, 249). In Tetouan, women supported the demonstrations with shouting and screaming, women were shot, and one woman was reported to have called for the replacement of King Hassan by a president as in Algeria (Clement 1986, 38). On the other hand, once the demonstrations had been brought under control and dispersed, women, even in the shantytowns from which most demonstrators came, offered tea and cakes to the army and spoke of their fear of reprisals and repression (ibid., 40).

In Sudan, where bread riots during late March 1985 evolved into mass protest and political opposition to the Numeiry regime, which led to a military coup in April and the overthrow of the government, women were actively involved in street demonstrations, protesting rising prices and austerity measures. Despite very real fears of heavy state repression, and despite the strength of patriarchal-religious ideology that stresses a woman's place in the home, over the weekend of March 30–31, "in Omdurman town, a part of greater Khartoum, hundreds of women took to the streets in a large demonstration to protest against rising prices; reports indicate that many were shouting down with the IMF" (Seddon 1989, 122).

Popular Protest and Women's Movements

In many instances, popular protest is demonstrably not simply a more or less spontaneous response to particular trigger events, but constitutes part of a rising tide of organized resistance and protest, associated with the emergence of new social movements. A consideration of the relationship between women's involvement in forms of collective action, such as riots or demonstrations, and their involvement in emerging women's associations and groups, as well as in more conventional political movements, would be particularly relevant to our understanding of these movements. The class basis of popular protest and that of the organized women's movement in different countries at different times requires further examination. It should, however, be recognized that, as Pickvance (1989, 73) remarks, "the existence of events (such as riots or demonstrations) does not *imply* the existence of a movement. . . . Nor does the simultaneous occurrence of riots throughout a country imply a national organisation. The presence of organisations behind collective actions is a matter of empirical investigation."

This chapter cannot begin to review the rise of organized women's movements throughout the Third World during the last decade. Some see women's movements as involving an "exponential increase in the number and types of women's groups in every country of the world, and the complex of networks and organisations which unite them" (Tinker and Jaquette 1987, 426). A review of women's movements would undoubtedly contribute to an appreciation of their significance and provide the basis for a better understanding of the relationship between those dramatic forms of popular protest that are so often referred to as "outbreaks" and those less immediately visible forms that are part of sustained and organized movements—between protest movements and more systematic resistance and organized movements for progressive social and political transformation. Such a task remains to be undertaken.

Empowerment Strategies of Poor Urban Women Under the Chilean Dictatorship

Joseph L. Scarpaci

Informal networks of reciprocity have long helped the poor survive in urban Latin America (Lomnitz 1978). A special dimension of household survival surfaced during the recent rash of military dictatorships, particularly in the Southern Cone. These military regimes, with their austere domestic programs and their need to search out and destroy shantytown organizations considered a threat to state security, made such organizations even more vital to local residents. The activities of shantytown organizations ended abruptly after the military coups d'etat in Argentina (1976), Uruguay (1973), and Chile (1973) (Ramos 1985; Ebole, Mitjavila, and Alonso, 1986; Hardy 1987). By 1990 civilian rule had returned to all three countries.

With few exceptions, the military state provided inadequate human services and terrorized the poor and disenfranchised. We are gaining much new information about how informal networks fill the gap in human services delivery and offer protection against state terror (Pion-Berlin 1989; Zwi and Ugalde 1989). More often than not, women form the bases of neighborhood networks. We know, for instance, that the decision making about how scarce household resources are allocated for food, clothing, and health care rests mainly with women (Leacock and Safa 1986; Nash and Safa 1985). Much feminist research on women's organizations is pessimistic, dwelling on the obstacles women face in organizing and creating a political consciousness (Babb 1990, 244). Although women's organizations are now legal and less subject to harassment by the civilian governments currently in power, the state is more concerned with macroeconomic policy matters, such as inflation, balance of payments, and foreign debt,

Partial research for this study was made possible by a grant from the National Science Foundation, SES–87–228464.

than with local, small-scale issues. That policy focus notwithstanding, improving the quality of life through support of grass-roots women's organizations remains an untapped and potentially useful social policy.

This chapter examines two women's organizations in Chile, the last Southern Cone country to restore democratic rule. A brief review of Chilean women's activities in the public sphere and of the political economy of the Pinochet dictatorship (1973–90) precede a description of the empowerment strategies used by these organizations. The next section provides background on the activities of organized Chilean women at the national and local levels. The main body of the chapter studies a sewing collective and communal kitchen (*olla común*) that formed under military rule. The purpose is to show the logic of these two women's organizations and to discuss the empowerment strategies they employ. The phrase *empowerment strategy* is used two ways in this chapter. One way refers to how these women's organizations marshal resources to satisfy immediate material needs—food and cash from the sale of artisan goods. A second meaning refers to how the quality of life can be improved in women's households and how the roles of women might change through their collective actions under democratic rule. This latter aspect of empowerment includes how women preserve group autonomy and remain independent of the local state. At risk is the possible co-optation of these groups by the new (democratic) municipal or national governments who seek political (electoral) support.

Several advantages would accrue to these two organizations if they were to broaden their organizational bases beyond their neighborhoods. Women of the communal kitchen could receive food subsidies from the government. More volunteers and household affiliates for preparing meals and financing the kitchen would generate economies of scale. Women of the sewing cooperative work in literacy campaigns, consciousness-raising groups, and the human rights movement. They have even started a men's group. Literacy outreach is one program that the new local government might wish to elaborate. Possible cooperation between neighborhood and municipality would, from the vantage point of the local state, complement the formal education system and encourage decentralization. The extent to which these empowerment strategies offer a marriage of interest between women volunteers and the newly elected democratic government poses several questions about social policy and planning that are discussed in the final section of this chapter.

CHILEAN WOMEN IN THE PUBLIC SPHERE

Chilean women's organizations reached national attention in 1913 when they organized to protest their working conditions in the nitrate and copper mines of the Atacama Desert. Beginning in the 1920s and 1930s, health care benefits and work laws have afforded Chilean women who work outside the home in formal sector jobs with relatively generous medical care and maternity benefits (Covarrubias and Franco 1978; Scarpaci 1987). Suffrage activities mounted in

Figure 2.1
Street Pamphlet from a Women's Protest, Tuesday, 12 July 1984

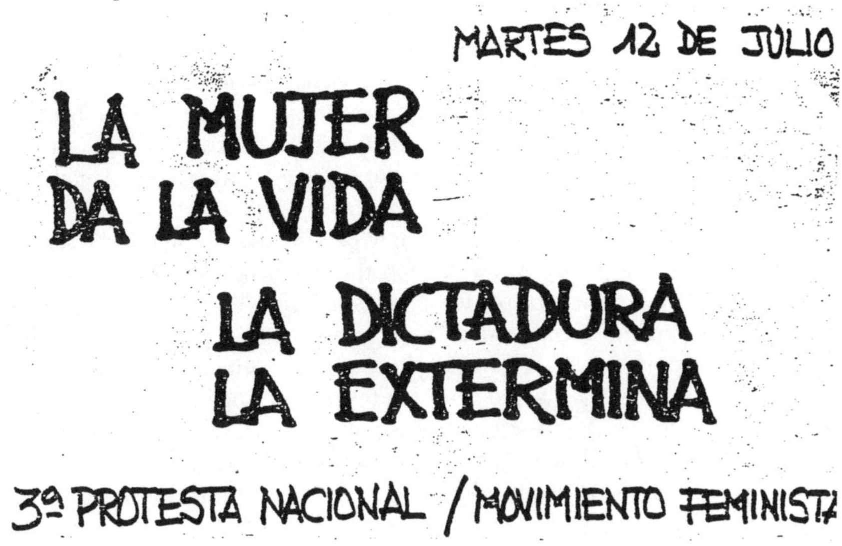

MARTES 12 DE JULIO

LA MUJER
DA LA VIDA

LA DICTADURA
LA EXTERMINA

3ª PROTESTA NACIONAL / MOVIMIENTO FEMINISTA

the 1930s and 1940s and culminated in the right to vote in 1949, a relatively late date within Latin America.[1]

As an electoral group, women's organizations have determined the fate of presidential administrations. For example, thousands of women demonstrated in the streets of Santiago and hurt the credibility of the socialist government of President Salvador Allende Goosens (Sigmund 1977). The famous women's pot and pan march in 1973 in the final months of Allende's tenure underscored women's important role in weakening his government. Kirkwood (1983) argues that women realized during the United party years that their efforts to reverse the oppression of poverty and social injustice should start with the elimination of oppression against women. Between 1983 and 1988, Chilean women held several national protests that facilitated the departure of General Augusto Pinochet from the presidential palace (see Figure 2.1).

Chilean women have also been active in local organizations. This activity stems, in part, from the larger political context noted above. It also derives from the popular mobilization that began with the administration of Eduardo Frei and continued under Allende. These administrations cultivated women's organizations in the fields of housing, agrarian reform, health care, literacy, day care, and many others (Castells 1983). Between 1973 and 1990, the Pinochet dictatorship sought to promote the traditional duties of women: obedience, allegiance to the homeland (*patria*), the family and motherhood, and a stridently apolitical view of the world. The economic crisis brought on by the regime's free-market policies created new survival strategies, called popular economic organizations (*organizaciones populares económicas*). For example, in 1982 there were 34 *ollas comunes* and by 1985 there were 232 (Hardy 1987).

Despite the many national and local women's organizations in Chile, it would be incorrect to characterize all Chilean women as politically and socially active. Participation varies by class and place of residence. Within the shantytowns (*poblaciones*) of Chile, for example, Campero (1985) estimates that perhaps 10 to 15 percent of the adult population participates in some sort of local organization. He portrays the typical shantytown dweller (*poblador*) as holding moderate political views and as conservative regarding family matters.

Razcynski and Serrano (1985) also portray poor Santiago women as reserved. Whether *pobladoras* (shantytown women) participate in activities outside of their homes depends on spouse or partner approval. Valdes's (1988, 145) in-depth study of poor women in southeastern Santiago found that "few [women] participated in some type of social organization. . . . The principal obstacle is the husband who reserves the right to permit or to prohibit whether women go out." Socially active women are subject to gossip and rumors circulated by women neighbors. "Fear of comments based on neighbors finding out about one's problems pressures [women] not to participate. . . . Organizations must be of vital importance for women to participate in them" (ibid., my translation).

Summing up, Chilean women are relatively active in the public sphere as compared to their Latin American sisters, although enfranchisement was awarded fairly late. The country's attempted transition to socialism in the 1960s and 1970s provided women with a wide array of outlets for both national and local participation in social organizations. Military rule severed this activism during the first decade, but the political opening (*apertura*) of 1983 rekindled interest in women's participation in social organizations. Although the majority of poor women in Santiago are not participants in groups outside the home, this should not be interpreted as apathy. Rather, competing demands intervene because of their multifaceted roles as mothers, sisters, spouses, partners, daughters, homemakers, and workers.

THE POLITICAL ECONOMY OF THE CHILEAN DICTATORSHIP

Chile began a unique social and political experiment during the governments of Frei (1964–70) and Allende (1971–73). Competition for the 1964 presidency brought Marxists and Christian Democrats into caustic debates about the role of the state. Both groups challenged the assumptions of liberal capitalist democracy. Perhaps the only point of consensus was that the state had a constructive role to play as an allocator of resources and a corrector of market imperfections. The Marxist-controlled *Frente de Acción Popular* (FRAP) proposed the creation of a socialist society.

Though the Christian Democrats agreed that Chile required fundamental structural change, they argued that this was best achieved through peaceful, institutional means. As an alternative to socialism and the dangers of capitalism, the Christian Democrats offered a communitarian society based on the writings of the French philosopher, Jacques Maritain. This philosophy, coupled with Catholic social doctrine, expanded state welfare and ownership of industries and services in the 1960s (Loveman 1988, 270; Scarpaci 1990). A well-developed infrastructure of neighborhood organizations of all types flourished during this period. Allende extended the socialist path of his predecessor, but his experiment was cut short by a military coup d'etat on 11 September 1973.

Between 1973 and 1990 the Chilean military regime restructured the economy in several key ways. It drew upon a political economy envisioned by the neo-classical economics school of Milton Friedman and Frederich von Hayek. Scaling back public services became a hallmark of the regime (Scarpaci 1989). Public investment in human capital projects such as education, health care, and housing were discouraged. In line with International Monetary Fund (IMF) and World Bank policies, the Chilean regime reduced public expenditures by privatizing state companies and by charging more for education and health services. Although the regime did not publicize it, one outcome of reducing the welfare state was freeing up public funds for payment of interest on the national debt. By 1983, Chile was in the dubious position of holding the second highest per capita debt in Latin America.

Significantly, this restructuring and indebtedness did not adversely affect upper income consumers in Chile. Rather, it triggered an unprecedented rise in the importation and consumption of consumer durables. Consumption and decollectivization were encouraged, even celebrated, in Pinochet's unfettered market economy. However, a pattern of increased consumption did not trickle down to the poor. Macroeconomic indicators revealed strong growth because of high levels of borrowing in the late 1970s (Ffrench-Davis 1986). A deep recession in 1981 ended the economic boom and triggered a broad-based challenge of the regime by the popular masses. In 1983 unofficial unemployment figures stood at 35 percent (17 percent officially). The recession lasted until 1986. Presently, Chile has one of the lowest levels of inflation in Latin America. Also, perhaps a third of Santiaguinos work at some time during the year in the informal sector (Hardy 1987; Scholnik and Teitelboim 1988). As we shall see, although women's unpaid work outside the household is undervalued in models of capitalist development, it becomes indispensable in the daily lives of poor urban women.

The regime's emphasis on decollectivization meant breaking up unions, professional associations, and neighborhood organizations that began before 1973. Political parties, vestiges of organized labor, and neighborhood groups took advantage of the apparent "crack" in the economic system in 1983 and forced a political opening. In October 1988, a national plebiscite asked whether Pinochet should continue in power until 1996. Mass mobilization and heated public debate led to his defeat at the polls. A year later a former Christian

Democratic Senator, Patricio Aylwin, won 55 percent of the presidential vote. His sixteen-party coalition and antiregime stance helped him take office in March 1990.

CASE STUDY ONE: EXCHANGE AND RECIPROCITY IN A WOMEN'S SEWING COOPERATIVE

This study of a women's cooperative is based on field research in 1987 and 1989. In the former year, I participated in a human-rights fact-finding mission with a team of three lawyers (Laureda et al. 1988). Our charge was to report on the activities and concerns of nongovernmental organizations (NGOs) in the area of human rights. I was introduced to a women's organization that, ostensibly, sewed *arpilleras* (tapestries and appliqués) to offset the judicial costs of filing appeals before the Ministry of Interior. These women initially organized because a husband, brother, or father was missing or detained by the state security forces. It quickly became apparent that the rights of women were tied to human rights and that the fight against the dictatorship mirrored the struggle against patriarchy in the home. Like many other urban social movements in Chile under military rule, activism in one sector frequently carried over into participation in other organizations (Frühling 1989).

The sewing collective is located in the shantytown (*población*) of Lo Hermida, in the municipality of Peñalolen in southeastern metropolitan Santiago. Lo Hermida is a poor neighborhood at the urban fringe, abutting the foothills of the Andes. Most of the homes are self-built, yet many have been upgraded over the years by the owners. Core blocks of the shantytown were settled after a land invasion in the 1960s. The built environment varies between what Griffin and Ford (1980) call "peripheral squatter settlements" and "zones of maturity" (older and upgraded squatter areas and low-income housing stock), though the bulk of the homes would be classified in the latter. Most homes are one-story wooden plank and plywood structures with zinc roofs. Over the years, the municipality has extended public lighting, sewers, and utility poles throughout most of the *población*. A small portion of the community is not connected with public infrastructure as evidenced by illegal tappings of electricity from utility poles and by outhouses in backyards.

After several conversations with a few of the women about their activities in the human rights movement, we spoke about a wider range of events and video-recorded unstructured interviews.[2] Conversations with the women in this co-operative explored the military dictatorship, the women's movement, female illiteracy, and other topics. Their testimonies show that the struggles of the women in this *población* are different from those of wealthier women in Santiago or in North America. Their collective actions are a response to the forces of patriarchy, machismo, and economic survival.

History of the Collective

In November 1986, a group of women met to discuss some common problems. Each had a husband or partner who had been detained, tortured, exiled, or sent to a concentration camp. As an act of solidarity toward women in Lo Hermida who were alone raising children, a few women decided to form a women's collective. Their goal was to monitor some of the changing needs of these women and their households. Preliminary meetings and discussions among women of the cooperative identified common forces that had repressed them. The women sponsored workshops to examine a variety of themes such as sexuality, women's health and hygiene, substance abuse, and human rights. They also sewed *arpilleras* while they met and talked. Funds from the sale of the *arpilleras* are used to defray the legal costs of filing petitions with the Ministry of the Interior in cases concerning detained and missing loved ones.

The primary objective of each workshop was not the community or group; instead, workshops encouraged the personal development of each participant. A secondary objective was tied to the collective's belief that Chile "should have new leaders" to sustain the changes (redemocratization) that were coming. The collective wished to explore these questions from a women's perspective. In the words of Negra, a founding member of the collective, mother of four, and spouse of a tortured husband who was left disabled, "We wanted something that would really be a part of our lives."

The interests of the twenty-two women in the cooperative emerged at a time of considerable social and political oppression in Chile. To many residents of the community, these women were a "danger" because they wanted to build a house and tried to organize. To be sure, these behaviors are uncommon among poor women in Chile. To state security forces, they were a threat because many women belonged to human rights organizations and leftist political parties. Despite these antagonistic views, the completion of a meeting house (*Casa de Mujeres*) was a tangible statement that their organizational efforts were taking root in the community.

Collective Activities

Three general activities characterize the bulk of the collective's activities: female literacy campaigns, sewing *arpilleras*, and women's issues and encounter groups. The women's testimonies enable us to understand the collective better.[3]

Literacy. Much effort is directed toward eliminating illiteracy among the women of Lo Hermida shantytown. Volunteers use the methods of Brazilian scholar and educator, Paolo Freire, which emphasize community-based instruction that depends less on traditional classroom instruction typical of public education. Networks of instructors who teach reading and writing to adults have developed throughout Chile. So well received was the literacy campaign that Magdalena, head of literacy programs in the sewing collective, traveled to a meeting of educators in Southern Chile in October 1987. Yet the obstacles she has encountered within Lo Hermida and elsewhere are formidable. Magdalena explains: "There is a myth that the *poblador* is ignorant. . . . The woman is the most important part of the literacy campaign. . . . Some of the professional teachers are very well trained and that's fine, but we [*pobladoras*] need to get involved as well. . . . So we have a representative from the *población*, and that's me, that's what I do here." One of the outreach activities of the collective is to publish an occasional newsletter called *Las Brujitas* (The Little Witches). It includes articles about women's health and hygiene, reproductive issues, community activities, and political and social commentaries.

Sewing. The women of this and other collectives are publicly known for making the *arpilleras*. They meet regularly in a sewing workshop and use scraps of old clothing and cloth to create *arpilleras*. These works of art depict scenes of women doing laundry together, women working in jobs programs, and protests of human rights violations (see Agosin 1988). Each woman sells two *arpilleras* monthly to the Roman Catholic Vicarate. The church then sells them to tourists and foreign retailers. Revenues earned by the women in the cooperative are used mainly for the costs of building and maintaining the house. Unused funds are spent on travel by the literacy instructors.

Arpillera workshops are more than just a place for sewing and exchanging materials. Teresita, the coordinator for sewing supplies and *arpillera* sales, says that the workshop is "a place where women can find out about themselves." It serves as a women's forum. Teresita explains: "I was one of those women who was 'enclosed,' you might say, but I decided to come to the workshop and break out into the world. The only way we women can really get ahead is to learn how to be independent, whether it be in our work, newsletters, or artistry."

Women's Issues and Encounter Groups. Women throughout South America organized to fight economic and political pressure in the 1980s. The Mothers of the Plaza de Mayo in Argentina, women who rallied behind the "glass of milk" efforts in Peru, mothers' clubs in Brazil, and the hundreds of popular economic organizations in Chile represented women's resistance against an oppressive environment. Women's organizations fostered group discussions which, in Chilean sociologist Claudia Serrano's (1989, 4) words, "became as or more important than the material benefit that characterized the organization. Self-esteem, self-expression, the discovery of the ability to contribute [something worthwhile to the group] . . . sexuality, were themes explicitly developed, sought, and evaluated by the workshops and [women's] groups."

The issues of gender and exploitation are perhaps the most unifying themes of the Lo Hermida sewing collective. Encounter groups explore ways that emancipate women and their families in some fashion from the injustices of sexism. Beatriz explains her reasons for coming to the collective and examining these issues:

It was tough dealing with my husband because he is really a "super macho." When I began participating in the women's collective I realized that I was a woman and that I am capable of learning, developing as a woman. You know that just because I wash dishes at home and feed my kids and all, doesn't mean that's all I can do. I realized that my role as a woman means that I have to share and work for things that I think are just.

This realization conflicts with the traditional role she had accepted and that her husband demanded in the home. Beatriz adds:

When I began working I realized that I contribute to my household. I contribute eco-nomically and therefore I don't find it fair that my husband should get upset because I participate in this [cooperative] and that he tells me that I should do the wash and other things. I get upset, damn it, because I don't think only women should do these household chores.

At this point, we see the risks noted earlier by Valdes (1988): participation in activities outside the home carries great costs. Pressures from within the home and the community work against women's collective actions. Beatriz goes on to explain:

But I'll tell you, it has been a real war. But now [my husband and I] are getting along well because I began to protest and object to his attitude. I was really getting tired [of his attitude] because I wasn't the only one who brought this child into the world. Learning all of these things has been very valuable and rewarding as a woman. I feel really well trained and I now recognize that we [women] have certain rights. I know we are able to do things for ourselves.

The collective also serves women by redefining their roles in social protest and politics. Angelica, a political activist, sees the virtues of the collective beyond the household and the community. With an eye toward the legitimate removal of the dictatorship in 1987 [three years before Pinochet's departure], Angelica's testimony underscores the oppression of military rule.

I think the collective is also a means to allow us to confront the life we live. It isn't only an organization for women: we deal with the *barricadas* [construction of barricades in street protests against the dictatorship]. And what we have learned is also how to defend this country and to change things, change this system. . . . This organization is important.

Angelica recognizes the role of women as educators and catalysts of change within the household. Her analysis goes to the heart of empowerment strategies that alter the traditional role of women in the home and community.

We can teach our children how to differentiate between one thing and the other and [therefore] it is important that women are in the middle of this struggle. It doesn't matter that men come down hard on us. It doesn't matter. We don't want to yank the man out of his role; we want men to be our companions, our equals. We want them to understand the daily lives of women, and we are going to work with him. Men have a lot of things to learn. Men are all wrapped up in themselves. This women's organization is forming a men's group and the men are working on seeing their own problems as men, not just as job-related problems.

So, I think it is important that men are learning and growing as people so they can express their feelings. That's really essential because we're all human beings with feelings and we have to show them.

To that end, the sewing collective in Lo Hermida began a men's group in 1987 to sensitize the other sex about household responsibility and changing gender roles. The men's group serves two key functions for the women's sewing collective. First, it suggests that the women are not antimale, which could, in the long run, compromise future relations with the community and local state. Second, the men's group of the Lo Hermida collective legitimizes some of their activities. Yudelman's evaluation of women's development organizations in the Caribbean and Latin America is insightful: "In several cases they have integrated men into their organizations and programs far more successfully than women have been integrated into many male-run institutions" (1987, 112). Thus the sewing collective demonstrates that their agenda is not sex-selective.

In brief, then, the women's sewing collective has broadened its activities since its inception in 1983. Original concerns about human rights violations and the status of disappeared men in their families still remain. Yet their activities in the sewing workshop, literacy campaign, and women's encounter groups have widened the scope of the collective. No single empowerment strategy exists. Rather, their feminist struggle employs several methods to cope with poverty, oppression, and sexism.

CASE STUDY TWO: A COMMUNAL KITCHEN

Olla comunes (communal kitchens) are private voluntary organizations of women who pool their resources to prepare meals. Though survey data on their prevalence in Santiago are scarce, Hardy and Razeto (1984) estimated that thirty-four communal kitchens existed in 1982 and that by 1984 there were forty-one. By buying in bulk, they feed themselves and their households for less than the cost of preparing individual meals in their own kitchens. This form of reciprocity and self-help activity is common throughout Latin America (Leacock 1979) and offers women and their families an empowerment strategy.

I observed one *olla común* in the municipality of La Florida in southeastern Santiago. About twenty hours of interviews and observations were gathered over four separate visits. My aim was to understand the operations of the communal kitchen, the role the kitchen played in the lives of the women workers, and to consider its continuance under the future democratic government. I prepared no structured survey. I introduced myself as a professor who hoped to learn from their organization.

The *olla común* is located at the extreme end of the Nuevo Amanecer *población* in the backyard of Señora Ana's house. Situated at the urban fringe, adjacent to pastures and vineyards, it is an older community than Lo Hermida, just five kilometers from the sewing cooperative. Originally built in the 1950s, the community has a sturdier housing stock than Lo Hermida. Squatter settlements in Nuevo Amanecer began in the late 1960s and early 1970s. The *población* is well connected with public transportation and more retail stores operate throughout Nuevo Amanecer than in Lo Hermida.

Señora Ana has one of the largest lots on the block and she heads her household where she lives with her four children. The oldest daughter was eighteen years old and had a fourteen-month-old son. The young mother and son had a separate room in the four-room house. Ovens and the food preparation for the *olla común* area are located in the backyard next to several chicken coops with assorted fowl; these animals are for her family's consumption and are not used by the *olla común*. Adjacent to the ovens is a storage shed that houses four large, institutional-sized cooking pots. Sacks of flour, oil, sugar, ladles, and thick wooden paddles for stirring are stored in the shed. The new storage shed is a source of pride for the women and is a marked improvement over the original shed, which was burglarized in 1985. No break-ins have occurred since the new shed was built.

In the winter of 1989 (June and July) the *olla común* prepared and served 130 meals daily for about thirty families. Like many shantytown organizations, the meals program began in the early 1980s during the severe economic crisis brought on by the neoconservative experiment of the dictatorship which, indirectly, was condoned by the IMF. Lunches are served Monday through Friday and are the only meals prepared by the kitchen. The cost of food and fuel for preparing twelve days of meals per month was covered by a donation from the Roman Catholic Archdiocese of Santiago (*Vicaría de la Solidaridad*). Users finance meals for the remainder of the month at a cost of about U.S. $0.60 daily per household. At its peak level of operation in 1986, the kitchen provided up to 420 lunches for about eighty-five households. Participation has declined since then because slum eradication projects have moved many *pobladores* to high-rise public housing in the southernmost edge of the metropolis. Relocation has disrupted local social networks and increased travel time and costs to jobs in the city center (Scarpaci, Gaete, and Infante 1988).

Eight women regularly work in the kitchen in exchange for free lunches for themselves and members of their households. Retaining a steady group of volunteers is a problem for the *olla común*. Women are often unable to come because of illnesses in the family, remunerative work outside the home, or visits to the public health clinic. Two of the eight women regularly bring their children with them. Caring for infant children while working at the kitchen is difficult. There are not enough childcare staff nor is there any reduction in domestic and childcare activities to offset work outside the home. Thus they carry the dual burden of labor (see also Brydon and Chant 1989, 153; Anker and Hein 1986). *Olla común* workers are concerned about the impact of inclement weather on children's health because the work area is outdoors. The Mediterranean climate of Santiago brings cold temperatures and rain during the winter. Only a thin zinc roof covers the work area around the storage shed and the wood-burning oven.

A typical work day at the kitchen begins at 9 A.M. after the women have prepared breakfast and completed their chores. Volunteers gather at Señora Ana's house to prepare the oven. Some kindling and firewood is gathered from nearby wooded lots, pastures, and vineyards, or else it is scavenged from garbage sites. Although this keeps operating costs down, most firewood is purchased from independent vendors who live in the neighborhood. Bread dough goes into the oven about ninety minutes after the fire is lit and the women have lined the floor of the earthen oven with a bed of coals. By 11:00 A.M. they have set large cooking pots used for preparing the main dishes on the grills.

Usually with a child or two astride on their hips or tagging along, women start to queue up for lunch at 1:00 P.M. They arrive at Señora Ana's house with buckets, pails, pans, or virtually any sort of plastic container. There are no males over the age of fourteen in the queue. All eight regular workers said that men rarely show up because it is shameful for them (le da vergüenza). Nonetheless, many men who are unemployed or who work in the neighborhood eat food prepared by the women's olla común. Luncheon staples are typically starchy dishes and include rice, pasta, macaroni, or a spaghetti-rice combination. Occasionally, these high-carbohydrate, low-protein dishes are served with a tomato sauce, but this is rare and is considered a special treat. Meat and fish are uncommon unless small amounts are used in soups or stews. Each child from participating households receives a small ration of milk.

The olla común has relatively little contact with outside institutions other than the church. For example, the police have never harassed the women. Publicly, the women claim not to be affiliated with any political party. On one of my visits, a church representative who delivered the monthly subsidy strongly denied affiliation to any political party. Subsequent conversations revealed that the women were sympathetic to several centrist and leftist parties. Volunteers stated that some pobladoras would object to political party support of the olla común. It would, they felt, leave the kitchen vulnerable to "outside manipulation" and "subject to volunteer work for a political party." This contrasted to another perspective told to me by Monica, a twenty-seven-year-old mother of three: "Sure we would be indebted to a political party for support. But many pobladoras are hungry and are willing to trade volunteer work for food."

Our talks often veered to the then upcoming presidential elections—an easy topic of conversation—and revealed what role the women thought the municipal government would play when the transition to civilian rule would resume in April 1990. Some women were optimistic that the municipal government of La Florida would supply them with flour and oil. They hoped that funds would come from the national government or else from sympathetic foreign governments. An older woman remembered food allotments provided under the Alliance for Progress in the 1960s. Three other women under thirty-five years of age had received food supplies during the dictatorship from Canadian, Belgian, and Italian NGOs. Most were optimistic that food supplies to the *olla común* would increase once a civilian government took office. Half said they would continue at the kitchen even if they had enough money to fix their own meals. They reasoned that the program was still a good way to maintain contact with the neighborhood and to share information about other neighborhood projects and organizations.

Although no comparable data are available for all women in the Nuevo Amanecer *población*, it was possible to gather information on other organizations with which the women of this *olla común* were affiliated (see Table 2.1). The most commonly cited neighborhood project was the neighborhood organization (*junta de vecinos*), which has some policy making input in municipal government. Less frequently cited activities were the women's health group, the soccer leagues, and the two evangelical churches in the area. None of the women felt her work was political. This coincides with Walker's (1986) study of another Santiago *olla común*, yet contrasts with the women in the sewing cooperative who viewed their work as political. The distinction between securing food for survival at the *olla común* as self-defined apolitical behavior versus the political activities of women in the sewing cooperative, suggests that the two types of empowerment strategies noted at the beginning of the chapter are present here. On the one hand, the *olla común* empowers women by satisfying immediate material needs. The sewing cooperative, on the other hand, changes women's roles vis-à-vis their Lo Hermida households, Santiago municipal governments, and machista Chilean society. This high level of feminist activity has implications

Table 2.1
**Other Organizational Affiliations of Nuevo Amanecer *Olla Común* Participants
(n = 42)**

Junta de Vecinos (Neighborhood Boards)	28
Grupos de Salud (Health Groups)	18
Soccer Clubs	12
Human Rights Organizations	9
Evangelical and other Christian churches	8
Other	3

Note: Although only about thirty households regularly participated in the daily preparation of lunches, often more than one woman per household would come to collect the meal. These adult women included grandmothers, aunts, sisters, or friends and relatives lodging with a family temporarily until permanent quarters could be secured. This accounts for a sample size greater than thirty and includes women fourteen years of age and older.

for development policy and women's empowerment strategies, which are considered in the balance of the chapter.

SUMMARY AND CONCLUSION

Shantytown residents in Latin America have long employed empowerment strategies to cope with poverty and oppression. Women organize because of their household responsibilities and frequent contact with the local community. During its sixteen-year tenure, the Chilean dictatorship was a catalyst to many women's private voluntary organizations. As Jaquette aptly observes, "Ironically, military authoritarian rule, which intentionally depoliticized men . . . had the unintended consequences of mobilizing marginal and normally apolitical women" (1989, 5).

Women's organizations are rational responses to the heightened economic and political crises under military rule. Salient policy questions remain: To what extent will the civilian government of Patricio Aylwin enlist these women's organizations into a base of political support? Similarly, can poor women's organizations continue providing local services to themselves and their families without being co-opted by the new government?

The two women's organizations reviewed in this chapter have relatively few physical needs that the new government can satisfy. The *olla común* relies on simple staples of flour, cereals, and oil, and the women's sewing collective seeks a market for their handsewn *arpilleras*. A decline in human rights abuses will change the type of *arpilleras* produced. Designs should shift to more community-based scenes of women and children working and playing. In fact, the women's sewing collective will likely require little money from the state. Their house is built and the women's encounter groups can be held without outside funding. Only reading and writing materials for the literacy campaign will be needed. The local government, however, could profit much from the literacy campaigns. Efforts to enlist the reading and writing teachers would complement existing adult literacy programs run by the state.

Thus there is no reason to assume that either women's group will have to seek a more formal relationship with municipal or national governments. Both organizations have considerable autonomy. Each was created to redress social and economic problems at the grass roots. Also, shantytown organizations throughout Santiago realize the advantages of neighborhood mobilization. Many of them pressed the Frei and Allende governments for more housing, schools, and health care. Making demands on local and national governments resulted in increased social services. There are disadvantages, however. The most active volunteers of these neighborhood organizations were the first to be sought out after the bloody coup d'etat that deposed Allende. Few have forgotten the house-to-house searches for community and political party leaders (often the same individuals) and the massive civil and human rights abuses that followed. Perceived as "enemies of the state," these local leaders were rounded up, detained, tortured, murdered, or sent into exile. State terror under military rule was gender blind. Rosa, a regular volunteer at the *olla común* studied above, aptly notes the fear that many women have about joining organizations even today.

There are women who are afraid. This is understandable. They remember very well what happened after the coup [of 11 September 1973]. To be active in a neighborhood organization was dangerous. [Security forces] searched for you and dragged you out of your house at all hours of the day. It was a real witch hunt, I tell you. Even though many women were not active participants, they attended meetings or else were *compañeras*. It didn't matter to DINA [the state security apparatus]; they looked for you anyway. . . . In all these years the dictatorship has treated us like naughty little girls. We've been scolded, even disciplined to a certain extent. Let's see what happens when the government of Mr. Aylwin comes.

To be sure, the Christian Democratic party of Mr. Aylwin and the sixteen-party coalition that brought him to office are steadfastly committed to respecting human rights. Still, Rosa's testimony reveals a very real fear that exists in the minds of at least a few shantytown women: should another coup d'etat result, will a similar witch hunt ensue?

Unlike Rosa's sense of caution, Isabel, a twenty-three-year-old mother of two who was just nine years old when Allende was overthrown, expressed optimism about the transition to democratic rule.

I hope the new municipal government comes and incorporates us [into their activities] a little bit. We do good things. The compañeras in the *población* and the [women's] collective have much to gain. We need to learn how to be women. That the government changes is one thing, but that the real problems [that afflict] women disappear, well, I don't think this will happen. If hooking up with the municipal government means better ties with other women of Lo Hermida [shantytown] or [the municipality of] Peñalolen, I think that is good.

The tension between maintaining strong local identity and benefiting from affiliation with larger organizations is ever present. The two case studies presented are by no means comprehensive. Yet they reveal the problems of local neighborhood organizations, especially women's organizations, that have been present in Chile and in other Latin American countries. Empowerment strategies employed here will likely continue (Scarpaci 1991). However, it is too early to tell to what extent the newly elected government will draw these organizations into its base of support. In the health care sector, for example, the Christian Democratic party circulated a position paper before the 1989 election stating that "community participation was essential in the delivery of primary care" (Concertación 1989, 17). The data reviewed in the *olla común* study show that women were also active in other neighborhood organizations such as health care. Although primary care activities are not particularly expensive programs to fund, the newly elected government must tread a careful line between satisfying the demand for social services, on the one hand, and repaying the foreign debt and keeping the rate of inflation low, on the other hand. This suggests that integrating neighborhood organizations into social delivery programs may be checked by fiscal constraints.

What are the implications of these case studies for international development policy? The need to address the concern of women in international development has been well publicized since the UN Women's Year (1975) and the following Decade for Women (1976–85). With the dictatorship gone, more international aid should be in the pipeline for Chile. NGOs would provide one way to avoid the politicizing of neighborhood women's networks and the attendant problems of co-optation and paternalism. A wide array of NGOs already exists in Santiago. Achurra and Salinas (1989) surveyed seventy-four NGOs in the health care field in greater Santiago. Scores of neighborhood associations operate in the primary care field and receive technical support from a large Italian- and U.S.-supported NGO, and Colectivo de Atención Primaria (Scarpaci 1991). This and other NGOs provide technical support to numerous private voluntary organizations (at the more-organized level) as well as to neighborhood associations (at the less-organized level). Though no firm evidence suggests that NGOs can completely insulate smaller neighborhood associations from manipulation by local elite and international agencies, they do offer small associations autonomy. NGOs in Latin America place fewer demands on their constituents than national and local governments (Smith 1989). To date, the church is the only NGO supporting the communal kitchen and sewing collective described in this chapter. Additional NGO support of these women's organizations would provide more resources and a buffer between the local state and community. Such support would guarantee that these organizations do not atrophy.

To what extent have the empowerment strategies noted at the outset of this chapter been achieved, and how might they change if conjoined with a democratic government? The food kitchen is satisfying some of the nutritional needs of participating households. Aside from food subsidies, it is unlikely that the role of these volunteers will change. The sewing cooperative will require few material needs from future NGOs or local governments. Significantly, their women's literacy program is a pragmatic and highly visible service in the community. It represents a type of voluntarism that is less stigmatizing than the receipt of free meals. Literacy campaigns require fewer material resources on a permanent basis than the food kitchen. Outreach programs can satisfy the sewing collective's desire to educate women, but the programs will also offer a forum for discussing a wide array of topics.

The experiences of these two organizations augur well for strategic gender projects as opposed to women-centered and family-centered organizations. Advantages of these two women's organizations are that they began without public support and they avoid the family-centered and women-centered perspectives that dominate male-controlled public planning. Family-centered perspectives include welfare projects in which women are the principal recipients of aid to enhance their roles as mothers and wives. Examples are education, hygiene, maternal and child health, and food distribution schemes. These top-down projects enhance pragmatic needs of women yet fail to alter their roles and power relations between the sexes (Buvinić 1984; Molyneux 1984; Moser 1987). Women-centered perspectives develop when government and international agencies regard women as individuals with needs beyond their roles as homemakers and mothers. To their credit, these programs often include antipoverty strategies, which function with the premise that poverty determines the social relations between women and men. Job training, access to credit, and fund raising are examples of these antipoverty projects. Thus, enhancing the material conditions of women, especially women-headed households, allows women to gain some independence economically and to realize potentials beyond those tied to marriage and child rearing. Normally, though, these antipoverty and women-centered projects are limited to cooking, sewing, handicrafts and other traditional, gender-related activities. As such, they fail to change gender stereotypes or alter the balance of gender roles and relations (Moser and Levy 1986).

The two case studies in this chapter are best described as examples of strategic gender activities, which result from "the analyses of women's subordination and the formulation of an alternative, more satisfactory set of arrangements to those that exist" (Molyneux 1986, 284). Put another way, strategic gender projects challenge the sexual division of labor by empowering women to make key decisions about the nature and direction of their organization. For example, the setting of the costs of meals, contracting out for food delivery, and scheduling worker/volunteer shifts are handled exclusively by women in the *olla común*. Women in the sewing cooperative design and sell their *arpilleras* to other women and they financed and built their own meeting house. They have not been constrained by expensive, long-term community projects which, Buvinić (1984) argues, are unlikely to support women's groups that radically alter sexual inequality. Yudelman's (1987, 112) warning about the ingrained cultural attitudes that women's development organizations face throughout the Caribbean and Latin America is particularly germane here.

Any hint that these organizations harbor feminist tendencies raises a red flag and makes it still more difficult to gain government support, raise private-sector funds, or in general establish credibility within the society. It is critical to understand that these women's organizations were spawned by related urban social movements that struggled against the political and economic oppression of the Pinochet dictatorship. Longitudinal studies will allow us to monitor changes in these women's empowerment strategies. Thus far, Chilean women have not been passive bystanders, trapped in urban poverty, and surrounded by a field of changing events. Rather, they have translated their concerns about survival, gender roles, and the household into action. Immediate needs are much more pragmatic: procuring enough food and fostering an intimate forum to discuss personal and household needs. Overtures by the local state will be approached cautiously. The challenge in the 1990s will be to what extent development policy can draw on these and other voluntary organizations without co-opting them. Independent of those outcomes, the empowerment strategies reviewed here will continue to make a difference in the quality of life of the women and their dependents.

3

Women's Work and the Urban Household Economy in Developing Countries

Briavel Holcomb and Tamar Y. Rothenberg

INTRODUCTION

Boserup (1990) defines economic development as the gradual change from family production to specialized production of goods and services. Production is moved from the household to disparate workplaces with new hierarchies of control. Yet while the role of the household in the larger economy changes with development, it is always an integral part of economies from the local to the international scale. It is only with the rise of concern with women in development that there have been serious efforts to place economics and politics at the household level in developing countries into larger contexts of economic development (see, for example, Brydon and Chant 1989; Momsen and Townsend 1987; Dwyer and Bruce 1988; Agarwal 1988).

This chapter sorts through the most common types of household and family arrangements in the Third World, placing them in the context of gender roles, gendered employment opportunities, the local economy and the international economy. We explore how women's work within and without the domestic space changes as household composition and roles within it vary with economic development and urbanization.

GENDER AND ECONOMIC DEVELOPMENT

There are several conflicting theories regarding the impact of economic development on gender inequality (Marshal 1985; Scott 1986; Tiano 1986). The older modernization hypothesis argues that the spread of industrialization and Western technology into the Third World liberates women from the restrictions of a patriarchal family, loosens religious restrictions, and widens the possibilities of employment. Society tends to become more democratic and offer more possibilities of upward mobility. Women's status is improved by greater access to education, contraception, and employment. Modernization theorists assume a reduction in gender inequality accompanied industrialization in the West and will also attend modernization in developing areas.

Critics of this hypothesis point to the withdrawal of women from productive labor during Western industrialization because of the improvement in male earnings (the family wage) and because of the spatial separation of the domestic and productive spheres. Lower rates of employment among women and gender occupational segregation persist. The marginalization or dependency thesis is that development further isolates women from production and political control, reducing their autonomy and increasing their dependence on men (Scott 1986). Thus women's marginalization is a product of the capitalist organization of production and use of labor; it is an irreversible systemic tendency that cannot be remedied by appropriate policies (Scott 1986, 651). In addition to the separation between production and reproduction, basic elements of the process are the hierarchical structure of capitalist enterprises and the mutual accommodation between capitalism and patriarchy, resulting in women's confinement to the home, to inferior jobs, and to the reserve army of labor (Scott 1986).

In a critique of marginalization theory, Scott finds contradictory evidence and concludes that the thesis cannot be proved or disproved. For example, cross-sectional studies of Peru show a high degree of gender segregation and of economic inequality of men and women, but they do not suggest that women were expelled from the labor force or that they constitute a reserve army of labor.

Building on the marginalization thesis, the exploitation thesis posits that women's labor is essential to industrial production in the Third World but that the competition for employment and the scarcity and fluctuation of employment opportunities makes the female labor force docile and powerless. Industrialization facilitates the extraction of surplus capital from female labor and, although it provides jobs for women, ultimately increases women's exploitation.

Socialist feminists and Marxists concerned with the material basis of women's subordination attribute the origins of women's poverty and inequality to their limited access to land, employment, cash, and credit. Women's economic position worldwide is bluntly demonstrated in the 1980 UN statistic that women perform two-thirds of the world's work hours yet receive only 10 percent of its income and own less than 1 percent of the world's property. As Sen and Grown (1987) note, "If the goals of development include improved standards of living, removal of poverty, access to dignified employment, and reduction in societal inequality, then it is quite natural to start with women."

THE TRIPLE ROLE OF WOMEN

In discussions of women's roles and men's roles, it should be remembered that gender roles are societally ascribed and, as such, vary according to place and time. While this variation among gender roles makes generalizations tricky, it also leaves room for optimism in the possibility of change. On the other hand, despite the fluctuations among ascribed gender roles, women are unequivocally the subordinated gender in every society. And although women may not be confined to child rearing and domestica, these roles act as constants to be added on to by productive and other roles.

Moser (1987, 1989) goes beyond the more standard characterization of women's role as dual—reproductive and productive—to describe the triple role of women. Particularly in low-income households, "women's work" consists of reproductive, productive, and community-managing work. "Reproduction" includes biological reproduction (child bearing), physical reproduction (cooking, cleaning, and other activities involved in the daily maintenance of the household), and social reproduction (the maintenance of ideological conditions upholding the social and economic status quo). Consumption is an integral part of reproduction (Brydon and Chant 1989).

Reproductive work, long associated with women's work, has been consistently undervalued by just about everyone, but (for the purposes of this chapter) particularly by economists. Much of the work of the past twenty years on women and labor/development/economics has sought to redress this deficiency and reassess the role of reproductive work in economies of scales ranging from local to international. "If we have understood housework, then we have understood the economy," maintains von Werlhof (in Mies, Bennholdt-Thomsen, and von Werlhof 1988, 168).

Joekes, however, warns against focusing on women's work in the reproductive sphere. Writing for INSTRAW (1987, 20), she argues that "as long as women remain confined to and identified with household work, their economic contribution will remain underrated, their contribution to material progress needlessly limited, and their civic authority undermined by their lack of access to money."

Productive work consists of work that generates income, or more generously and less frequently, work that has an exchange value. While the distinction between production and reproduction tends to be assumed in much of the literature, many feminists find the split problematic. Moser (1989, n.8) notes that it is critical "to acknowledge that reproductive work is also productive, but [that] because of the production of use value under nonwage relations it is not identified as 'productive' work." Focusing on productive work as one of women's roles, however, and distinguishing it from reproductive work, does help to illuminate the often hidden and unrecognized income-earning work that women do.

Community-management work is largely an extension of women's domestic role. It includes mobilizing for and maintaining local facilities—whether infrastructural services such as water and sanitation, or social services such as schools and clinics—and organizing activities such as childcare at a community level. Moser (1989) differentiates women's role as community managers from men's role as community leaders, the former being informal and unpaid, the latter formalized by way of local politics and positions of direct authority, and paid. Distinguishing women's community-managing role from their reproductive role not only makes it easier to see the different arenas of women's work and the time devoted to them, but becomes particularly useful in evaluating development policy. For example, a UNICEF urban basic services program in India provided paid employment for men in official positions but relied on women's voluntary labor in the community to make the program function (Moser 1989, n. 11). A grass-roots women's collective in Chile formed to monitor human rights also taught literacy (see Joseph L. Scarpaci, chapter 2, this volume).

DEFINING THE URBAN HOUSEHOLD

Study of the household economy incorporates all three of women's roles. The household is almost by definition the arena of reproduction. Schmink (1985, 140) focuses on the household's reproductive nature by rephrasing it as "domestic unit." She defines the domestic unit as a group of people who live together and share most aspects of consumption, maintaining and reproducing themselves and their unit by pooling resources (including labor). Momsen and Townsend (1987) take care to point out the danger of treating the household as a *cohesive* unit, however. Members may not only have different and even competing interests, but income and other resources are not necessarily pooled efficiently or distributed equitably within the household.

The household is not just a group of people, but a group of people *someplace* (or, it could be argued, *some places*). The location of the household largely defines the community in which women may function as community managers.

The household's position in the productive arena—within the assumption that there is a discernable division between production and reproduction—is perhaps less obvious than its position as reproductive center. Yet while urban households generally do not maintain the holistic mesh of production and reproduction characterized by precapitalist and subsistence rural households, women in particular do a fair amount of productive work within urban households. Such income-generating activities include self-employment or cooperative-based work in the form of handicrafting, petty trading, and food and drink processing and vending, as well as factory-subcontracted outwork (Momsen and Townsend 1987). The prevalence of income-generating activities in the household is one of the reasons why Momsen and Townsend prefer Pahl's (1984) less detailed definition of household: "units for getting various kinds of work done, 'work' including production and reproduction."

URBAN HOUSEHOLD STRUCTURES

The most common urban household arrangement in the Third World is the nuclear family, which consists of the shared residence and consumption of a married or cohabiting couple and their children (Brydon and Chant 1989). "Nuclear" does not mean that the male is the head of the household, although most governments and policy makers assume male dominance, and indeed in the majority of nuclear households, the man is the chief income-earner and, in some spheres, decision maker.

A growing number of households have no male heads and so are unquestionably female-headed. The term *female-headed* is usually applied to families consisting of a woman and her children, although it may also cover other arrangements, such as a three-or-more-generational family, a woman living alone with her grandchildren, or sisters or unrelated women living together. Female-headed households are not restricted to urban areas, but they do tend to be more numerous in cities than in rural areas. Statistics on the number of female-headed households in the world or in individual countries are notoriously unreliable; however, one estimate holds that as much as a third of the world's households are female-headed, about half of these within the Third World (Buvinić, Youssef, with Von Elm 1987). As an example of how variable such data are, Moser (1989, n.12) notes that a senior administrative official estimated that 3 to 4 percent of the households in one Indian city were woman headed; a social worker working in one of the city's slums estimated the proportion of women-headed households to be 70 percent. Acknowledging the disparity between the two reporters' standpoints—one working in a middle-class environment, the other in a poverty-stricken area—raises an important point about female-headed households: They tend to be among the poorest of the poor. In Calcutta, for example, the more a household relies on female income, the more likely it is to be poor (Standing 1989). During a recent visit to the Working Women's Forum in Madras, one author was told that over three-quarters of the women members were the sole adult supporters of households, yet none of the approximately fifty women present was divorced. One assumes that most husbands were either unemployed or had left the family.

Brydon and Chant (1989) distinguish between de facto female heads, whose male partners are either temporarily absent or do not play a major economic role in the family, and de jure female heads, who have either never established a household with the father of their children or who have been divorced, deserted, or widowed. It should be noted that household structures are not static; a nuclear household can easily become solely woman headed, newly migrated relatives can turn a small nucleus into an extended family, children grow up and leave or bring their spouses and children into the household.

Types of female-headed households and the reasons for their occurrence vary by culture and region, and even a focus on regional tendencies masks complexities. In parts of West Africa, for example, where kinship arrangements have traditionally favored women heading their own households or living with other female relatives, female-headed urban households are common. Widowhood is the main cause of female-headed households in much of Asia. Women tend to have longer life expectancies at birth; in societies where young women marry older men, the likelihood of widowhood increases. Unstable unions are the predominant cause of female-headed households in Latin America and the Caribbean (Momsen and Townsend 1987; Bruce 1989). In Latin America, which has a long history of male desertion, at least one-fifth of all urban women head their own household (Brydon and Chant 1989). Studies indicate that divorce or its extra-legal equivalent is on the rise in many other societies as well. Chances of widowhood and marital dissolution increase as women get older, so that by age forty to forty-five, 20 percent of African women and 10 to 29 percent of Asian women will be separated, divorced, or widowed (Bruce 1989).

Differential gender migration is a major catalyst for the increasing incidence of female-headed households. International migration is a dominant factor in North Africa and southern Africa and is gaining ground in Asia. High intra-national migration rates are also found in central Africa and Latin America. In one squatter settlement near Nairobi, an estimated 60 to 80 percent of the households were woman headed (Momsen and Townsend 1987). In rural Africa, the outmigration of men and the practice of polygamy results in many women carrying the major responsibility for the household. In ten African countries, women and children together make up 77 percent of the population; in only 16 percent of the households in these countries do the women have the legal right to own property (Perlez 1991).

Civil war and related forms of organized violence account for an additional portion of female-headed households. Roughly half the households in Managua, Nicaragua, are female headed, and in some Central American refugee camps, as many as 90 percent of the households are female headed (Momsen and Townsend 1987). Indeed, Bruce (1989, 989) predicts "an increasing sub-nu-clearization of families to the mother-child core."

Is it possible that there are parallel trends of shrinking and expanding households? Evidence suggests that the number of extended households, which consist of a core nuclear or one-parent family living with other relatives who share daily consumption and financial arrangements, may be increasing. A common belief supported by both modernization theorists and Marxists (although for different reasons) is that industrialization and urbanization have converted the rural extended family into the urban nuclear family. While acknowledging that the range and number of relatives within an extended household tends to be smaller in urban areas than in rural areas, Brydon and Chant (1989, 141) argue that "the extended-to-nuclear trajectory is in no way a universal, let alone inevitable outcome of 'urbanization.' " Extended households are common in Third World cities. Studies indicate that up to 25 percent of Mexican low-income urban households, 50 percent of Taiwanese urban households, and as much as 75 percent of the households in one Sierra Leone city are extended (Brydon and Chant 1989).

In urban as well as rural areas, extended families have more members— generally adults—to help out with domestic, childcare, and income-earning tasks. Brydon and Chant (1989) hypothesize that it is the difficulty of being a low-income working mother that is prompting the continuance, if not an actual increase, of extended households in urban areas. In a study of shantytown families in Querétaro, Mexico, Chant (1987) found that many women would have liked to have another relative living in the house, but that most male heads of nuclear households did not want an additional relative living with them. Extended families allowed for greater stretching of gender roles. Males were more likely to help with the housework, and women, with the domestic burden eased and with more members to support, were more likely to get productive work outside the house. Brydon and Chant (1989) see a likely connection between the rise of women's labor force participation in Third World cities and an increase in the number of extended households.

In addition to the extended households in which the participating members reside together, there are the households in which members reside in different locations yet still share financial and reproductive resources. Much of the growth of this quasi-extended family can be attributed to the increase in women's rural-urban migration. In West Africa and the Caribbean, working urban women who migrate within or outside the country often send their children, particularly those of preschool age, to live with grandparents or other relatives in rural areas (Bolles 1986; Brydon and Chant 1989). Young unmarried women in southeast Asia, in their role as daughters, leave their rural homes for employment in the cities and export-processing zones; often much of their income is sent back to their families. In Thailand, young daughters are bonded to houses of prostitution in Bangkok and typically must work for several years to repay their family's loan (Phongpaichit 1982).

Noting the prevalence of residentially dispersed family networks in the Philippines, as well as in Indonesia and Peru, Trager (1988, 183) questions the spatially confined concept of "household" in the context of migration:

If "household" means, as is generally accepted, a residential group sharing a common pot, then how should one interpret the position of a family member who resides elsewhere but who (a) visits home every weekend and thinks of the place as home; (b) contributes a substantial portion of his or her income; and (c) whose contribution affects the possibility of others in the family to eat, go to school, etc. The migrant is not a resident of that household but is in many ways part of it, and is perceived as part of it by other family members.

GENDER, HOUSEHOLDS, AND MIGRATION

The process of development is almost always accompanied by migration, usually from rural to urban areas, but also from small towns to big cities and sometimes from one country to another. There are often significant differences between men and women both in their motives for migration and in the volume of movement. The consequences for the people who migrate and those who remain also differ.

Involuntary migration—the plight of refugees, the majority of whom are women and children—is usually the result of political conflict. Marriage migration is common, particularly for women, in both Africa and south Asia (see Turshen, Bretin, and Thébaud-Mony, chapter 5, this volume). The motivations for voluntary migration most commonly related to development, however, are economic. People leave rural areas because they are unable to earn a living in agriculture, which results when mechanization displaces farm labor and when land reform fails and small farms no longer support new generations of peasant families. The possibility of obtaining employment, of finding markets for one's labor or its fruits, and of improving one's standards of living is a primary reason for the migration of people from rural to urban areas and for the movement of labor from less developed areas to industrialized countries.

Although economic pressures for migration are frequently the same for men and women, men commonly migrate in larger numbers than do women. According to 1979 UN data, only the United States, Argentina, and Israel have had greater annual numbers of female migrants than male migrants, and have since at least the early 1950s. Charlton (1984) reports that historically the proportion of international migrants who are female is highest in Europe, particularly from such southern European countries as Yugoslavia and Turkey. Women are a significant proportion (38 percent in 1975) of immigrant populations of West African countries, but a much smaller proportion in the Middle East; less than 2 percent of immigrants to Saudi Arabia are female. Over the last fifteen years, however, there has been a dramatic increase in the labor migration of women from Sri Lanka, the Philippines, Indonesia, Bangladesh, and Thailand to the more prosperous Asian countries of Japan, Hong Kong, and the Persian Gulf nations. Women, many of whom are wives and mothers, migrate in search of paid domestic employment, leaving their children in care of *their* mothers and other female relatives (Matsui 1987; Basler 1990). By 1980, an average of 14,000 Sri Lankan women a year were leaving for employment in the Middle East alone (Heyzer 1989). Brettell and Simon (1986) note a significant correlation between female migration and the substantial global increase in the female labor force.

Women are a dominant share of the rural to urban migration in Latin America as well as in the Philippines, a proportion that has intensified with urbanization and is encouraged by the growth of employment in domestic service for women in cities (Jelin 1977; Orlansky and Dubrovsky 1978; Trager 1988). Khoo, Smith, and Fawcett (1984) plotted urbanization levels by gender and for two age groups and report two distinct patterns of age-sex migration: In Western Europe, Latin America, and other "areas of European settlement" (North America, Australia, and New Zealand), there appears to be a predominance of women in migration to urban areas, whereas a male-selective process is apparent in Africa, the Middle East, and south Asia.

Sex differentials in rural to urban migration result from gender differences in economic opportunities and in cultural expectations. In parts of Latin America, for example, there are fewer employment opportunities in agriculture for women than for men, while urban areas offer considerable service and industrial work opportunities for women. Similarly in the Philippines, men tend to stay in their rural area to do farm work while women migrate to urban centers for work. In addition to finding better work opportunities away from home, women—daughters—in Latin America and the Philippines are expected to be more dependable than sons in fulfilling family obligations and supporting their parents and other relatives (Butterworth and Chance 1981; Trager 1988). Both women and men sometimes migrate to escape social restrictions, but the limitations and sanctions may be more severe for women, such as the opprobrium of unmarried motherhood (Whiteford 1978; Youssef, Buvinić, and Kudat 1979).

In many African countries, women are more involved in agriculture and there tends to be a paucity of employment opportunities for women in cities. When women do migrate, they are most likely to join husbands already settled with jobs. While comparatively low, however, the proportion of African women moving to towns is increasing (Sudarkasa 1977; Wilkinson 1987). Gender roles are strong and the female migrant influx small and recent; women who migrate, especially single women, are assumed by some to be prostitutes (Thudani 1978; Obbo 1980).

GENDERED IMPACTS OF MIGRATION ON THE HOUSEHOLD

On the flip side of migration lie those who remain behind. Where men outnumber women in the urban and international migrant streams, the differential gender ratio results in heavier workloads for rural women. Although often perceived as temporary, with the assumption that the male worker will return to the family periodically, in reality male migration has a periodicity and permanence. In southern Africa, where male labor migration is decades old, the chronic absence of men makes it continually more difficult to maintain a nominal level of agricultural production (Gordon 1981; Perlez 1991; Wilkinson 1987). Male oscillating migration is the chief cause of the significant change in Botswana marriage patterns; some women, including single mothers, never marry and those that do get married do so at an older age (Brown 1989). For low-income women in Cairo, the prolonged absence of their husbands working in Persian Gulf countries has meant an essential diminishing of traditional male financial control (Hoodfar 1988).

Migrants of both sexes within developing countries and from less developed to more developed countries all face challenges not faced by nonmigrants. To leave the relative security of the known and of kin, however materially deprived the conditions, and to migrate to a novel environment, however rich in possibilities for improving one's quality of life, requires adaptation to new expectations, mores, values, skill requirements, languages and ways of communication, daily habits, and so forth. International migrants face the confusion and corruption surrounding visas, passports, and employment agencies (Heyzer 1989; and see Meredeth Turshen, Hélène Bretin, and Annie Thébaud-Mony, chapter 5, this volume).

The difficulties of migration, of course, vary greatly by circumstances. Many migrants, particularly those following an oscillating migration pattern, are bolstered by close ties to the places from which they came. Others join family or other former placemates in the place to which they migrate. Trager (1988) finds that rural-based women living and working in Dagupan City in the Philippines move back and forth between town and country with considerable ease, adjusting their behavior accordingly.

The contrast between the place left and the place to which one migrates often may be greater for women than for men because the destination is usually more modernized, and thus the societal expectations about gender roles has begun to change. Obviously, this may result in greater ultimate advantage for women, but it also creates greater challenge to adapt.

While both women and men in Egypt, for example, may be caught in the transition from traditional rural to modern urban life, the consequences of the shift are often harsher on women. According to Hoodfar (1988), modernization and social change have made women more dependent on men, but men more independent from women. Men living in low-income Cairo neighborhoods do not come home much, preferring to spend time and money on leisure activities outside the home and neighborhood, which they feel is unmodern. With many goods and services previously provided by women now bought for cash, the perceived value of women's reproductive role has decreased, while lingering traditional ideology and minimal labor opportunities prevent women's productive role from expanding. Men's lack of respect for the neighborhood also weakens women's power, for the neighborhood is their base.

In Zambia, the contrast between rural traditions and a relatively recent urban society can be even more severe. The sexual division of labor in cities is dramatically different from the rural tradition of husband-wife teams working together in the fields; in town, women—particularly those in customary marriages—are economically dependent on their husbands. When women do earn money, they run up against the recent convention whereby a man "owns" his wife's earnings, an urban amendment to the tradition of marriage payments a man makes to his wife's family. Widows in urban areas face the disintegration of rural customs that had the husband's heir "inheriting" the widow and assuming responsibility for the children, but they have not gained new rights of inheritance from their husbands (Munachonga 1988, 1989).

In other situations, particularly in which women migrants have had at least some exposure to modern ideas of gender roles, advantages that may ensue from the change are more forthcoming for women than they are for men. Pessar (1988) finds that as Dominican women in the United States, many working for the first time (at least since marriage), prove that they can share material responsibility with men on more or less equal terms, they begin to expect to be copartners in heading the household. The women, many of whom have urban middle-class backgrounds and limited education, tend to want to stay longer in the United States, while their husbands want to return to the Dominican Republic and a more traditional financial arrangement.

Economics is, of course, a critical determinant of the condition of migrants' lives, and poverty is what prompts many people to migrate in the first place. For the poorest migrants, many of whom are women, the only work accessible to them tends to be the most precarious jobs with few prospects of upward mobility (Standing 1989). Although migrants may be seeking industrial employment, they are more likely to join the growing ranks of the service sector. Domestic service, which often puts the worker at the mercy of her employer and for which there is little training, is a particularly common option in Latin America, South Africa, and southeast Asia. Three-quarters of Sri Lankan women working outside their country are domestic servants; many have complained of harassment, and runaways are not uncommon (Heyzer 1989). Other informal service occupations prevalent among female migrants include petty trading and food and drink vending.

Poor rural women in India and Thailand, sent by their families or on their own initiative, go to cities to work as prostitutes. In some countries the sex trade is by far the most profitable occupation for young women (see Catherine Hill, chapter 8, this volume; Heisoo Shin, chapter 7, this volume). A recent ILO report on prostitution in Thailand, which took evidence from fifty women who had moved from rural areas to Bangkok to work in massage parlors, found that "the migration gave them an earning power which was simply outstanding relative to normal rural budgets. A couple of years of work would enable the family to build a house of a size and quality which few people in the countryside could not hope to achieve in the earnings of a lifetime" (*The Economist* 1989, 30).

GENDER AND THE CASH ECONOMY

Women in urban areas are far more likely than their rural counterparts to work for wages or sell goods and services. Even semiaccurate statistics, however, about the number of women in income-earning activities are just about nonexistent. Momsen and Townsend (1987) note that one of the main problems in studying the geography of gender is the serious incongruity in the calculations of work done by each gender. Each country has its own definitions of work and its own system of measurement, and nonwaged income of the informal sector, in which women are well represented, often is not calculated as "direct production."

Inconsistency of employment statistics in mind, a recorded 42 percent of adult women in developing countries were labor force participants in 1985. Between 1950 and 1985, women's share of the total recorded labor force rose from 28 percent to 32 percent, although women's labor-force participation in oil-rich Middle East and North African countries declined as incomes there rose in the

1970s and 1980s (Joekes 1987). Assumptions about women's appropriate role as confined to the domestic sphere continue to preclude or strongly inhibit women's possibilities of nondomestic employment in some places, for example Bengal and Indonesia (Caplan 1985). Women's share of urban employment is increasing fastest in Latin America and southeast Asia, the most industrialized regions (Seager and Olson 1986). Growth of services tends to follow industrial growth; while industrialization attracts people in search of work to urban areas, many do not find industrial employment and instead join the service sector. The entry of women to the paid labor force and the cash economy has many implications, but a constant is that it seldom changes the gendered division of domestic work and in most cases their income-generating work is added to their reproductive and community work.

Schmink (1985) notes that not only are men and women concentrated in different occupations, but women's occupations are more clearly polarized by age. In Brazil, female workers under thirty represent more than 70 percent of all women in the recorded labor force, and while the majority are self-employed in low-paying informal jobs or employed in unskilled white-collar jobs, women— mostly as teachers and nurses—show higher proportions than do men in the technical and professional occupations. Most women over thirty are not in the recorded labor force, and the majority of those who are do unskilled manual work or are informally self-employed (ibid.). In South Korea, women under age twenty-five working in electronics, textiles, and toy manufacturing compose a third of the entire industrial labor force (Agarwal 1988). In determining employment patterns, age is linked with marital status. In Querétaro, Mexico, 66 percent of unmarried women of all ages are in paid work, while only 10 percent of married mothers are. The highest participation among married women, about 50 percent, is among those forty to forty-four years of age (Chant 1987, 285). Little has been written and even less has been done about older women workers, those in their fifties and sixties. Standing (1989, 1094) notes that

with urbanization and industrialization, kinship support networks are being eroded, yet very few women workers have pension rights; nor do women have employment security or access to retraining or labor market assistance in times of recession or structural adjustment. . . . Given today's flexible, insecure labor processes, and weakened social support systems, the needs of older women have never been greater.

Types of employment can be divided into two broad groups: formal sector and informal sector employment. While generally distinct, the two sectors are dependent on each other and the occupations within them often overlap. The formal sector covers activities in privately or publicly owned enterprises or in the civil service, which conform generally to tax and labor laws and other state regulations (Grown and Sebstad 1989). Although conditions vary widely, formal sector employment tends to provide better incomes, job security, and legal protection than informal sector employment. Informal sector work consists of a wide range of enterprises falling outside the bounds of social and labor legislation (Brydon and Chant 1989). People who work in small-scale and often home-based manufacturing or commercial enterprises, provide personal services such as domestic work or sewing, or who are self-employed as, for example, petty traders, vendors, casual laborers or prostitutes are considered part of the informal sector.

WOMEN IN FORMAL MANUFACTURING

Outside of civil service, factory work is probably most easily identified as formal sector labor, although as it will be noted, there is an increasing trend toward the informalization of manufacturing. Women in the Third World comprise an average of a quarter to a third of the recorded manufacturing labor force, with ranges from 4 percent in Malawi to 56 percent in Singapore (Momsen and Townsend 1987). In South Korea, Taiwan, the Philippines, Singapore, Thailand, Tunisia, and Haiti, the share of women in the manufacturing labor force is more than 40 percent, a greater share than in any developed countries (Joekes 1987).

Women are typically concentrated in labor-intensive light industries that produce consumer goods. Although proportions vary widely by country, women tend to be most represented in food processing, textile, garment, electronics, chemical, rubber, and plastics industries, with clothing and electronics the most feminized branches (Joekes 1987). Women tend to occupy the lowest ranks of the manufacturing hierarchy, unskilled routine jobs that are repetitious and offer little chance of promotion. Women who work in factories often earn lower wages than their male peers. A survey of nine developing countries found that among comparably employed men and women, women's wages were from 50 to 80 percent of men's wages, the former figure in South Korea, the latter in Burma (Bruce 1989). African women who secure jobs in urban-based industries usually work at the lowest levels in textiles, confectionery, and food processing, which are the lowest paying sectors and have the poorest working conditions. In part, their placement in these industries arises because few African women have any technical knowledge, but also microelectronics is not yet a major industry in most of Africa. In microelectronics, some women earn substantial sums as computer operators and programmers, but they play no role in the higher echelons (Rogombe 1985). In Korea women are disproportionately concentrated in the more labor-intensive textile and chemical manufacturing sector, and in all industries, they generally occupy low-paying jobs of production workers, transportation equipment operators, laborers, and sales workers (Lele 1986, 209).

Women tend to have less education than men, which contributes to their placement in low-skilled, low-paying jobs, but even when women are more educated than men, they still are paid less. One study showed that educated women in Brazil, carefully selected and trained by their companies, were placed in lower-ranked jobs than men who had been hired without regard to training or entry qualifications. The women's jobs required more skills, but the ranking was linked with pay scales and constructed in such a way that the women would earn less (Humphrey 1985).

Employers' prejudices about appropriate jobs for women, and their assumptions concerning absenteeism and turnover, are reflected in lower wages for women. Even when the demand for labor is high, as in Mauritius, employers limit women's jobs to daytime and pay differential wages based on the assumption that the male is the family breadwinner (Anker and Hein 1986). Given the high proportion of women-headed families and the fact that women's earnings are far more likely than men's to be devoted solely to household expenses, the prevailing notion of only the male earning the family wage is absurd (Afshar 1985; Dwyer and Bruce 1988).

The availability of cheap female labor has been crucial to the rapid growth of developing countries' manufactured exports. As Joekes (1987, 81) notes, "Industrialization in the postwar period has been as much *female* led as *export* led." Young women predominate in the world market factories of multinational companies. Wages that Third World women earn in these factories may be as little as a tenth of those earned by workers in developed nations, and Third World women may work up to 50 percent longer (Momsen and Townsend 1987). World market factories generally forbid their employees to join unions, but even factories in which unions are not illegal have a low rate of female unionization (Matsui 1987; Enloe 1989). One of the reasons why women are less unionized than men may be the traditional male domination and orientation of unions. Joekes (1987) suggests that because of their subordinated position in society, women are more likely than men to be used to deferring to superiors. Conformance to conventional notions of the feminine among Malaysian women workers has impeded organized demands for improvement in working conditions (Armstrong and McGee 1985).

WOMEN IN THE SERVICE SECTOR

While there has been a good deal of attention paid recently to women workers in multinational factories, more women in the formal sector work in services than in industry. In 1980, 70 percent of Latin American and Caribbean women in the recorded labor force worked in the service sector, and women comprised nearly 40 percent of the sector's total labor. Africa and Asia have smaller service sectors employing fewer women, who make up 27 percent of the service sector in Africa and 24 percent in Asia (Joekes 1987). Government and public services are significant employers of women, although generally to a lesser degree than in developed countries; in 1980, 50 percent of urban Indonesian women and 72 percent of urban Mexican women were so employed (Brydon and Chant 1989). In the service sector, women are probably most heavily represented in commerce. Forty-five percent of urban Indonesian women employed in services in 1980 worked in wholesale and retail commerce, restaurants, and hotels (ibid.).

Again, women tend to fill the lower-paid ranks of each occupation—more nurses than doctors, more primary school than secondary school teachers, more secretarial than managerial civil service positions (Joekes 1987; Seager and Olson 1986).

Statistics on the service sector are probably less accurate than those of other sectors, as many personal services are small-scale and informal (Joekes 1987). Informal activities account for a larger proportion of total female employment than formal work in the Third World (Sen and Grown 1987). About 30 million Latin Americans work in the informal sector; approximately three-quarters of the informal workers in Chile, Brazil, and Costa Rica are women (Tokman 1989). Nearly 90 percent of employment in India is in the informal sector, and women comprise an estimated 60 percent of that portion (Bhatt 1989). Studies of major cities in Africa and Latin America found that women comprise from 25 to 40 percent of informal sector business operators and owners (Grown and Sebstad 1989).

The informal labor market is generally easier to enter than the formal labor market and often requires fewer skills. For women, a major impetus toward informal labor is their need to perform reproductive tasks. Informal work has no time card and, as such, allows more time or more flexible time for women to take charge of their reproductive work. Employers in formalized factories often require overtime work in peak periods of production, and workers may fear losing their jobs if they refuse overtime. As women are clustered in the unskilled jobs, they are easily replaced; there are always others willing to accept sixty- and even eighty-hour weeks in return for needed extra income (Ibrahim 1989). Female heads of households tend to be overrepresented in informal labor. In Caribbean territories, most women workers in the informal sector are their households' major or sole supports (Massiah 1989). In Belo Horizonte, Brazil, 85 percent of women heading households worked in the informal sector, compared to just 25 percent of male household heads (Merrick and Schmink 1983).

Women's typically higher relative participation rates in the informal than formal sector may also be partially attributable to cultural mores concerning appropriate roles and work (Hill 1983). Domestic outwork—subcontracting parts of the production process to home-based workers—can be a compromise between a woman's need to earn income and the ideology that says that women do housework while the men earn the family income. Because it is "invisible work" and provides a smaller income than the more formalized jobs that men are likely to have, Mexican husbands tended to be less likely to oppose their wives' involvement with outwork than with more visible factory or domestic service jobs (Roldan 1988).

Outwork is a growing trend that involves disproportionate numbers of women. Employers tend to use subcontracting and outwork to cut costs and avoid paying minimum wages and other benefits to workers (Ibrahim 1989). In their study of industrial outwork in Mexico City, Benería and Roldan (1987) describe a complex process of subcontracting, with home-based workers doing the labor-intensive, lower paid, more informal activities. The workers, mostly women, pay for their own tools, machinery, and other materials, saving employers these costs as well as the rent that would have to be paid if these workers were doing their activities in a factory. The circumstances of outwork also impede coalition-building or class consciousness: "The isolation, dispersion, and secrecy dependent in domestic outwork, coupled with women's knowledge that there exists a reserve of wives and mothers ready to take their place if they fall into disgrace with an intermediary, make collective organization extremely difficult and usually impossible" (Roldan 1988, 246).

Although the general lack of labor organization is a significant feature of informal sector work, labor organizations for informal workers do exist. One of the best known and best established of these groups is India's Self-Employed Women's Association (SEWA). Established in 1972 by a group of garment vendors, head-loaders, junksmiths, and vegetable hawkers, SEWA has since organized more than 40,000 poor women workers in the state of Gujarat and has expanded into five more Indian states. Informal workplaces are homes and public spaces, and unlike traditional labor organizations, SEWA does not make distinctions between productive and reproductive arenas. SEWA helps vendors get licenses, organizes industrial and service cooperatives, agitates for better and more accessible health services, provides legal support for informal workers, offers poor women loans and banking services through the SEWA Co-op Bank, and fights women's economic and political invisibility at local, national, and international levels (Bhatt 1989). A similar organization, the Working Women's Forum (WWF), was founded in Madras in 1978 and has expanded to three southern Indian states. Its membership of over 100,000 women are mainly employed in the informal sector. The WWF provides small loans, employment support services, health care, and birth control and has had considerable success in empowering and improving the lives of women workers (*Decade of the Forum* 1988; Azad 1986).

The immense value of organizations such as SEWA will only grow as formal jobs become increasingly "informalized." Since the 1980s, large centralized work forces have been giving way toward more decentralized, flexible systems, increasing the use of women as workers but weakening their income and employment security. The industrial labor force is becoming informalized though extensive subcontracting, outwork, and flexibility's decreased demand for vocational skills (Standing 1989). The trend of privatization also bodes ill for women, as women's wages and employment conditions are generally better and the gap between men's and women's wages is smaller in the public sector than in the private sector (Standing 1989).

THE URBAN HOUSEHOLD IN THE CASH ECONOMY

Women who earn an income do not necessarily have more power than women who earn no money for their labor. In many parts of the world, women do not control the household finances unless they are the sole heads of households. In addition, women in poor households allocate greater proportions of their incomes than men do to everyday subsistence needs such as food, rent, clothing, and fuel. Married women generally earn significantly less than their employed husbands, yet while they will spend the entirety of their income on household needs, the men—many of whom do not tell their wives how much they earn—keep some of their own income as personal pocket money. In an ironic twist on the conventional idea of a married woman earning a small income so that she can have spending money for herself, the reality in many cases is that the women's "extra" earnings contribute instead to their husbands' spending money (Dwyer and Bruce 1988).

In many cases, however, earning income does have a clearly positive effect on poor women. Evaluation studies of income-generation projects often mention women's increased self-confidence and assertiveness, although Buvinić (1989) notes that if the self-confidence is triggered by a project, it may also be reversed. As far as development projects are concerned, since women are more inclined than men to spend money on the household, increasing women's income is likely to make more of an impact in raising the household's standard of living than is the traditional route of increasing men's income. Several studies of the employment of young mothers in the Third World find that maternal employment has a positive effect on child nutrition (Leslie 1988; Tucker and Sanjur 1988; Pryer 1987).

CONCLUSION: UNDERSTANDING LIVELIHOOD SYSTEMS

Income-earning mothers, particularly sole heads of households, must grapple with the simultaneous tasks of managing childcare, domestic work, community activity, and their income-producing labor. The difficulty of this endeavor accounts for the prevalence of part-time work, outwork and types of self-employment based in the home and in public spaces such as open markets to which small children can be brought. Another management tactic is "granny fostering," in which working mothers have their small children raised by the children's grandmothers or older female relatives (Brydon and Chant 1989).

Any effort to improve women's income-earning opportunities requires an understanding of the range of women's work activities—productive, reproductive, and community-managing—and the way in which women balance each activity against the others (Massiah 1989). This involves understanding the patterns and problems of male and female migration, the variety and significance of household structures and the management and control of household finances.

Grown and Sebstad (1989) elucidate the need for a more holistic approach to the analysis and practice of gender and development: "Conventional definitions of enterprise, employment, and income are inadequate; much greater attention needs to be given to the *livelihoods systems* concept because it more fully captures the nature of women's participation in the economy and their contribution to household, community and national income" (ibid., 939). A livelihoods system is the mix of individual and household survival strategies developed over a given period of time that seeks to mobilize available resources such as skills, time, and property—common, collective or individual—as well as opportunities like kin and friendship networks and group and organizational membership (ibid., 941).

A livelihoods system approach to development could be put to good use by governmental and nongovernmental policy makers as well as by researchers. For example, both Singapore and South Korea have based their development on labor-intensive, export-oriented industrialization, much of it dependent on female employment. The Singapore government located the factories near workers' homes; between the extended family households and their proximity to the workplace, the young women workers were able to continue their employment after getting married and having children. Since their presence in the work force was continuous, the women were able to learn new skills as the production process changed and had the tenure necessary for advancement. South Korea's workers, on the other hand, were drawn from the wider rural hinterland. Young women workers did not have family support in the vicinity of where they worked, and many stopped working after they had their first child. With outdated skills and little education, poor married women in their thirties and forties are left out of the industrial labor force and have little choice but to find work as domestic servants or in other low-paying informal jobs (Phongpaichit 1988).

Women's work—the extensive range of it—is integral to the international economy, and women's livelihoods are greatly influenced by the international economy. Although developmentalists, governments, and policy makers may find the enormity and interconnectedness of a livelihoods systems approach overwhelming, its depth of field is what is needed for assessing and finding ways to improve the lives of women and of all poor people.

4

The Impact of Population Control Policies on Health Policy in Bangladesh

Betsy Hartmann

The main cause of ill health is poverty. Other causes are malnutrition, which greatly increases susceptibility to disease and, in the case of women of child-bearing age, to reproductive complications, and poor sanitation and unclean water, which facilitate germ transmission. Patriarchy also contributes to ill health. In many cultures, including Bangladesh, women eat last and least, even when they are pregnant or nursing and need extra food. Girls too frequently receive less food and medical care. Women's poorer health is reflected in sex ratios: for every one hundred males in Bangladesh, there are ninety-five females (World Bank 1988, 286).

The same basic force that underlies poverty and patriarchy—elite and male control of economic, social, and political resources—also helps to determine the nature of health care services. In Bangladesh, the government's lack of commitment to popular welfare has directly affected the quantity and quality of its health programs.

Today, only 30 percent of Bangladesh's population has access to primary health care. For every 6,000 people there is only one doctor, for every 15,500 only one nurse or midwife (World Bank 1987a, 183, 187). While Bangladesh's doctor ratio is similar to the average for low-income economies, its nurse ratio is considerably worse than the average and over triple that of neighboring India.[1] Moreover, because medical personnel are concentrated in the cities, these ratios are far worse in the rural areas where 85 percent of Bangladesh's population lives.

The poor quality of health services takes its greatest toll on women and children. By 1987 only 2 percent of children had been immunized against the common infectious diseases; almost half of infant deaths and one-third of child-hood deaths are caused by such illnesses as tetanus, measles, and diarrhea, which could be avoided or readily cured. The virtual lack of antenatal, delivery, and postnatal care, as well as the absence of decent family planning and abortion services, means that women face unacceptably high risks of maternal death. Maternal mortality rates range from 510–770 deaths per 100,000 live births, and maternal morbidity is also extremely high. Up to 70 percent of pregnant women are anemic and malnourished (World Bank 1987a, 187–189).

Better nutrition would greatly improve the health profile of both women and children. In theory, the Ministry of Health and Family Planning is supposed to implement nutrition programs; in practice, according to the World Bank, "few initiatives" and "only minor expenditures" have been made for this purpose (World Bank 1987a, 187). Indeed, the nutritional status of the poor is deteriorating in Bangladesh, with young children the worst victims. Nutritional studies indicate a 14 percent decline in food intake among children under five between 1962 and 1982, so that now three-quarters of these children suffer from secondary and tertiary malnutrition (van Praag 1988).

Why do health services in Bangladesh have such a poor record? The reasons involve internal and external resource constraints and political forces, which interact to create an inefficient bureaucracy pursuing misguided policies.

ON THE INSIDE

On first inspection, one might be tempted to blame the failure of Bangladesh's health system on the country's poverty. According to this logic, the country simply does not have the resources to devote to health, especially given the size of its rapidly growing population. In reality, the government's budget priorities are skewed toward the military. From 1973–85, defense expenditures rose in real terms a staggering 400 percent, while over the same period, expenditures on health (including population) rose only 18 percent. In 1973, health expenditures were slightly higher than defense, whereas by 1985, defense expenditures were more than three times those for health (Asian Development Bank 1986, 93–96).

In general, the level of public expenditures for human development in Bangladesh—health, education, training—is among the lowest in the world and well under half the estimated minimum expenditures required to fulfill the most basic of human development needs in low-income countries. Moreover, as a percentage of gross domestic product, human development expenditures actually declined from 2.4 percent in fiscal years 1976–80 to 2.1 percent in fiscal years 1981–86 (World Bank 1987a, 184–186). Clearly, more resources could be spent on health and other human services, if that were the government's priority.

Poverty, of course, takes other forms besides financial constraints. The colonial legacy of inadequate infrastructure and lack of trained personnel present very real problems to the development of health services in Bangladesh. But in the almost two decades since independence, little has been done to overcome this legacy, not because of lack of resources, but because successive regimes have been more concerned with staying in power and enriching their allies than with developing the country.

On the local level, the government maintains an elaborate patronage system, whereby friends of the ruling party are rewarded with government jobs, contracts, and other favors in return for bribes and political support. These friends are usually drawn from the rich peasant, landlord, and local commercial classes— the suppression of popular, democratic institutions has created a situation in which poor people have little opportunity to enter government service (except for the military and police). In the health field, this means that many of the basic field workers come to the job, not out of any sense of interest or commitment to the local communities they are supposed to serve, but because of their political connections.

The effect is predictable. According to an article in *Studies in Family Planning*, the political patronage system leaves health and family planning workers immune to managerial control. At the same time:

Politicians view the program as a valuable source of employment for their constituents but not as a set of activities that deserve their vigilant encouragement. As a consequence, the program is as much a target for resource extraction as for the mobilization of energies directed at performance goals. Low work effort and infrequent client contacts are a logical outgrowth of these conditions (Simmons, Koblinsky, and Phillips 1986, 263).

According to one international consultant, the sterilization incentive system was originally envisioned as a way to combat this "low work effort," to encourage workers to get out in the field! (Personal communication.)

It would be wrong, however, to place the entire blame for poor performance on the workers. Low salaries coupled with the pressure to fill quotas for sterilizations and intrauterine devices keep morale low. At the same time, there is no system to reward good performance in the delivery of maternal and child health (MCH) services.

Unrealistic worker-client ratios also make the regular interpersonal contact that is necessary to promote health and family planning virtually impossible. For example, the basic female field worker, the family welfare assistant, is supposed to service 1,500 to 3,000 households. In practice, most family welfare assistants are able to see only a small number of neighboring families on a regular basis; they see the others maybe once every six months or every year or not at all. Currently, more family welfare assistants are being recruited to improve the ratio, although a recent Dutch report expresses considerable doubt over the quality of the recruitment process (van Praag 1988, 15–16).

The widespread practice of female seclusion, or *purdah*, in Bangladesh, whereby a woman's movements are restricted to a close radius around the home, also hinders the work of family welfare assistants. The family welfare assistants' travel between neighborhoods and villages opens them to allegations of misbehavior, which is a detriment to performance and morale. Yet, *purdah* means that home visits by family welfare assistants are essential, since many village women have difficulty traveling to clinics.

Most local level health workers also receive inadequate supervision and training. The government's lack of commitment to health means that at all levels managerial positions, especially those that involve oversight and training responsibilities, are empty. Health and family planning are not considered prestigious fields, and there is a lack of salary differentials to make service in the rural areas more attractive.[2]

Meanwhile, clinics are in a state of disrepair, with many buildings experiencing "a complete breakdown of essential services such as water and electrical supply, severe roof and wall leakage, structural cracking . . . and acute security problems involving the loss of equipment" (World Bank 1987b, 8).

As a result of all these problems, health facilities in rural Bangladesh are actually underutilized—a tragic irony in a country where so many people desperately need access to basic care. Time and again, the foreign donors chide the government for this sorry state of affairs. The cofinanciers (Australia, Canada, the Federal Republic of Germany, the Netherlands, Norway, and Great Britain) of the World Bank–coordinated Population III project in Bangladesh issued a particularly harsh aide memoire that noted the "poor performance and very low quality of care, both in terms of health care and FP [family planning]," and "a pattern of serious qualitative and quantitative mis- and under-utilization of the existing facilities . . . throughout the system" (cited in van Praag 1988, Annex 1:3).

However, many of the donors, particularly the U.S. Agency for International Development (USAID) and the World Bank, bear a large share of the responsibility for the failure of the health system. Foreign funds and pressure have been instrumental in making population control, instead of primary care, the centerpiece of health policy.

FROM THE OUTSIDE

In 1978 at a historic international conference in Alma Ata, the governments of 134 countries called for "Health for All by the Year 2000." The means to achieve this end was the provision of primary health care, defined as "essential health care made universally accessible to individuals and families in the community by means acceptable to them, through their full participation and at a cost that the community and country can afford" (Morley, Rohde, and Williams 1983, ix–x). Primary health care was defined broadly to include health education, proper nutrition, safe water, adequate sanitation, maternal and child health, family planning, immunization, prevention and control of endemic diseases, provision of essential drugs, and medical treatment.

There were many different opinions, however, on how to implement such programs. Many grass-roots health providers, as well as some international professionals, pointed out how in the presence of poverty and the absence of equity, it is difficult to establish a popularly based health care system. "In virtually all countries primary health care implies a very fundamental social revolution," observed Halfdan Mahler, former Director-General of the World Health Organization (*New Internationalist* 1983).

In order to circumvent this political reality, many governments and international agencies narrowed the definition of primary health care to emphasize the delivery of selected cost-effective targeted interventions such as immunization and oral rehydration therapy for diarrhea, which would not upset the status quo. The emphasis differed from year to year, according to the current fads in the international community, so that one year community participation might be the focus, the next the training of traditional birth attendants. Nevertheless, the articulation of primary health care is a step forward because it recognizes that poor people have a right, even if narrowly conceived, to some form of basic health care.

However, in Bangladesh, in the decade following the conference at Alma Ata, even the most limited concept of primary health care did not take hold for the simple reason that population control remained the central focus—indeed obsession—of USAID and the World Bank, the agencies that largely determine the direction of the country's health policy. There were voices raised in protest, of course. Bangladeshi health activists; UNICEF; Scandinavian, Dutch, and British official aid agencies; and various nongovernmental organizations tried over the years to alter the agenda in favor of primary care. But their efforts were consistently thwarted by the more powerful agencies.

The dominance of population control has meant that discussions of primary health care services, particularly maternal and child health, have centered around how they can best be integrated with family planning. In theory, some sort of integration between health and family planning makes sense. The delivery of quality family planning services depends, above all, on an adequate health care network, and the practice of family planning has the potential of contributing to the improvement of women and children's health. However, in Bangladesh, where family planning means population control, the debate over integration has taken place in an extremely limited context.

USAID, which is by far the largest single bilateral aid donor to Bangladesh, strongly encourages the government to implement population control programs independent of the development of health services. According to a 1983 USAID "Emergency Plan for Population Control in Bangladesh," the integration of family planning with maternal and child health services "requires unnecessarily costly and long term efforts to establish a Primary Health Care (PHC) system instead of focusing on the quick delivery of birth control services to meet the unmet demand. . . . A population control program does not depend on a functioning primary health care system" (quoted in Akhter 1984a). This document dismisses the positive association between reductions in infant mortality and increased interest in family planning on the grounds that Bangladesh cannot afford to wait for infant mortality to come down.

Similarly, the former UN Fund for Population Activities (UNFPA) representative in Dhaka, Walter Holzhausen, wrote in 1984 that no one seriously believes "that Bangladesh has the money or the time to establish better maternal and child health services and better educational facilities as a precondition for making voluntary family planning more successful" (quoted in Hartmann and Standing 1985, 37–38).

A second competing point of view, more widely embraced by the donor community including the World Bank, is that selected maternal and child health services can be very useful in promoting and conferring credibility on population control efforts, and therefore some kind of limited integration is desirable. This view is largely based on research undertaken in the Matlab area by the International Center for Diarrhoeal Disease Research, Bangladesh. In fact, the center's Matlab model has had considerable influence not just in Bangladesh, but on the international health and family planning fields generally. As a result, it warrants a closer look.

UNCONTAMINATED OBSERVATION

The Cholera Research Laboratory was the precursor of the International Center for Diarrhoeal Disease Research, Bangladesh. The Cholera Research Laboratory was set up during the early 1960s by the U.S.–dominated defence alliance, the South East Asia Treaty Organization (SEATO). After Bangladesh gained independence from Pakistan in 1971, plans were set in motion, primarily by the U.S. government, to transform the Cholera Research Laboratory into a major international health institution.

These plans met with a negative response from both Bangladeshi and foreign health activists. Dr. Zafrullah Chowdhury, head of the People's Health Center outside of Dhaka, warned that "Bangladesh people will serve as guinea pigs for experiments from which they may or may not benefit" (quoted in Keysers 1982, 216–218). The main beneficiaries, he pointed out, would be U.S. professionals in the fields of medical and demographic research. John Briscoe, a foreign researcher who had been working at the Cholera Research Laboratory, cautioned that the main aim of population studies at the new center would be to " 'prove' that population growth can be reduced without any change in the health conditions, poverty or social (in)justice" (ibid.).

Ten years later their predictions proved all too correct. On the population front, the International Center's Matlab project area is the most thoroughly studied region in Bangladesh, with the highest density of family planning workers (not health workers) relative to local population. It has become the prime location for U.S. research to undertake social experiments on the integration of maternal and child health and family planning.

The International Center's researchers recognize that many villagers distrust family planning workers because they rightly suspect that these workers are less concerned with meeting their health needs than with meeting sterilization and contraceptive quotas. As a result, the International Center's Family Planning Health Services Project introduced selected maternal and child health interventions, such as oral rehydration for diarrhea, tetanus immunization of pregnant women, antenatal care, and training of traditional midwives, into its family planning program in different "packages" in order to see which ones had the greatest effect on enhancing field worker credibility and thus increasing contraceptive use.

"Opportunities for researching the integration issue that are comparable to the FPHSP [Family Planning Health Services Project] are rare," write the researchers. "Experiments involving the uncontaminated observation of integrated versus single-purpose service systems are usually impossible to carry out, because national integrated programs have long been functioning" (DeGraff et al. 1986, 229). In other words, the Matlab area has not been "contaminated" with an integrated national health care system.

What are the results of the experiment? Through a series of regression equations, the researchers concluded that only a minimal maternal and child health package was needed to achieve the desired result and that further expansion of maternal and child health services to include, for example, antenatal care and midwife training was not essential to increase contraceptive use. In fact, some maternal and child health interventions were deemed harmful to family planning. For example, when oral rehydration therapy was introduced for diarrhea, the study found that this had the "negative" effect of diverting "attention away from family planning to new and complex health education and community organization activities" (Phillips et al. 1984). This was especially true when the locally available salt and molasses rehydration method was promoted because more training and motivation were required for this method than if the villagers were simply given manufactured rehydration packets.

The International Center's priorities are clear: Family planning comes first, and nothing should stand in its way. This single-minded approach has yielded results. Contraceptive prevalence rates in the Matlab project area are much higher and birth rates lower than those in neighboring villages, which have similar socioeconomic conditions but are served only by the government health program. The reasons are not hard to fathom: The International Center's female family planning workers receive far better training and logistical backup than government workers. As a result, they are better able to meet women's real demands for family planning (although the intense promotion of injectable contraceptives raises very serious questions as to whose interests the workers are really serving).

Measured by narrow population control standards, the International Center's program is a success—but how real is that success for the local people, who are just as poor as ever? For the International Center, reducing poverty is not the issue. Indeed, as four of its top researchers note, their findings that a well-organized family planning program can reduce birth rates in Bangladesh "have a significant bearing on one of the central questions in the population field: Can family planning programs in the developing world succeed in the absence of extensive socioeconomic development?" (Koenig et al. 1987, 123). The implication is that the answer is yes, even in Bangladesh, a country that Koenig et al. characterize as static with possibly even deteriorating economic conditions.

In theory, there is nothing intrinsically wrong with providing (voluntary) family planning services to a poor population, but there is something ethically questionable about promoting those services not only in the absence of desperately needed basic health care, but at its expense. When faced with this question, population control advocates usually fall back on the position that their narrow focus on family planning is justified because contraception is one of the most important health interventions to reduce infant and maternal mortality.

Lately, however, this assertion has come under increased scrutiny from demographers. John Bongaarts (1987) of the Population Council demonstrates, for example, how changes in family building patterns that accompany increased contraceptive use (for example, a higher proportion of first births and births after short intervals) offset the decline in infant mortality that would be expected as women adopt contraception and have fewer high risk teenage births and births after the sixth child. As a result, infant mortality rates remain virtually the same with high levels and low levels of contraceptive use. Bongaarts points specifically to the Matlab project area, which has witnessed little improvement in infant mortality despite a dramatic rise in contraceptive use. "What little decline [of infant mortality] that did occur," he writes, "was probably due in large part to maternal and child services introduced at the same time" (ibid., 331). As we have seen, it is precisely those services that the International Center is striving to keep to a minimum so as not to interfere with family planning.

Similarly, increased contraceptive use seems to have had only a limited effect on maternal mortality in the Matlab project area. Maternal mortality is typically expressed either as a ratio or deaths per 100,000 live births or as a rate of deaths per 100,000 women of reproductive age. By reducing the absolute number of pregnancies and births in the project area, the International Center's family planning program has achieved some reduction in the maternal mortality rate. However, the maternal mortality ratio has remained roughly the same because there has been no reduction in the health risks associated with each individual pregnancy (Koenig et al. 1988). The International Center's researchers attribute this phenomenon to the fact that increased contraceptive use has shifted the distribution of births from one high risk category, older women who have already borne many children, to another, younger women who are pregnant for the first time. (To their credit, they also recognize that the lack of safe abortion services in the project contributes to the persistence of high maternal mortality.)

At first glance, their analysis may seem compelling, but it ignores the International Center's own role in perpetuating the high risks associated with pregnancy in rural Bangladesh through its conscious decision not to provide basic maternity care as part of its family planning program. According to its own study, direct obstetric causes, such as postpartum hemorrhage, toxemia, and postpartum sepsis, accounted for 77 percent of all maternal deaths in the project area. Many of these could have been avoided with basic maternity care, including the training and equipping of traditional midwives, one of the "packages" the International Center has decided is not necessary to increase contraceptive acceptance.

Clearly for the International Center, preventing pregnancy takes priority over protecting the pregnant woman. One can only hope that a change is in order, for at least the study by Koenig et al. (1988, 79) admits that for real progress to be made in reducing maternal mortality, "family planning must be offered as only one component of a broader intervention strategy, that includes antenatal, delivery and postdelivery care" (ibid., 79).

The family planning approach toward reducing maternal mortality also fails to take into account that many contraceptives have associated mortality risks. Indeed, many feminists in the population field are calling for a wider definition of maternal mortality ("reproductive mortality"), which would include not only deaths associated with pregnancy, but those related to contraceptives. They are also challenging the efficiency of family planning alone in reducing maternal mortality. "Provision of health care seems to offer a more certain ability to prevent most fatalities from pregnancy," conclude Winikoff and Sullivan (1987). They point to the example of Sweden, where they estimate 97 percent of the reduction in maternal mortality between 1911 and 1980 was due to improved socioeconomic conditions and general health care, including maternity services, while changes in the age/parity distribution of births typically associated with increased contraceptive use accounted for only 3 percent.

Not surprisingly, within Bangladesh there is widespread disillusionment with the Matlab model. Local International Center staff as well as government health officials are reportedly very critical of the project's neglect of maternal and child health services and overemphasis on data collection. Yet the Matlab project still exercises considerable authority within the international population field and will no doubt continue to influence health policy in Bangladesh, unless there is a radical change in direction.

INTEGRATION OR DISINTEGRATION?

Attempts to integrate family planning and health, or more precisely to append a few health measures to population control, have wreaked havoc over the years with the Bangladesh health care system. They have led to five major reorganizations of the health bureaucracy, causing, according to the World Bank (1985, 7), "a legacy of program disruption and staff demoralization." Under the current system set up in 1983, family planning and health are joined in the Ministry of Health and Population Control, with family planning and selected maternal and child health services forming one semiautonomous wing and broader health services the other. Although the two are separated at upper levels of the bureaucracy, health and family planning are functionally integrated at the local level, with various personnel from the two wings supposedly assuming aspects of both duties.

The shift toward greater integration of the two at the local levels stems, in part, from the increased emphasis on sterilization and the intrauterine device, both of which require clinical infrastructure (see Akhter 1984b). Although the population program has benefited from the use of medical facilities and personnel, basic health care has suffered. A study of a UNFPA-funded maternal and child health/family planning project in Bangladesh makes this revealing observation:

This problem of orientation (which still persists), has resulted in placing undue emphasis on sterilization performance at the cost of other family planning methods and MCH services. (The Director of MCH reports that this aspect of service delivery is badly neglected because of lack of conviction on the part of programme managers: the sterilization activities are kept up largely as a result of external aid.) (Miyan 1984, 19).

In financial terms, population control (which includes some maternal and child health services) now absorbs over half of the annual health budget (World Bank 1987a, 186). Meanwhile, in purely operational terms, the latest functional integration has been nothing short of a disaster.

Dr. M. R. Khan (1986) of the Bangladesh Institute for Development Studies describes how functional integration "was introduced in great haste and without any field trial," leading to the "creation of enormous administrative problems." With different bosses and different budgets, local level health and family planning workers have little incentive to cooperate with each other. Instead, according to Khan: "Friction, tension, conflict, distrust and rivalry permeate at all levels. . . . Under the integration there is an anarchy in the subcentres . . . there is practically no supervision and no accountability. It appears that one group vies [with] the other only with respect to malpractices." This competition has had especially negative effects on the delivery of maternal and child health services, with no one willing to take adequate responsibility for their oversight.

In 1986–87, the government announced new measures that are supposed to improve the situation. These include greater integration of staff at the upper levels of the health bureaucracy and giving the *upazilla* chairmen (local elected officials) greater control over health and family planning workers in their areas. A Dutch evaluation of the Population III project notes how this latter measure may lead to more problems because it introduces "a highly politicized cadre in these activities" (van Praag 1988, 6). Indeed, it could strengthen local patronage networks, which already undermine the health system.

On the donor side, there appears to be a change in attitude as to what precisely integration means. The failure of past policies to reduce birth rates substantially, much less to improve people's health, has finally convinced the population hardliners in the aid community, notably USAID and the World Bank, of the need to strengthen and expand maternal and child health services, as well as to improve the quality of family planning. The Dutch evaluation of the Population III project notes that this recognition is rather late in the light of experiences elsewhere because of two related inhibiting factors: "The separation of the health ministry into two sub-ministries, and therefore two separate bureaucracies of population control and of health; [and] the strong emphasis of certain donors on singular, independent and vertical population programmes" (van Praag 1988, 5–6).

According to the evaluation, donors now realize a reduction in infant mortality is the key to motivating people to have fewer children. As a result, a universal child immunization program has been launched. So far it has been very successful in eight pilot areas, with local level family planning and health workers cooperating well for the first time. Other positive developments are increased recruitment and training of local midwives and expansion of diarrheal disease control. Even USAID is beginning to channel more funds into infant survival and is financing scholarships so girls can attend secondary school because of the link between literacy and control over one's fertility.

These measures are to be welcomed, but we must wait and see how far this increased commitment to maternal and child health extends because population control still remains the centerpiece of health policy. For example, the aide memoire written by the cofinanciers of Population III refers to the Bangladesh government's "insufficiently visible overall commitment . . . to population policy" (quoted in van Praag 1988 Annex 1: 4, 11). It also states explicitly that the main goal of the women's development projects organized under Population III is fertility reduction of the targeted women and not, by implication, improvements in their welfare or economic condition. Similarly, maternal and child health services continue to be perceived as an adjunct to family planning, not as a basic health right.

A LOOK AHEAD

The first step toward the establishment of a popularly based health care system in Bangladesh must be the abandonment of population control as the organizing principle. However, population control is itself an outgrowth of the larger technocratic model of development, in which modern technology is expected to solve social problems and leadership is vested in the managers, who substitute top-down social engineering for democratic self-determination. Inequalities between sexes, classes, and nations are typically ignored. Development, according to the technocratic definition, can occur without a fundamental change in power relations.

Even if there is a genuine shift away from population control in Bangladesh, the technocratic approach to health is likely to persist. In terms of maternal and child health delivery, donors increasingly emphasize, in Bangladesh as elsewhere in the Third World, the identification of a few select health problems and the introduction of cost-effective technological interventions, notably oral rehydration for diarrhea and immunization, rather than address the social roots of ill health and build a lasting health care system. "Means have taken the place of ends," writes Wisner (1988, 965) in his critique of this approach: "Are we really supposed to believe that oral rehydration therapy is an acceptable substitute for the clean water which would prevent diarrhea, to which parent and child have a right?"[3]

It will be interesting to see how the international community's current (and long overdue) concern for maternal mortality is translated into concrete programs in Bangladesh. Certainly, the conceptual framework of the World Bank's "Safe Motherhood Initiative" is extremely limited. It proposes a few specific interventions, such as family planning, pregnancy risk screening, and emergency referral capability, which can be implemented at a minimum cost, to reduce maternal mortality. The basic assumption is that poor countries simply do not have the resources to implement more comprehensive maternity care. According to the World Bank, the dilemma is whether to provide:

"a little for the many" versus something more for somewhat fewer people. Unfortunately, the evidence so far suggests that substantial reductions in maternal mortality are difficult to achieve without some minimum [health] system. . . . The problems of pregnancy require a certain amount of health technology and referral capacity that carries a cost (Herz and Measham 1987).

This approach raises a number of serious questions. Why just "a little for the many"—why can't resources be redistributed so there is more to spend on people's health? One only has to look at the level of military expenditures in Bangladesh, and indeed throughout the world, to see where precious resources are being wasted. The debt burden draining Third World economies also represents a tragic waste of resources. The World Bank and International Monetary Fund are forcing Third World countries to make drastic cuts in social programs so governments can service their debt. The result is that in the last ten years spending per person on health has dropped nearly 25 percent in the thirty-seven poorest nations of the world (UNICEF 1989, 17), and it is women and children who have suffered the most from such cuts.

One also has to ask why it is "unfortunate" that a minimum health system is required to reduce maternal mortality? And that it "costs" something? Once again, as in the case of family planning, the World Bank would like to divorce women's reproductive health needs from their needs for general health care. And of course reducing maternal mortality will cost money, but it is money well spent. Money spent on basic health care, including reproductive health, is a productive investment in the future. High levels of chronic ill health are a brake on development and a further drain on a country's resources.

Fortunately, feminists in the population field are challenging this narrow concept of "safe motherhood" and calling for a health strategy that meet women's needs from the moment they are born because that is when their problems begin.

International and national feminist organizations, such as the Women's Global Network on Reproductive Rights, are also drawing attention to the social forces that condemn women to high risks of maternal mortality and morbidity: malnutrition, poor living standards, illiteracy, low wages, lack of control over sexuality, illegal abortion, and male violence in the family, to name but a few (see, for example, Winikoff 1988; Women's Global Network . . . 1988). Not even the best health care system can cure these social ills.

Ultimately, the politics of health must become the politics of transformation: transformation at the international level, so that technocratic models are challenged and replaced; transformation at the national level, so that resources are redistributed and allocated toward meeting people's genuine needs; and transformation at the local level, so that poor women and men have the power to assert and win their rights.

In Bangladesh today, many people are involved in the politics of transformation. The People's Health Center (*Gonoshasthaya Kendra*) in Savar has taken the lead in building a popularly oriented health care system that serves the surrounding villages. Making use of its experience in training village women as paramedics, the center has also worked to redesign medical education in Bangladesh, so that medical staff are more responsive to the needs of the rural population. In addition, it has set up its own nonprofit pharmaceutical factory to produce essential drugs at low cost, challenging foreign multinationals' dominance of the Bangladesh market.

The center also provides family planning services, but only on a strictly voluntary basis. It has long been critical of population control in Bangladesh. As far back as 1977, it made this statement:

We believe [family planning] should be one part of a general, permanent, primary health service, where women can be assured of constantly available advice and supplies, and where family planning is a means towards the emancipation of women. We must resist an attitude where pregnancies and babies are treated as an epidemic that has to be eradicated once and for all (quoted in Keysers 1982, 246).

Through its network of clinics, the Bangladesh Women's Health Coalition has shown how family planning, menstrual regulation, and general reproductive health care can be offered safely, sensitively, and effectively. The coalition and its international counterpart, the International Women's Health Coalition, have played a major role in shifting the terms of the family planning debate away from population control toward women's reproductive rights (see, for example, Germain 1987).

The independent research organization, UBINIG, has also played a vital role in analyzing health and population policy in Bangladesh and exposing abuses. UBINIG has demonstrated how important it is to do local level research and to record the experiences of poor women and men in order to find out how family planning programs function in reality.

   Throughout Bangladesh, there are also many other groups, whether they be
unions of landless laborers or women's organizations, working to transform the
social, economic, and political conditions that lie at the root of ill health. Medical
care alone can never cure malnutrition or dirty water or lack of shelter. Land
reform, employment generation, mass education, the emancipation of women,
and democratic political structures are the best medicines against the most serious
diseases of all in Bangladesh: poverty and inequality.

5

Migration, Public Policy, and Women's Experience

Meredeth Turshen, Hélène Bretin, and Annie Thébaud-Mony

INTRODUCTION

Although theoretically acknowledged, international migration is a relatively neglected aspect of demography. The majority of demographic studies are devoted to fertility and mortality. Most research on fertility patterns is about women, whereas research on mortality trends is traditionally about infant and adult populations, though there is some interest in differential male/female mortality rates (Lopez and Rudicka 1983). Migration studies are for the most part about men, although women and children may account for 80 percent of one group of migrants, namely refugees (United Nations 1991, 74). There are few statistics on women's migration, and we must turn to the sociological literature for estimates and trends.

Migrants fall into four groups: settlers, labor migrants, refugees from catastrophes such as drought and war, and political refugees. Whatever their reason for leaving home, all contemporary migrants find that their lives are shaped by public policy. Our focus in this chapter is labor migration.

In recent years, increasing numbers of Asian and Latin American women have migrated in search of work. Sassen-Koob (1983) describes the phenomenon in terms of the new international division of labor. She is particularly interested in two circuits—from the periphery to centers of high economic growth in the Third World (countries with large oil-export processing zones), and from southeast Asia and the Caribbean to London and New York City. Jelin (1977) was the first to draw attention to the migration of young Latin American women; she studied women looking for work as domestics. Since then, Berlin (1983) has studied Colombian female workers in the Venezuelan garment industry. Matsui (1989), a Japanese journalist, has interviewed Filipinas working in other parts of Asia. The majority of studies remain concerned with internal rather than international migration. Some researchers focus on the impact of men's international migration on the women left behind (see Gordon [1981] and Wilkinson [1987] for studies of the impact of men's migration to the South African mines on women in Lesotho).

This chapter is about African women who migrate to France because their husbands are migrant laborers there. It considers the impact of male labor migration from North and West Africa on the lives of African women and their families in France and the ways in which French immigration policy conditions those experiences. Little has been written in English about the migration of African women to Europe. There is a small body of unpublished academic literature in French, which appeared in the 1970s and 1980s, concerning the migration of North African women to France (Tauzin and Virolle-Souibès 1990). France, like the United States, has long been confronted with the need to integrate newcomers (Noiriel 1988). Several French government studies have appeared recently on the question of immigration and national identity (Haut Conseil à l'Intégration 1991). The government has felt a new urgency since the influx of sub-Saharan Africans in the 1970s concluded with the beginning of a long economic decline. The growing confrontation between the older French population and the younger migrant populations from North and West Africa, incited by the racist National Front party line of Jean-Marie Le Pen, erupts periodically in riots (Commission Nationale Consultative des Droits de l'Homme 1991). Although the French government recognizes that immigrant women are subject to the double discrimination of racism and sexism, only two pages of the 1991 report by the National Consultative Commission on Human Rights are devoted to this problem (ibid., 163–164). The High Commission on Integration passes over the subject of women's integration in silence.

BACKGROUND TO LABOR MIGRATION

In general, public policy determines the circumstances in which men migrate in search of work, and it therefore shapes the lives of the women who are their wives, mothers, and daughters. If labor immigration policy prohibits the entry of family members, then the women left behind must take on additional responsibilities, often tasks that only men assumed in the past, and husbands and wives must cope with the loss of daily emotional support and with intermittent sexual relations. If immigration policy permits families to accompany male migrant workers, then women will face the problems of adjustment in a new land, for which they rarely have the necessary language or educational skills.

The economic needs of industry and agriculture tend to govern public policy on immigration in most countries, and the flow of workers expands and contracts with business cycles. Schematically, when the business cycle is on the upswing, all sectors of the economy expand and require more workers. If the national labor force is too small, as in countries with small populations, or if the country has large numbers of people too young or too old to work, or if the population is too well-off to want to do menial jobs, or if the labor force is highly unionized and workers are able to command high wages, then employers have recourse to an immigrant work force. They petition government to encourage immigration and may even organize recruitment missions abroad. Their success depends on development policies in the countries in which they recruit.

These employers are interested in units of labor: Generally, they prefer single young men. They are not concerned with families and do not want to pay a family wage or extend benefits to family members. They prefer to regard married men as bachelors and to recruit them without their wives and children. In the colonial period, European administrations maintained the fiction that "native" families were self-supporting and that women could sustain themselves and their children on the land.

When the business cycle swings down into a recession, the economy contracts and workers are laid off. The colonial hope was that migrant workers would return home, to be absorbed by the subsistence economy, kept viable by women, children, and the elderly. There was no need for employers to pay unemployment insurance or for the government to pay the dole. Subsistence economies, it was thought, do not expand, nor do they experience recessions.

In these periods of contraction, employers may signal the government that they no longer require an open door policy on immigration. If the recession is severe, national workers may petition the government to stop immigration because they perceive foreign workers as a threat, in competition for the few remaining jobs. If the downturn drags on for several years, right-wing political forces may manipulate the unemployed and whip up xenophobia, putting recent immigrants in danger of verbal abuse and physical attack.

In the colonial period prior to World War II, women were left behind by the men who migrated in search of work. These women struggled with increased responsibilities (usually not compensated by broadened authority or sanctioned by society). The breakdown of family life often occurred when their men took second wives and started second families in the town where they worked. Some of the rural areas in which women lived became so underdeveloped that the women fled, too, leaving only children and the elderly in what became rural slums.

In recent years, Africanists, especially feminist historians, have turned their attention to the women who lived on the fringes of male encampments. For example, Parpart (1988) writes about the women who lived in copper mining camps in Zambia; she is interested in the response of these women to patriarchal coalitions of colonial officials and rural chiefs that tried to bring them under control. The sex ratios of cities were so imbalanced that they were virtually male camps. Luise White (1988) describes the women who migrated to Nairobi and supported themselves selling food, lodgings, companionship, and sex to migrants.

The stories of the women who worked on plantations are only now being recovered (see Matsui [1989] on Malaysian plantations; Loewenson on Zimbabwean plantations [1991]).

Although simplistic and inaccurate, colonial authorities described the women who left their villages as prostitutes. Binary thinking divided women into two categories: the "good" married women who were not permitted to accompany husbands in migration, and the "bad" single women who left their father's or brother's protection and must be prostitutes.

Some of the same problems arose in the postcolonial period in Europe. After World War II, as most African countries agitated for independence and as the European economies prospered in the postwar boom, African workers began taking jobs in the metropolitan countries, and many sent for their wives and children to join them. This was the pattern in France. From 1955, French industrialists were once more actively recruiting foreign workers, with official sanction. As the usual hunting grounds—the poorer nations of southern Europe (Portuguese and Italians remain the largest national groups in France)—no longer produced enough workers to meet the needs of the expanding economy, recruiters turned to northern and western Africa.

From the mid–1950s, North Africans—Algerians, Moroccans, and Tunisians—brought their wives and children to France; at a later date, starting in the mid–1970s, West Africans—Senegalese, Malians, and Mauritanians—did the same. By 1984, the Interior Ministry estimated that immigrants accounted for 7 percent of the population of France: There were 770,000 Algerians, including 305,000 women, and 156,700 sub-Saharan Africans from French-speaking countries, including 55,100 women (Brucker 1989, 785; Rahal-Sidhoum 1988, 356). These women found themselves even less welcome than their menfolk; few of them spoke French or were educated in their mother tongue; many from rural areas had no experience of waged work and were perceived by the French to be costly to the welfare state. Even women from West African cities who left jobs had trouble translating their skills into the requirements of the metropolitan capital and could not find comparable work.

When the postwar expansion ended and the present economic crisis began in the 1970s, France's public policy changed quickly. In 1974, the French government decided to halt immigration (Brucker 1989, 782). Noiriel (1988, 24), the French historian of immigration, explains the change in government policy: "In periods of crisis, the interests of society and of those who govern it are necessarily displaced from production to reproduction (as the Marxists would have it); that is to say from the foreign worker to his family and his children."[1] It seems paradoxical that, just at the moment when the government has virtually halted all immigration (some aliens still enter the country illegally), there is a popular perception that immigrants are more numerous than ever.

From the viewpoint of migration, one of the great paradoxes of crises is that they cause a stabilization of the foreign population in the receiving society at a moment at which that society is shaken by fundamental structural transformations. Each of these periods of stabilization brings the realization of the irreversible nature of the settlement of new-comers. As the number of women and children rises, their new visibility in workplaces, in neighborhoods, in schools and hospitals can be traced to their permanent settlement (ibid., 250).

MIGRANT WOMEN

Changing societal expectations about gender roles and the changed expecta-tions migrant women have of their roles as mothers, wives, and workers in their new homes are of special interest. In the course of our research on women's use of contraception in family planning centers in a *département* of the Paris region, we conducted interviews that turned out to be rich in information on the impact of migration on marriage and family life and on women's personal development. In this study, which is reported on elsewhere (Bretin et al. 1991), 38 percent of the 1,035 participants were from thirty-two foreign countries. Algerians were the single largest group, and one of us (HB) contacted eight women through the teams of public health workers who staffed the clinics. In 1987 and 1988, interviews were conducted in the centers or at the women's homes by HB, a medical sociologist, accompanied by Zohra Medjahed, an Algerian medical doctor. The women recounted their life histories, including their contraceptive practice. Women from sub-Saharan Africa represented 6 percent of the 1,035 participants in the study and came from thirteen countries. Again using the clinic staff as intermediaries, in 1989 and 1990, we interviewed six women from Mali, Mauritania, and Senegal. We also spoke with clinic staff, doctors and nurses, and with an association defending African women, *Association Soleil d'Afrique*. All interviews were conducted in French and translated by MT.

INTERVIEWS WITH AFRICAN WOMEN

Our interviews with African women in France showed a complex picture; migration often emerged as a turning point in their lives, sometimes as a point of no return.

For many women, the experience of migration begins with a husband's de-parture. (There are variations on this theme: Some men are already migrants before they marry and only come home for the wedding ceremony and then are off again; others migrate only after several years of marriage.) Life changes for those women whose husbands migrate and leave them behind. They find them-selves alone with their in-laws, and some complain that they become maidser-vants to their husband's often aged parents. This is the experience recounted by Fadela, about when she was nineteen years old and pregnant with her first child:

It was not a life. I stayed at home all day long with my in-laws. We did not go out. I could not leave the house alone. The wall surrounding the courtyard was ten feet high, and the iron gate was locked. If someone knocked, I was not allowed to answer—only my mother-in-law or my father-in-law could go to the gate. There was no one to confide in, no one to speak to, no one to tell what was on my mind. I was disgusted with my life.

Fadela's marriage was arranged by her family; she was betrothed to a migrant worker who returned during a vacation for the wedding ceremony. Zahwa was chosen by a migrant worker who came back from France looking for a wife. After her marriage, Zahwa lived with her in-laws for two or three years before joining her husband in France. She describes her situation at twenty-three:

He was working in France; he sent money to his parents. I was like a slave; I worked for them, like a maid! In France maids are paid. I ate, I slept, that's all. I had no right to leave the house unless my mother-in-law said, "We are going to see your parents." We were neighbors; they lived one block away, yet I might not see my mother for three or four months. For my husband's sake I put up with it, with two years of suffering. My mother-in-law was in charge. She made me do the laundry for the whole household. If I began at 9 am, I did not finish until 4 pm. There was no washing machine.

Some women find life more restricted and more isolated in Paris than in their native lands. Saïma, twenty-five years old, married a man born in France and did not meet her mother-in-law until she joined her husband in Paris.

When I heard that he had parents here, his sisters and all his family, I wasn't afraid. I said, his mother will become my mother, his sisters will be my sisters. I won't have any problems; I won't be lonely; I won't be distressed. If I become troubled, I will just tell my mother-in-law, as I would my own mother, and she'll take me out and we'll have fun. This is how I reckoned. In many families that I know, there are daughters-in-law, but I wasn't aware of their situation. I imagined that if my mother-in-law were told, your daughter-in-law is distressed, she has no one here, she lives alone, that my mother-in-law would take me out. But not my mother-in-law. I hadn't reckoned on this. I didn't think things would go wrong. At least if I were in my country, it would be only half-bad. Near my parents, it would be only half-bad. If my parents were here, a friend or someone, perhaps I would not be so depressed. When I am within these four walls, there are problems, and I don't even have a friend I can go out and visit, which would do me good. I am homesick. There I had family, friends, everything. Now I live like a prisoner between four walls.

Saïma's mother-in-law accompanied her everywhere, even to the maternal and child health center, which is usually the one place women can go alone. Her mother-in-law exercised control over everything, including the couple's bills and their budget. Saïma suffered from her husband's inability or unwillingness to defend her, and the conflicts were so sharp that she even spoke of leaving him.

The women complained frequently of the loss of friends and the extended family. Zahwa regrets her life without deep and faithful friends, "Friends here are not like friends in Algeria. The difference is that here one says, 'good morning, good evening' and that's all. Here, if one falls ill, no one comes to see you. Sometimes I stay in bed one or two weeks and no one comes, other than my husband." Fatoumata said that in sub-Saharan Africa, "even if you have many children, everyone helps you and the house is large; there is always someone to look after a child, it's a different family structure." She is pregnant with her fifth child and is also taking care of three children that belong to her cowife who is back in Mali, but "here there's no help."

Violence Against Women

Coumba's marriage was arranged in France by her mother; her husband is an older man (not polygamous) who was previously married three times. There were violent conflicts between them and he beat her; she showed us a scar in her neck from a hot iron he had thrown at her, and she said she had broken his arm.

Does the absence of family and friends isolate immigrant women and expose them to domestic violence? The relationship between isolation and domestic violence is well established. According to Marchev (quoted in Sidel 1986, 40), battered women are particularly isolated. They are isolated by their husbands often because of men's extreme jealousy. And they isolate themselves; they are isolated by their shame. Battered women may not see people outside the family for months at a time.

Fainzang and Journet (1988, 140) confirm the observation that immigrant women are isolated. Their study of Senegalese women in Paris showed that the possibilities of divorce are reduced in the context of immigration: women without an income have no economic autonomy, and their social isolation does not give them an avenue of escape. Customarily, a married woman in trouble would return to her parents' home. If her family and friends are in Africa and she has no money for airfare, a wife cannot easily leave a conflictual situation.

The knowledge that a woman is his virtual prisoner probably adds to a man's sense of power over his wife. Many analysts attribute domestic violence to the structure of the patriarchal family, which institutionalizes the subordination of women and their subjection to male authority and control (Sidel 1986, 45).

The Division of Household Labor

The traditional sexual division of labor may or may not be maintained in France; some men help women with domestic tasks. Zahwa, mother of seven, recounts:

When my husband was working, he helped me out. When he worked, yes, but now that he is unemployed he's changed. When he takes off his clothes, he drops them on the floor, and I have to pick them up. Before he used to put the children to bed, he put

them in their pyjamas, he even fed them. He helped me a lot. Now, nothing. I even
have to wash up his shaving things and put them away. I'm the one who takes the children
to the doctor, supervises their homework, me, everything is on my shoulders.

Both Zina, a second-generation Algerian born in France, and her husband
work, she during the day, he at night. They have three children and share the
domestic tasks: "We divide the tasks according to who is home at the time. One
or the other of us washes the dishes, starts the washing machine, takes the wash
out of the dryer; if I'm not there, he wakes up the children, cooks for them at
noon."

Karidiatou says her husband is helpless, doesn't know how to change diapers,
can't cook. "I was at the maternity hospital for a week, and he lost weight because
he didn't eat."

In general, immigrant women take on added responsibilities; they have to deal
with the state on the issues of an all-encompassing bureaucracy that administers
their daily lives, no matter how limited their ability to speak and read French.
One of us (MT) went through the immigration process and experienced the
frustrations of the time-consuming paperwork involved in securing a medical
examination, a visa, an identity card, permission to stay and work in the country,
a social security card, and health insurance.

Fadela complains,

I'm tired. I tell you that right away, I'm tired. I have five children and no help. My
husband does nothing at home. He works, he brings us food, that's it. If it's a question
of shopping or paperwork, he doesn't lift a finger. His days off are Saturday and Sunday,
when offices are closed. So for the post office, city hall, for papers, for social security,
it's me; I take care of everything.

Paid Work

In most of sub-Saharan Africa, women are self-sufficient, paid for their work
or sell on their own account. Except in northern Nigeria, West African women
often work outside their homes as traders. Aïsha, forty years old from rural
Mauritania, told us through an interpreter, "In Africa, it's different; women work
like men." She resented having to ask her husband for everything, for the daily
allowance that allowed her to feed and clothe six children as well as for big
purchases like the washing machine that liberated her from washing eight people's
clothes by hand every day. Coumba, twenty-four years old, a divorced mother
of two from Senegal, said, "In Dakar, you are free, you have a trade [she is a
dressmaker and ran her own business in Dakar]. In Paris, it's hard." Coumba's
family was well off in Senegal, employing a cook and a housemaid. In Paris, it
is likely that the only work she will find is cooking or cleaning for a French
family. We found these women angry about the changes in their status.

Few Algerian women work outside their homes: In 1982, 3.5 percent of women were in the paid labor force in Algeria (Bernard 1990, 96). Nadia was one of the few. She had eleven years of schooling, which qualified her to work first as a secretary and later as a computer operator for SONATRACH, the Algerian national oil company. She worked for nine years before her marriage to a migrant worker. In France, she was unable to find a job. She looked, soon after her arrival, but was discouraged by the long lines at the employment offices. "I would like to go back, get back my job. There's work for me in Algeria, but not for my husband."

Algerian women are confronted with a different model in France, where 45 percent of women work (United Nations 1991, 104). The contact with working women leads some of them to aspire to finding a job, but they encounter obstacles: either their husbands object, or they have no marketable skills, or the bureaucracy stands in the way.

At thirty-four, Zahwa has seven children, the youngest an infant, the oldest ten. "He doesn't want me to work," she said of her husband.

After my last child was born, I said, I will stop having children, I will work. As I saw he didn't earn a lot, I suggested that I take a job. He said, "You will never work." He said, "What would you do?" And it's true, I have no training. I could work in a school canteen, but he doesn't want me to work. If tomorrow we found something, like a restaurant to run, I would help him.

At twenty-six, Fatima had one child and wanted to work. Her husband was unemployed. "If I had papers, I would be able to work a little, housecleaning, child care, anything."

Personal Development and Cultural Conflicts

For some African women, life in Paris is full of deceptions. Zahwa says,

I have been here for ten years and I have seen nothing. I have no memories of my years in France, as if I wasn't living. I think about my life in Algeria, I begin to laugh. I remember which families came to our house, which feasts we celebrated. I phone home and I begin to cry. I cry each time because I remember the warmth there. I am alone here. It's no life. I don't know what keeps us here. I can't see this life. I just can't see it.

Some West African women imagined France as offering them greater educational opportunities—and it is true for their daughters and for a different population of single women sent to France by well-off families to complete their studies, often at the university level. For wives of the migrants who work as street sweepers and in commercial cleaning services, even the completion of primary school is impossible. Karidiatou, twenty-three years old from Senegal, left school after eight years; she wanted to continue, but her husband was opposed to having anyone else look after the children. She thought she could take up her studies again when she came to France but, she said, "with children it is not possible; one cannot do both."

Zina, a second-generation Algerian, is caught between two cultures; the conflict is expressed in the differences between her life and her mother's and in the distance between them. Born, raised, and educated in France, Zina bowed to her mother's wish that she marry; she returns regularly to Algeria, where the family has a house. But, she says,

there are many things my mother doesn't understand. She finds it normal that a woman works, but she doesn't understand that I have lots of girlfriends, both French and Algerian. She thinks that when a woman finishes work, she should return home and stay there, taking care of her children, her husband, and her parents. Above all, it is important not to forget one's parents.

Zina is expected to be the guardian of a culture of which her knowledge is imperfect and from which she has broken on certain points.

The Racist Encounter with French Norms

Expectations of motherhood—of childbearing, child rearing, and family size—change dramatically for migrant women in France. On the one hand, women come with expectations based on African norms: total fertility (which represents the number of children that would be born to a woman if she were to live to the end of her child-bearing years and bear children at each age in accordance with prevailing age-specific fertility rates) is 5.4 in Algeria, 7 in Mali, 6.5 in Mauritania, and 6.5 in Senegal (World Bank 1990, 231). On the other hand, women confront the realities of reduced living space, lack of aid from members of the extended family left behind, reduced time between pregnancies (which the women attribute to lack of work outside the home), and above all pressures from French society, which has experienced a dramatic decline from 2.8 total fertility in 1965 to 1.8 in 1988 (ibid.).

Women encounter the pressure to reduce and space their pregnancies in their contacts with the medical establishment; they are made to feel guilty and ignorant by the staff of the maternal and child health centers. Zahwa explains:

When the staff in the clinics see a woman with many children, they don't like it if she is pregnant again. They ask me whether I have help—someone to clean and care for the children; I say no. If I want an abortion, I'm the one who knows. If I don't want a child, I'm the one who knows. If I am pregnant, I'm the one who has come to see the gynecologist. I don't want a lecture. I know what I'm doing. . . . When I returned from Algeria with the twins, I was embarrassed about going to the maternal and child health center. I don't know if they don't like it because it's not good for a woman's health or what. I'm in very good health. When the doctor saw me, I'm in such good shape, she asked, "Is this your first?" . . . The gynecologist doesn't tell you directly, the doctor doesn't question you, why are you having another child; but the staff let you know.

At the maternity clinic, Noura confronts the same attitude. The staff takes it for granted that she will use a contraceptive after the birth. "They didn't even ask my opinion. They asked whether I wanted the pill or an IUD [intrauterine device]. I said the pill. I wouldn't say neither because, you know, they say that Arabs want babies right away."

Zahwa feels that her treatment at the maternity clinic was different from what a French woman would have received; she realizes she is used as teaching material, that students are learning obstetrics on her body:

I'm not a racist but when they see an Arab, they take advantage. Not just a little, a lot. If it had been a French woman they wouldn't have done that. They call all the interns, they come to touch; they have no right to come and touch. It hurts when they insert their fingers. You take them out, another one puts them in. It was a breech presentation; I understood it was to learn. One doctor said "See how it feels," the other said, "I feel its dick." I didn't say anything. Only now. I'm not a bad person, I figured if they don't know they have to learn. At least ten, men and women, inserted their fingers.

Saïma is more direct in her condemnation; she recounts this experience of childbirth:

The day of the delivery was terrible because of a midwife. I had planned on a normal delivery, not a Caesarian. She asked the doctor to perform a Caesarian. I didn't even know what it was. The doctor didn't agree. When she asked me, I thought it was "points" [episiotomy], so I said yes. The next morning when I woke up I saw the Caesarian, tubes, serums, and everything; I said oh, so that's a Caesarian. Later I saw my stomach, it was terrible! . . . I don't know. Afterwards I asked myself whether she was racist. She doesn't like Arabs. There are racists everywhere. That's the truth. That's what I'm thinking, because there was no reason for a Caesarian. I had all the tests—the midwife said they were good, the sonogram was good. The doctor gave me an oxygen mask, but as soon as he was out of the room, she removed it. When the doctor came back, I asked for it and he gave it to me; as soon as he leaves again, she removes it. Really, I fell into the hands of a woman. . . . I'll never forget that day. I was so scared. I am absolutely certain she is racist.

Children

For the nostalgic Zahwa, her seven children are the only reference point in a life without memories, in a life that escapes her control and that she cannot make her own. "I had my children. I can see them. I know that I had them. If it weren't for them . . . "

Noura, illiterate and uneducated, was married at eighteen to the son of an Algerian migrant worker. Her husband has lived in France since he was eight years old. Noura wanted to space her pregnancies but her husband said, "I brought you here to have children, and it is better to have them right away so that they can grow up together. . . . If I didn't intend to have children, I would have left you in the village and I would have married a French woman or an Algerian woman living in Paris." Noura sighs, "He was happy to hear about my first pregnancy. I was ambivalent. I was not well adjusted to life in France." (Ten years after her arrival, she still speaks through an interpreter.) "I was ill with my first pregnancy. I wasn't aware of anything, didn't even know I was pregnant. I couldn't speak French or anything. I knew no one. He went to work each day and left me all alone in the apartment."

The Second Generation

Parents fear for their children's future in France and some Algerians think it would be better to return to Algeria. Noura's husband says, "The day my oldest son turns fifteen, we go home. I've had it. I've seen what it's like, I don't want my children to get hurt. Not for nothing did I buy a house in Algeria, it's obligatory. We must return."

Zahwa describes her conflicting and contradictory feelings:

It's hard. We have to save our children. If they grow up here, they will never go back. They get used to this place and they won't follow their parents home. I know of many families who have returned to Algeria, but the children came back to France because they couldn't live there. When they are small they can do it. I don't think there's a future for them in France. They have no work and hang out around the housing projects. When my oldest turns eighteen, he won't find work, and I'm going to feel sorry for him, sorry that we stayed in France.

CONCLUSION

Just as the stabilization of foreign populations in periods of crisis increases their visibility in the host country, the discontinuation of labor migration accentuates the arrival of family members. People seem to believe that the number of families arriving to join established migrants grows annually, that many workers wait and postpone the decision to bring their families over. A 1983 study of a sample of workers asking permission to bring in their families showed that transformation of male migration into family migration is not a new phenomenon; it had been masked by a period of massive male labor migration. Public concern with the entry of families coincides in reality more with the arrival on the political scene of the second generation of immigrants than with the mass arrival of families (Silberman 1990). In the same way, the often remarked upon high birth rate of foreign women appears in reality to be varied when one approaches the question from the profiles of individual migrating families.

The situation of migrant women does not weigh heavily in the deliberations of the French government, nor are women's participation and opinions solicited, as the list of consultants to even the most recent reports reveals. The first annual report of the High Commission on Integration for 1991 makes no specific reference to women. The 1990 report of the National Consultative Commission on Human Rights finds it sufficient to note that the mission of the Secretary of State for the rights of women is to help migrant women with social and cultural integration and with employment and training.

The integration of foreign women encounters multiple obstacles linked to government family immigration policy. In 1981–82, there was an exceptional amnesty that allowed 23,000 clandestine female workers to regularize their situation; 67 percent of them were unmarried and 75 percent lived alone. Of those who were married, 76 percent had a husband in France, and 50 percent of married women who had a husband in France said their husband could not or would not obtain papers authorizing their stay in France (Rahal-Sidhoum 1988, 359). Until 1981, men were required to bring their whole family, but now they can bring whichever members they want. If the family comes and the husband does not procure for his wife the legal documents required by the government, she may find herself without a visa or permit to stay.

In addition, family immigration is conditional on the rental of an apartment of sufficient size, on the husband's ability to document his rental (with a lease or landlord's certificate), on his savings, and on his work contract. In 1976, a government decree permitted families already in France that fulfilled these conditions to regularize their stay. This permission was revoked in 1984. Now only the entrance procedure functions. Family members in France for several years must leave and re-enter the country. They must pass the medical exam required by the Office of International Migration in order to obtain an entry visa. The sheer number of requirements ensures limited family immigration and, paradoxically, favors clandestine and precarious situations for many people who give up hope of legalizing their stay.

In this context, women can find themselves in absolutely dramatic predicaments, especially single mothers living alone. One social worker attached to the Department of Health and Social Affairs in Paris, which receives requests from such women, said,

Mothers living alone can regularize their situation under the Nationality Code, if they have been in France for more than five years, by claiming French nationality for their child. But to benefit from article 54 of the Code, women must produce proof of stable employment. Since these women hold only the receipt acknowledging their request for a visa, they cannot obtain regular work, [which is dependent on a visa]. Before, article 54 was not applied so strictly and the problem of single mothers was not so critical. . . . I see more and more single mothers, six or seven a day, who have no legal right to be here. When they give birth, they stay at the hospital only three days before they are discharged. I have seen Algerian women with three children, for example, each of the children holds a French identity card, but the mother still has no papers" (GISTI 1990, 13).

Immigrant women have organized a number of associations to help each other: *Les Nanas Beurs*, created in 1985, offers help with the everyday life problems of second-generation Algerian women in France. *Association Nouvelle Génération Immigré(e)s* does similar work in a suburb of Paris. *Expressions Maghrébines au Féminin* is involved in the education, training, and employment of young North African women in France. *Association Soleil d'Afrique*, an organization concerned with West African immigrants, initially limited its assistance to women, but now offers to help men and women with their problems (employment, housing, legal and administrative questions, and the education of children). These groups give aid to individuals, but they also speak out in behalf of their communities, especially on issues of racism and sexism (see, for example, *Carnets des Nanas Beurs*, 70 rue Casteja, 92100 Boulogne Billancourt, France; *Mousso: Mensuel de la femme immigrée noire en Europe*, 39 rue de Romainville, 75019 Paris, France). Their aim is to represent an organized constituency that can influence French immigration policy.

In the absence of access to official channels through which citizens normally apply political pressure at local, parliamentary, and state levels, these associations are forced to confine their influence to the communities in which they work. Immigrants do not have the right to vote in France. Male immigrants have some access to power through participation in trade unions at their workplaces. Female immigrants are totally excluded from any expression of citizenship in French society. Forms of resistance and solidarity exist, but they do not amount to an alternative power structure. The inability of immigrants to influence the policies that control their lives illustrates the limits of democracy in France in this last decade of the twentieth century.

Part II

Sex and Marriage, Violence and Control

6

Violence Against Women: An Obstacle to Development

Roxanna Carrillo

Human development is a process of enlarging people's choices. The most critical of these wide ranging choices are to live a long and healthy life, to be educated and to have access to resources needed for a decent standard of living. Additional choices include political freedom, guaranteed human rights and personal self-respect. Development enables people to have these choices.

—UNDP, *Human Development Report 1990*

The United Nations Decade for Women (1976–85) helped to bring attention to the critical importance of women's activities for economic and social development. However, after fifteen years of efforts to integrate women into development, women are still only marginal beneficiaries of development programs and policy goals. Various studies show that women remain in a disadvantaged position in employment, education, health, and government. There is no field of activity and no country in which women have obtained equality with men (Sivard 1985, 5).

In spite of the slow process of change, the UN decade and women working in the international development community have been successful in identifying issues critical for women's development that were not traditionally understood as central to the development process. One such area is gender violence. Violence against women was previously seen, if seen at all, as a private matter, a cultural and family issue, or at best, pertinent to social welfare policies. Those concerned

The basic research for this chapter was done under the sponsorship of the United Nations Development Fund for Women (UNIFEM).

with the general position of women have addressed gender violence within the framework of promoting peace and, increasingly, as part of the human rights agenda. These approaches underscore the multiple aspects of such violence but they in no way exhaust our understanding of the problem. There are still large gaps in our knowledge of the dimensions and effects of gender violence on the development process. Lack of statistical data is one of several problems in documenting the issue. We have reached a critical point in understanding how violence as a form of control affects women's participation in the development process.

Rather than being dictated by outside authorities or international agencies, the subject of violence emerged organically as a crucial issue for Third World women's development because it arose from grass-roots women's endeavors. Projects from various regions of the world funded by the United Nations Development Fund for Women (UNIFEM), for example, increasingly identify violence as a priority concern or as a problem that limits women's participation in development projects or their capacity to benefit from them. Women are taking leadership in making violence against women visible and in addressing its causes, manifestations, and remedies. From the Uganda Association of Women Lawyers, to the Asia and Pacific Women Law and Development Network, to the Trinidad Rape Crisis Center, and the Fiji Women's Rights Movement, leading women's groups in the developing world are struggling to include issues of violence against women on national agendas and to demonstrate the ways in which violence blocks development. They confirm that gender violence, whether in its most brutal or more subtle forms, is a constant in women's lives. In Latin America, Isis International (1990) identified 109 women's projects dealing with various aspects of violence against women. In this region, women's movements have institutionalized 25 November as a day to denounce violence focused on females and to call for action against it. In other parts of the world, women are taking similar initiatives as well.

In a 1988 global survey of women's groups in developing countries, MATCH International, a Canadian nongovernmental organization (NGO) devoted to issues of women and development for two decades, found that violence against women was the most frequent concern raised by women. Women's groups identified the impact of such violence on development in concrete terms, leading MATCH to conclude:

Violent acts against women, the world over, attack their dignity as human beings and leave them vulnerable and fearful. Conditioned to undervalue their skills and abilities and paralyzed by real fears of violence and retribution, women are marginalized in society and forced out of the decision making processes which shape and determine the development of their communities. . . . Violence against women is not limited to any one country. The acts range from battering, incest, assault, and rape worldwide to female circumcision in Africa, dowry deaths in India, and militarization in the Philippines. Along this continuum one must also include the limited employment opportunities for women, the lack of access to education, women's social isolation and the sexual harassment that women experience daily. The manifestations of violence against women simply alter their forms according to the social, economic, and historical realities in which they occur (Amin 1990).

MATCH has since launched a program on violence against women in relation to development as one of its top priorities.

THE EXTENT OF THE VIOLENCE

Violence against women is not a problem that affects only the poor or only Third World women; women in industrialized countries are also affected. Yet, even among industrialized countries, few researchers have undertaken the empirical studies that could provide a solid basis on which to map the true dimensions of the problem. In the developing world, with few exceptions, such as Papua New Guinea, statistics are even more scant. The seriousness of the problem should not be underestimated. When available, statistics powerfully document and make visible the pervasiveness and extent of violence against women globally.

Official statistics and survey data in the United States, for example, dramatically convey the endemic nature of gender violence. A rape occurs somewhere in the United States every six minutes. Domestic battery is the single most significant cause of injury to women, more than car accidents, rapes, and muggings combined. Yet a 1985 FBI report estimates that wife assault is underreported by a factor of at least ten to one. Researchers produce chilling numbers: Roy (1982) indicates that violence occurs at least once in two-thirds of all marriages; Strauss, Gelles, and Steinmetz (1981) reveal that one in eight couples admitted there had been an act of violence between them which could cause serious injury; and in a study at a Connecticut hospital, Stark and Flitcraft (1979) report that battery accounted for 25 percent of suicide attempts by women. Three different studies show that significant numbers of women are battered even when pregnant. Police report that between 40 and 60 percent of the calls they receive, especially on the night shift, are domestic disputes.

A study done in Kansas City showed that the police had been called previously at least five times in the two years preceding 50 percent of all homicides by a spouse. In Cleveland, Ohio, during a nine-month period, police received approximately 15,000 domestic violence calls, but reports were filed for only 700 of them and arrests were made in just 460 cases (National Center on Women and Family Law 1988).

Statistics from other industrialized countries are equally disconcerting. Reports from France indicate that 95 percent of all victims of violence are women, 51 percent of these at the hands of their husbands. In Denmark, 25 percent of women cite violence as the reason for divorce. A 1984 study of urban victimization in seven major Canadian cities found that 90 percent of victims were women. One in four women in Canada can expect to be sexually assaulted at some point in their lives, one-half of these before the age of seventeen (MacLeod 1990, 12).

While there are fewer studies in the Third World, the pattern of gender violence there bears a remarkable similarity to that of advanced industrialized societies. Its manifestations may be culturally specific, but gender violence cuts across national boundaries, ideologies, classes, races, and ethnic groups. A Mexican NGO estimates that domestic violence is present in at least 70 percent of Mexican families, but most cases go unreported. The Mexican Federation of Trade Unions reports that 95 percent of women workers are victims of sexual harassment and complains that the impunity of these crimes limits women's participation in the work force.

The *Servicio Nacional de la Mujer* of Chile has chosen as one of its priorities the prevention of intrafamily violence; according to a survey in Santiago, 80 percent of women acknowledged being victims of violence in their homes (ILET). A national survey on domestic violence undertaken by the Papua New Guinea Law Reform Commission showed that an average of two-thirds of rural wives in that country have experienced marital violence (Bradley, 1988).

A report of the Asian Women's Research and Action Network (AWRAN) indicates that in Korea over two-thirds of the women are beaten periodically by their husbands (AWRAN 1985); while in Nicaragua, 44 percent of men admit to having beaten their wives or girlfriends regularly (ILET). A Thai report found that at least 50 percent of all married women are beaten regularly.

In a study of child prostitution in Cochabamba, Bolivia, 79 percent of the girls said they became prostitutes because of economic need when they ran away from violent homes in which they were victims of incest and rape by male relatives (ILET). Another study published by the Indian government shows that crimes against women are "an increasing trend in the last decade," while the rate of conviction has declined; meanwhile, the female suicide rate in that country doubled from 1987 to 1988. A newspaper survey done in Pakistan revealed that 99 percent of housewives and 77 percent of working women were beaten by their husbands and listed the following types of violence committed against women: murder over land disputes, blinded by husbands frustrated on some issue, kicked to death, burnt in anger, abducted, sold, sexually harassed, raped (AWRAN 1985). Other reports also found a high incidence of family violence in countries as different as Bangladesh, Colombia, Kenya, Kuwait, Nigeria, Vanuatu, and Uganda (United Nations 1989, 20).

Violence against women not only maims and debilitates but femicide is responsible for the deaths of women on a large scale from before birth and throughout life. Sen (1990) points out the deadly cost of social and economic inequalities between men and women by analyzing the sex ratio of females to males in the least developed countries (LDCs). Whereas there are 106 women per 100 men in Europe and North America, there are only 97 women per 100 men in the LDCs as a whole. In some areas, notably Asia, and especially India and China, when one applies the sex ratio of Africa (1.02), which comes closer to that of

Europe and North America (1.06), the equation yields chilling results. Given the number of men in those two countries, there should be about 30 million more women in India, and 38 million more in China. These missing females disappeared through gender violence ranging from female feticide to selective malnourishment and starvation of girls, neglect of health problems, dowry deaths and various other forms of violence. Sen (1990b, 124) reminds us that "since mortality and survival are not independent of care and neglect, and are influenced by social action and public policy" development strategies clearly must take more account of women's needs in this area.

THE SUBJECT OF VIOLENCE AGAINST WOMEN AT INTERNATIONAL CONFERENCES

The United Nations Decade for Women led many people to begin to recognize the problem of violence against women. At all three world conferences on women and at the parallel nongovernmental fora which took place at each, in Mexico City (1975), Copenhagen (1980), and Nairobi (1985), women's advocates raised the issue of gender violence and demanded special attention to the constraints it places on women's full participation in society. The official documents produced at these events are powerful indictments of the discrimination that women face in all countries, regions, and cultures, and they provide a useful foundation for a different understanding of gender-related violence. The record establishes the concerns of the international community and acknowledges the responsibility of governments and all members of society for its eradication. The documents constitute the building blocks for framing new strategies and policies to address these issues.

One of the most significant UN documents addressing gender violence in relation to development goals is the "Forward Looking Strategies" paper produced at the 1985 Nairobi world conference. It includes Resolution 258, which calls for elaboration of preventive policies and institutionalized means of assistance to women victims of the various forms of violence experienced in everyday life in all societies; and it acknowledges that "women are beaten, mutilated, burned, sexually abused, and raped" and that such violence is "a major obstacle to the achievement of the objectives of the Decade and should be given special attention" (United Nations 1985). Other sections of this document (e.g., paragraphs 76, 245, 271, 288) insist on the special training of law enforcement officials who deal with women victims of violent crimes; urge legislation to end the degradation of women through sex-related crimes; stress the priority of promoting female human rights, specifically in relation to issues of domestic violence and violence against women; insist on favoring a preventive approach that includes institutionalized economic and other forms of assistance; and suggest the establishment of national machineries to deal with the question of domestic violence. In addition to assisting victims of violence against women in the family and in society, paragraph 288 demands that:

governments should undertake to increase public awareness of violence against women as a societal problem, establish policies and legislative measures to ascertain its causes and prevent and eliminate such violence, in particular by suppressing degrading images and representations of women in society, and finally encourage the development of educational and re-educational measures for offenders (ibid.).

Other UN divisions, such as the Economic and Social Council, also address the issue. The report of the UN Secretary General at the thirty-second session of the Commission on the Status of Women defined violence against women as "physical, sexual, emotional, and economic abuse within the family; rape and sexual assault; sexual harassment and trafficking in women; involuntary prostitution; and pornography" which all share a common denominator "the use of coercion to make women do things against their will" (n.p.).

HUMAN DEVELOPMENT AND VIOLENCE: A CONTRADICTION

When speaking of development, this chapter relies on the approach adopted by the United Nations Development Program (UNDP) (United Nations 1990) in the Human Development Report (HDR). Reassessing the approaches that marked the three previous UN development decades, this document questions the ability of statistical indicators, such as growth and national income, to measure development adequately. Rather, it suggests the need to focus on other aspects of development that provide more accurate and realistic indicators of human development: nutrition and health services; access to knowledge; secure livelihoods; decent working conditions; security against crime and physical violence; satisfying leisure time; and participation in the economic, cultural, and political activities of one's community. From this perspective, the goal of development is to create an environment that enables people to enjoy long, healthy, and creative lives.

Despite three decades of significant progress toward human development in the Third World, particularly in relation to life expectancy, education, and health, one has to examine cautiously the results from a cross-cultural gender perspective. Nowhere do females enjoy the same standards as males, and in some areas, gaps have widened so considerably that one must question whether development attempts are intrinsically gendered to the disadvantage of females. As the 1990 UNDP report states: "In most societies, women fare less well than men. As children they have less access to education and sometimes to food and health care. As adults they receive less education and training, work longer hours for lower incomes and have few property rights or none" (United Nations 1990, 31).

Discrimination against females extends to every aspect of life. If women are fed less, have poorer health and less education than males, and their contribution to society's production and reproduction is underestimated, it is no wonder that wide gender gaps between males and females persist in human development indicators.

Looking at development from a human-centered gender perspective requires that development studies focus on women as a demographic category and that development indicators be recorded according to gender. In order for women to benefit from the development process, a fundamental emphasis must be placed on increasing women's self-confidence as well as their ability to participate in all aspects of society. Violence against women is in direct contradiction to securing human-centered development goals. It disrupts women's lives and denies them options. It erodes women's confidence and sense of self-esteem at every level, physically and psychologically. It destroys women's health, denies their human rights, and hinders their full participation in society. Where domestic violence keeps a woman from participating in a development project, or fear of sexual assault prevents her from taking a job or attending a public function, or force is used to deprive her of earnings, development does not occur.

Women experience violence as a form of control that limits their ability to pursue options in almost every area of life from home to school, workplace, and most public spaces. Violence is used to control women's labor in both productive and reproductive capacities. For example, case studies of victims of domestic violence in Peru and of garment workers in the Mexican *maquilas* showed men beating their wives frequently to demand the income women had earned (Vasquez y Tamayo 1989; Bruce 1990). Indonesian female workers returning to their villages complain of their helplessness in the face of harassment and sexual abuse; quite often their wages are withheld for months, preventing possibility of escape or resistance. In the Philippines, women workers in export-oriented industries claim that male managers give female employees the choice of "lay down or lay off" (AWRAN 1985).

UNDERSTANDING THE CAUSES OF VIOLENCE

Explaining why gender violence is so endemic is a complex endeavor and here is best pursued as it relates to the question of prevention. There are innumerable theories ranging from biological and genetic explanations, to those that attribute causation to alcohol and toxic substance abuse, poverty, socialization, and even to women themselves (Commonwealth Secretariat 1987, 12). Although some of these theories may contain a grain of truth, none of them justifies violent behavior and all of these so-called causes are better understood as cofactors that concur with a violent situation. The major point here is to look at violence against women as learned behavior, which can be changed. Gender violence can be prevented or, at least, substantially reduced if the social and political will exist to make this happen. This discussion is not intended as an abstract investigation into the origins of violence against women, but as an effort to see how understanding gender violence helps to create preventive strategies that go beyond the social service response.

A Peruvian study by Vasquez y Tamayo (1990, 106) argues that causes of battery are many, including unequal relations between men and women; the sexual hierarchy; domestic isolation of women with male figures as the final authority; early marriages before women have developed a sense of autonomy; the family as the sole institution that shapes women's identity; the representation of masculinity via the domination of women; poor communication in family conflicts; and the privatization of conflict between men and women in a couple relationship. This suggests a number of important development objectives that might reduce such violence.

Jane Connors describes the pervasiveness of violent behavior in the report written for the Commonwealth Secretariat

[as] best understood in the context of social structure, institutions and codes of conduct. In this context, the abuse of women can be seen as naked display of male power, the outcome of social relations in which women are kept in a position of inferiority to men, responsible to and in need of protection by them (Commonwealth Secretariat 1987, 14).

The Papua New Guinea study agrees with Connors' assertion and states: "The essence of male violence against women is the sense of inadequacy, of vulner-ability, of helplessness, of weakness, and of sheer naked fear that men inspire in women when they threaten or use violence against women. The use of brute force by men makes women feel inferior" (Bradley 1988).

FEMALE DEPENDENCY

The socially constructed dependency of women on men is key to understanding women's vulnerability to violence. This dependency is frequently economic and results from various layers of sexist discrimination. First, much of women's work is unpaid labor at home and in the fields, which is not valued by society nor calculated as part of the gross national product (the productive work of a nation). Second, even in paid jobs, women work longer hours for lower pay with fewer benefits and less security than men.

Female dependency extends also to such other areas as psychological, social, and cultural. Women are trained to believe that their value is attached to the men in their lives—fathers, brothers, husbands, and sons. They are often socially ostracized if they displease or disobey these men. Women are socialized to associate their self-work with the satisfaction of the needs and desires of others and thus are encouraged to blame themselves as inadequate or bad if men beat them. This socialization process is reinforced by cultures in which a woman is constantly diminished, her sexuality commodified, her work and characteristics devalued, her identity shaped by an environment that reduces her to her most biological functions. Yet, women are still blamed for "causing" or deserving the abuse of men toward them.

Women's socioeconomic and psychological dependency makes it difficult for them to leave situations of domestic violence or sexual harassment. Often in rural settings it is physically impossible; women literally have no place to go or the means to get away, and there are no services available to them. The Commonwealth Secretariat report on domestic violence mentioned above cites the opinion of experts that a shelter or other safe refuge alternative is only possible in a city of at least 10,000 inhabitants.

But even in large urban settings, where it may be easier for women to leave abusive relationships, there is often nowhere to go, as illustrated by the links between domestic violence and homelessness. A shelter for homeless women in Boston reports that about 90 percent of its occupants are victims of domestic violence (*New York Times*, 26 August 1990), and New York City shelter workers note a similar trend. Australian sociologist, Robert Connell (1987, 11) sees the lack of alternative housing as one of the reasons women stay in, or return to, violent marriages. Further, violence makes women become even more dependent. Studies from several countries find that the escalation of violence undermines women's self-esteem and their capacity to take action diminishes.

EFFECTS ON FAMILY AND CHILDREN

Violence against women also affects the development and well-being of children and families. A recent study on children of battered women in Canada reports posttraumatic stress, clinical dysfunction, behavioral and emotional disorders in children from violent homes (Jaffe, Wolfe, and Wilson 1986). Some argue that children's socialization into accepting or committing violence starts at home when they witness their father beating their mother and sometimes abusing them as well.

It seems increasingly clear that the best way to reduce infant mortality is through the education of women (White House Task Force on Infant Mortality Report, cited in the *New York Times*, 12 August 1990; Buvinić and Yudelman 1989). The 1990 UNDP report underlines the high social dividend that comes with female literacy, as demonstrated by lower infant mortality rates, better family nutrition, reduced fertility, and lower population growth. Other studies show a connection between women's self-confidence and child mortality. Since the health and psychological well-being of children is connected to the future development of a country, the gender violence implicit in disproportionate female illiteracy is clearly contrary to development. Improving women's self-confidence and education are therefore crucial investments that may have long lasting effects on children and the future of a nation.

Gender violence also destroys families. A study of the Law Reform Commission of Papua New Guinea found that husbands, through their violence, were affected negatively in the long run by losing the very basis of their patriarchal control: A husband may be injured or even killed if his wife acts to defend herself; he fails to earn the love and respect of his wife and children; and he frequently loses his family altogether. In Papua New Guinea, as in many other countries, battery is one of the main reasons women give for filing divorce.

COSTS TO SOCIETY

Violence against women deprives society of the full participation of women in all aspects of development. Heise (1989) states:

Female focused violence undermines widely held goals for economic and social development in the Third World. The development and community has come to realize that problems such as high fertility, deforestation and hunger cannot be solved without women's full participation. Yet women cannot lend their labor or creative ideas fully when they are burdened with the physical and psychological scars of violence.

Many work hours are lost as a result of violence, not to speak of the costs of providing services to victims. In this we should include the work time lost by the victim, plus the work time of police and others in the legal, medical, mental health, and social services. It is almost impossible to quantify the total costs of the problem given the limited information available on the extent of such violence. Among the few estimates made, the Australian Committee on Violence calculated that the cost of refuge accommodation for victims of domestic violence for the year 1986–87 was $27.6 million Australian dollars, and in the province of Queensland alone, serious domestic assault cases cost about $108 million Australian dollars a year (Australian National Committee on Violence 1990, 15). However, the greatest cost is one of human misery:

Beyond such calculable costs lie the costs in human suffering, which are vast. The most significant long term effect and ultimate cost of wife battery, however, is the perpetration of the societal structure, confirmed by marital violence, that keeps women inferior and subordinate to men politically, economically and socially (United Nations 1989, 24).

Violence in an environment in which public safety measures are inadequate and public transport unprotected severely limits women's integration into the paid work force. Addressing this problem, a coalition of women's organizations in Bombay demanded the establishment of "ladies only carriages" in mass public transit after serious incidents of sexual harassment of women commuting to and from work. The Toronto Metro Action Committee on Public Violence Against Women and Children (METRAC) has raised awareness and affected public policy regarding the connections between transportation, safety, and women's participation in the work force. Based on an extensive survey of women's concerns about urban planning and design, METRAC lobbied city government to improve lighting, signs, mass transit, and suggested new criteria and guidelines for all buildings in the city. These initiatives are a reminder of how women's freedom in public spaces is often restrained by the way these are designed. Another example is the lack of adequate sanitation, water, and garbage facilities. Frequently, women have to go to desolate places to satisfy basic sanitary needs—a common experience for women living in shantytowns and in rural areas—and in such situations, they are specially vulnerable to violent crimes.

Violence against women is often a direct obstacle to women's participation in development projects. For example, in a Mexican project funded by the United Nations Development Fund for Women (UNIFEM) instances of wife battering increased with women's sense of empowerment through their participation. The project found that men perceived the growing empowerment of women as a threat to their control, and the beatings could be explained as an attempt to reverse this process of empowerment the women experienced in order to drive them away from the project. Similarly, a revolving fund project of the Working Women's Forum in Madras almost collapsed when the most articulate and energetic participants started to drop out because of increased incidents of domestic violence against them after they had joined (Noponen 1989). Faced with the same problems, the Association for the Development and Integration of Women (ADIM) in Lima succeeded in its work by initiating programs that combined income-generating schemes with legal aid to battered wives and women abandoned by their partners (Buvinić and Yudelman 1989, 44).

Even when women continue their involvement in development projects, concern about the problems caused by violence often diverts their energies from pursuing other goals. Sometimes women miss meetings because they fear beatings or already suffer physical disability from injuries inflicted on them or because they are taking care of another battered woman or her children. Some women decline public visibility due to shame over their injuries because society's "blame-the-victim" attitude does not create an environment sympathetic to them. In groups that discuss these issues, time spent dealing with violence and the problems accompanying it is time away from other project goals.

Another long-term effect of gender violence and the cultural atmosphere that demeans women by condoning such violence is the denial of the full talents of their female citizens to developing countries. Family control and violence encourage some of the best-educated women to leave their countries, contributing to the brain drain in the Third World and the loss of highly skilled women who could contribute to the development process. Women who stay often must comply with the subordinate role that society assigns them and they may be reluctant to be promoted for fear of upsetting their husbands. For example, with regard to Papua New Guinea: "Threats of violence control women's minds as much as do acts of violence, making women act as their own jailors. This means that a woman makes her choices not on what she wants to do or believes is best, but on what she thinks her husband will allow her to do" (Bradley 1988, 5).

HEALTH, AIDS, AND VIOLENCE

Health is usually recognized as an important development issue. One of the clearest facts about violence against women is that it is detrimental to women's physical and mental health, including women's very survival. A 1989 report by the then Surgeon General of the United States, C. Everett Koop, affirms that battered women are four to five times more likely than nonbattered women to require psychiatric treatment and more likely to commit suicide. He reports that each year some 1 million women in the United States are sufficiently injured to seek medical assistance at emergency rooms for injuries sustained through battering. These injuries include bruises; concussions; broken noses, teeth, ribs, and limbs; throat injuries; lacerations and stab wounds; burns and bites. Injuries are caused by being struck by fists and blunt objects as well as knives, kicks, strangulations, being thrown down stairs, and more. In view of the extensive evidence, Koop calls it "an overwhelming moral, economic, and public health burden that our society can no longer bear" (Koop 1989). He demands a major response from governments at the national, state, and community levels; legislators and city councils; police, prosecutors, judges, and probation officers; health professions and educational institutions; the communications media; the church and clergy; nongovernmental organizations, as well as "international organizations that must demonstrate a clear recognition of the problem and provide the necessary leadership to us all" (ibid., 5–6).

The AIDS crisis has cast unequal gender relations in a new light. In Africa, where the AIDS epidemic has reached staggering numbers, women are experiencing the effects of male control in multiple deadly ways. A report of the Health Ministry of Uganda reveals that there are twice as many cases of AIDS among girls between fifteen and nineteen years old as among boys of the same age group. These numbers reflect a common belief among men that possibilities of being exposed to the AIDS virus are lowered when they engage in sexual intercourse with younger women. In some areas where the control of women is reflected in traditional practices like female circumcision and infibulation, the risks of acquiring the disease have multiplied. Deeply entrenched attitudes and traditions around the world justify men's easy access to women's bodies and result in the transmission of the virus via rape, incest, and other forms of coerced sex as demonstrated by recent news reports. Thus, although hard data proving the connection between AIDS and violence against women are not yet available, this is a research area that would expand our understanding of the deadly impact of gender violence.

DIRECTIONS FOR POLICY

The problem of violence against women is systemic and common to all societies. This chapter specifically looks at strategies for combatting violence against women as related to development planning in the Third World. There are several levels on which those concerned with the consequences of development for women can take action in addressing the connections between gender violence and development. The overall question is how to make use of limited resources to support projects that take into account and challenge the limitations and constraints that violence places on women's full participation in development activities. The answer lies in the catalytic role that a development organization or project can play at both the programmatic and nonprogrammatic levels. Central to this catalytic role is a commitment to highlighting the obstacles that gender violence places in the development path and to identifying means of countering it in all phases of the project cycle: planning, implementation, documentation, evaluation, and dissemination of results.

ACTION AT MULTIPLE PROGRAM LEVELS

Awareness of the obstacles posed by gender violence in the formulation and implementation phases of a project can take several forms. First, an awareness of forms of gender violence that are specific to certain cultures can help identify and overcome obstacles impeding women's participation. The lack of safe transportation when women interact with unrelated males, for example, may require the identification of alternative means of travel that are sustainable in the local context. The reservation of "ladies only" cars in mass transit in Bombay or obtaining the protection of the local khan for female health extension workers in Northern Pakistan represent such strategies.

Second, at the formulation and implementation stages, sensitivity to situations in which changes in women's status makes them vulnerable to violence is essential. It is a cultural truism that change is threatening. Project activities might seek to strengthen women's self-confidence and ability to defend themselves as well as reach out to men in the community, win their commitment to the change, and even change their expectations. Project activities may need to change during implementation to address incidents of violence. The staff of a UNIFEM project in Tempoal, Mexico, had to take time to work with husbands and community members when violence emerged as a result of project participants' changing roles.

Third, in personnel selection for the implementation stage, awareness of violence as an obstacle should be an important consideration. Project management requires not just technical skill, but an awareness of the larger environment and how it must be altered to facilitate women's full participation.

Fourth, gender violence that obstructs development and its remedy—measures that reduce women's vulnerability to violence—need to be documented as they occur in the project cycle. Incidents can be noted in periodic reporting, in staff monitoring visits, or in evaluations. The findings can be collected and analyzed as part of lessons learned from project experience.

The integration of statistics on gender violence into data collection, planning, and training projects is central to the visibility and recognition of such violence as an obstacle to development.

Finding sustainable ways of deterring gender violence is also crucial. On a direct level, projects can experiment with techniques or interventions that focus on, and deal with, violence. With respect to deterrence, projects that document the extent and severity of violence against women, or that test one or more education campaigns and seek to make violence unacceptable within a society, can serve as models that demonstrate the possibilities and benefits of such approaches. In a similar way, projects dealing with the consequences of violence (rape crisis centers, training of police, magistrates, hospital personnel, etc.) should be supported, especially when they have some possibility of testing a new approach, or of influencing the government to initiate services and expand tested approaches to addressing gender violence.

It is important to increase the capacity of women to identify and combat violence. Projects that strengthen communication skills, raise women's awareness of possible actions, build management skills, teach self-defense, and strengthen women's organizations, and at the same time contribute to capacities to address gender specific violence, should be supported.

Nonprogrammatic Steps

The international development community, and particularly women's agencies within that community, can undertake important changes that are not related to projects and would not require additional expenditures beyond staff time. This approach involves making violence visible as a development issue in relation to many other themes. By disseminating reports of projects concerned with violence, women's advocates within the development community can highlight the impact of violence on program activity.

Overall, development agencies and organizations addressing women in development must conduct their program and project work with an increased sensitivity to the issue of violence and the ways in which development brings forth new forms of gendered violence. It is important to address gender violence as an aspect of many other development projects, such as income-generating schemes or housing plans, and not just those specifically focused on violence against women. International development agencies such as the United Nations Development Programme, UNIFEM, World Health Organization, and the International Labor Organization, which are concerned with the issue of women in development, need to use their leverage and prestige as international agencies to expand the legitimacy of and give voice to groups working on these areas at the national or community level.

CONCLUSION

Attempts to integrate women into development are doomed to failure if they do not address the issue of violence against women. This chapter has attempted to build the case for the international development community's support of projects that address the various manifestations of gender violence as legitimate development projects. It maintains that projects dealing with violence toward women are building blocks for a more comprehensive, empowering, and therefore sustainable effort that will tap women's full participation in the development process.

Countering violence against women not only eliminates an obstacle to the development of women but also actively addresses women's realization of their full potential. This quote from an interview with a popular education worker in Mexico illustrates the potential of this work:

Q. How do you address the issue of violence?

A. When women explore their social roles, if the issue of violence doesn't arise, the workshop methodology is not addressing the issues of gender. We ask women to choose which experience of violence they would like to explore of those they have mentioned—children dying of hunger, battering, economic hardships. They usually choose domestic violence as they already understand and confront the other kinds of violence. To confront economic violence, they sell food or demand government subsidies. But there are other aspects of violence that they can't even talk about in their family, with their neighbors or in their organization. These forbidden themes are the basis of work with gender. There is not much to discover about being poor. But as women look at what it means to be women (poor women), they gain the desire to live, learn to express themselves, they see how they are reproducing sexual roles in their children. They discover the causes of their oppression and are empowered to act (*Correspondencia* 1990).

7

Industrial Prostitution and South Korean Dependent Development

Heisoo Shin

On 14 December 1988, Korean Women's Associations United (KWAU), a coalition of twenty-four women's organizations in South Korea, held a press conference to issue a statement that they would fight against trafficking in women. They voiced their anger over the increasing numbers of women being kidnapped from the street and sold into prostitution. Many different women, including high school girls and housewives, were the victims of this crime. KWAU located the root cause of trafficking in women in the flourishing entertainment industry and the spread of a corrupt culture and they demanded goverment action against it (Korean Women's Association United 1988).

This phenomenon of outright kidnapping of female pedestrians and selling them to bars and into prostitution is rather new; a more common practice is to entice women, through newspaper ads or fake employment agencies, to take jobs in entertainment businesses and eventually to enter prostitution. Young girls migrating from the countryside, who were disoriented at the bus terminal or train station in the big city, were also easy prey to the pimps who pretended to offer them help. The recent phenomenon of outright kidnapping of women is a manifestation of the increasing demand for women in the entertainment industry.

The entertainment industry is generally understood to comprise businesses that make liquor and hostesses available to male customers; it includes liquor "room-salons," cafes, houses (taverns), beer halls, night clubs, bars, adult discotheques, massage parlors, turkish baths, tea houses, and cabarets.[1] The entertainment industry began to grow in the middle of the 1970s and by the mid– 1980s mushroomed and became socially visible. Journalists first exposed the problems of the entertainment industry in early 1984; they were followed by a few concerned academicians. So far, there is no clear conceptual definition of the entertainment industry (Won 1988). Terms such as *pleasure industry* or *corrupt industry* are used interchangeably.

Traditionally in Korea, since the tenth century, there were professional female entertainers called *kisaeng* (like *geisha* in Japan), who served government officials, foreign diplomats and upper-class men with songs, dances, and poetry along with sexual services (Kim 1976). This legacy continues into the present day with the job of hostess in the entertainment industry. The current Food Hygiene Law allows entertainment restaurants to employ entertaining receptionists, that is hostesses, whose job is to "drink with the customer and entertain the customer with songs and dances." Not only the entertainment restaurants but also many general restaurants are hiring hostesses illegally. According to the National Police Headquarters, the number of unlicensed premises is estimated to be three times the number of licensed ones.[2] Where these businesses are clustered, hotels and motels are abundant for short-time users. The entertainment industry also includes massage parlors and "corrupt" barber shops, where the masseuses and female shavers offer not only their usual services but also "special massages." After a raid by the Ministry of Health and Social Affairs of 150 corrupt barber shops in the southern part of Seoul, blood tests revealed that sixteen (5.2 percent) out of 307 female shavers were infected by syphilis, and of the 77 women who were examined by the nearby clinic, thirteen or 16.9 percent had gonorrhea (*Sae Gae Times*, 18 February 1989). These infection rates are higher than those of women who are working in the "special business," whose health is controlled through regular government examinations.

The reality is that many hostesses, masseuses, and waitresses working in the entertainment industry are also engaged in prostitution: Formally they are workers in service occupations but included in their duties is the provision of sexual services. Distinguished from the more traditional profession of prostitution, this type of sex work is referred to as "industrial prostitution" in South Korea. A 1989 study estimated that over 400,000 establishments offer industrial prostitution and that the number of industrial prostitutes was 1.2 to 1.5 million (Seoul YMCA 1989a). This latter figure corresponded to one-fifth of the total number of South Korean women in the fifteen to twenty-nine year age cohort and more than 10 percent of all women of childbearing age. Total entertainment industry sales were estimated to reach 4 trillion won (about $5.7 billion) or 5 percent of the gross national product in 1989 (Seoul YMCA 1989a, 7–10). Because tax reports are not correct and tips are not included in the reports, the actual figures are probably much higher. In a survey by the Ministry of Health and Social Affairs in 1988, tax reports were between one-quarter and one-twenty-fifth of their real value (Seoul YMCA 1989b, 17). Besides the nouveaux riches, businessmen are the main regular users of the services of industrial prostitutes. Business entertainment is a systematic extension of business activities in South Korea, and companies pay the expenses from an entertainment account.

This chapter first explores the structural conditions of the growth of industrial prostitution on the macrolevel. The relationship between the process of South

Korean dependent development and the growth of the entertainment industry is the focus of attention. Next, on the microlevel, the internal dynamics of industrial prostitution are examined. A close inspection of the room-salon, which is the most popular type of establishment for business entertainment, reveals the organization of women's work inside the entertainment industry. For this study, fifty-eight in-depth interviews—thirty with business people and twenty-eight with people in the entertainment industry—were carried out in Seoul during the thirteen-month period of October 1989 to November 1990.

SOUTH KOREAN DEPENDENT DEVELOPMENT AND THE EXPANSION OF INDUSTRIAL PROSTITUTION

South Korea represents a dynamic case of capitalistic dependent development. The miraculous economic growth rate is accompanied by enormous foreign debt and heavy dependence on foreign capital and technology, as well as on imported raw materials. The export-oriented, outward-looking development is built upon the sacrifices of the rural population and workers, who are under the tight control of a strong state. After three decades of intensive, but lopsided dependent development, South Korea is now categorized as semiperiphery in the capitalist world system (Wallerstein 1979), dependent upon the developed core countries but also investing and exploiting the peripheral countries of Asia, Africa, and Latin America. As a result, the trade deficit turned into a trade surplus in 1986 for the first time. Although the situation is precarious and income inequality among people is widening steadily, South Korea as a whole is now enjoying more economic prosperity than it did one or two decades ago.

Industrial prostitution is a direct product of South Korea's development path. More specifically, it is a product of state policies formulated within the framework of the country's structural linkage to the capitalist world economy. At the same time, industrial prostitution contributes to economic development. Businessmen use it widely as a strategy to obtain credits and secure favors as well as to increase sales in domestic and world markets.

South Korea depends primarily on Japan and the United States. Japan, as Korea's colonizer for thirty-five years until 1945, extracted natural and human resources and thus ultimately underdeveloped the country. During the last period of Japanese colonialism, Korean men and women were forcibly mobilized to work in factories and at the war front—men as laborers and soldiers in the Japanese army, women as entertainers for the comfort of Japanese troops at the war front.[3] After liberation, the United States and the Soviet Union divided the Korean peninsula in two. The presence of the U.S. military in the southern part for more than four decades contributed a great deal to the spread of prostitution.[4] The number of prostitutes who deal exclusively with the 43,000 U.S. soldiers currently stationed in South Korea is estimated to be more than 18,000 (Sturdevant 1988)—roughly one prostitute for every two to three American soldiers.

After the normalization of relations between South Korea and Japan in 1965, Japan reappeared as one of the primary core countries on which South Korea became economically dependent. Economic dependence on Japan created a new form of sexual exploitation of South Korean women by Japanese men. This time the South Korean state encouraged and condoned prostitution because it saw women as a valuable resource with which to earn badly needed foreign currency. The *kisaeng*, the professional female entertainer, is officially registered with the Korea International Tourism Association (KITA) through the party house to which she belongs. In 1973, eighteen party houses employed an estimated 24,000 women throughout the country. Among these party houses, Sam-chong-gak and Taewon-gak each have 800 women registered with them (Korea Church Women United 1984). KITA also sponsors an orientation program for these women, in which "renowned personages and college professors" give lectures and say such things as, "You girls must take pride in your devotion to your country, for your carnal conversation with foreign tourists does not prostitute either yourself or the nation, but expresses your heroic patriotism" (ibid., 26).[5]

In addition to structural links to the world system, which South Korea shares with other Asian and Third World countries, there are peculiarities in the South Korean development process that contribute to the proliferation of the entertainment industry and industrial prostitution.

Because the South Korean state is the main actor in allocating valuable resources and in controlling bank credit, the success or survival of any enterprise depends crucially on maintaining "good" relations with people in positions of power. Business entertainment—the use of *kisaeng* houses, where female entertainers serve individual customers—developed as a way to create or maintain good relations with the political elite. Companies also use business entertainment with foreign buyers in order to promote exports. Business entertainment spread into other sectors of South Korean society with power and resources, and there are now chains of business entertainment connected to the press, banks, police, and tax office.

Another characteristic of South Korean development is the excessive real estate speculation created by the pressures of physical development and urbanization. The price of land skyrocketed: During 1969–88, when consumer prices rose only 11.5 percent annually, the average annual increase in land prices was 25 percent (Kim 1990, 51–52). Big business conglomerates and others who had capital and succeeded in getting advance information on development plans became the nouveaux riches. They are the second group of people who regularly patronize women in the entertainment industry.

The need to curry favor and the sudden wealth from land sales combined with the already existing *kisaeng* culture, which considered women as sex objects, contributed to create the entertainment industry. There was a ready pool of potential workers among the poor because of the limited economic opportunities for women. South Korean women, unlike their Latin American counterparts, are relatively well incorporated into the development process. During the last three decades, women's economic participation rates rose from 27 percent in 1960 to 43 percent in 1986 (Korea, Economic Planning Board, 1960, 1986), and the proportion of women in the total labor force also steadily increased. Repressive labor control by a dictatorial state, however, left workers vulnerable to harsh working conditions. According to a 1986 international survey by the International Labor Office, South Koreans worked the longest hours of all workers—an average of fifty-four hours per week (Bello and Rosenfeld 1990, 24). South Korean women worked on average even longer than men and earned less than half of men's wages (Korea, Ministry of Labor 1987, 84–85). In recent years, manufacturers have found it harder and harder to recruit young female workers. Meanwhile, entertainment businesses are booming. Good looking young women seem to prefer the much higher incomes earned in the entertainment industry, even if it means losing respect in exchange.

THE DYNAMICS OF INDUSTRIAL PROSTITUTION: INSIDE THE ROOM-SALON

Room-salons are playing a leading role in the entertainment industry. They are the most expensive sites of entertainment, the ones most frequently used for business deals (Seoul YMCA, 1989c). A room-salon usually has ten to twenty rooms, each furnished with a table and sofas and equipped with a men's toilet. Groups of male customers are served hard liquor and hors d'oeuvres by an equal number of hostesses. A 1989 survey found that on average each person spent 125,400 won (about $170) at a room-salon, which was equal to 20 percent of the average monthly income of urban wage workers (Seoul YMCA 1989b, 12–13). Because the charges are so high at a room-salon, individual men usually do not use such places. All the businessmen interviewed said that they could not afford to use room-salons when they were with their own friends.

Expenses are usually covered by the company account. The official aggregate of an enterprise's spending on entertainment is 0.2 to 0.4 percent of the net sales; corporations actually spend much more, sometimes as much as 5 percent of sales. In comparison, they spend only 0.1 percent on research and development (The Bank of Korea 1987). The Office of National Taxation, after analyzing the tax reports of enterprises and entertainment businesses, estimated that about 70 percent of the money spent in high-class establishments comes from enterprises (*The Dong-A Ilbo*, 18 November 1990).

When a businessman wants to entertain his clients, he usually makes a reservation beforehand, explains what kind of an occasion it is, and asks for beautiful hostesses. If he is entertaining foreign buyers, he will request hostesses who can communicate in another language. The madam understands that she should select women who are willing to spend the night with the clients if asked to. The hostess's job is to sit next to her partner and serve him, putting ice in his glass, pouring his drinks, lighting his cigarettes, arranging his food so that it is convenient for him to eat it, sometimes feeding him, conversing with him, and singing and dancing with him. If the client seems to like his partner, the patron asks the madam to arrange for a sleep-out. In business entertainment, it is not rare for patrons to demand that the hostess "report" (meaning to show her private parts) and play the game of strip poker. In an interview, the president of an electronics company recalled that his former boss used to enjoy the "pubic hair pulling game" whenever they had a chance to go to the entertainment establishment.

Because a room-salon is a business, it is not surprising that its organization resembles that of an enterprise. There is a president (sometimes copresidents in the case of a partnership) who provides the capital; a few managers with different titles in hierarchical order, who supervise and manage the business; madams and waiters who are responsible for hostesses and bill collection; hostesses who are unpaid, daily employees (they collect tips); and other auxiliary personnel such as busboys, a one-man bank, a chef and his aide, a bartender, a cashier, and a couple of chauffeurs. At a medium-sized room-salon with ten to fifteen rooms, the total number of employees can easily reach one hundred: one madam and one waiter per room (each room takes one group of patrons at a time), about half as many busboys (two waiters share one), five to ten hostesses per madam, and a dozen other people.

The president may have enough capital to cover the initial expense of starting the business and maintaining it for a few months, but the success of the business depends on enterprising madams. The two main functions of a madam are to attract patrons and to secure hostesses. Because madams are vital to the business, other establishments will try to hire an able madam who has many big patrons.

When a madam takes a job in a new room-salon, the new employer assumes whatever debts she has with her former employer; the new employer presents her with a bill, specifying the date by which the sum must be repaid. The new employer may even offer her an advance, depending on her situation. Unlike the hostess, the madam signs a contract, which specifies the amount she must take in during a set period of time, for example, 60 million won (about $82,000) over six months. Then the madam receives 5 to 6 percent of the contract amount as "public relations (PR) expenses," which she can use to advertise her new job to her patrons. If she sells more within the contract period, she can sign a new contract and receive the PR expenses again. If she sells less, she has to return a portion of her PR expenses which corresponds to the shortage of the contract money.

The madam's share is 30 percent of sales. Even when she is not paid by her patrons, she has to pay the room-salon the other 70 percent. If she sells on credit, which happens quite often, it usually takes a month to collect. Therefore, the big patrons are those who not only come often and run up big bills by consuming many bottles of liquor and many hors d'oeuvres, but who also pay cash or, if on credit, pay within a short time. It often takes much longer to collect the money, sometimes from six months to a couple of years. In addition to the slow cash flow, other deductions eat up a madam's 30 percent share of her sales. If the expenses are charged on a credit card, the bank deducts a 5 percent commission from the madam's 30 percent share. Patrons may also ask for a discount. Sometimes the madam cannot collect the money at all, for example when the patron's company goes bankrupt or she loses contact with the debtor patron. For all these reasons, madams are constantly in debt and forced to stay in the business even when they want to leave. Under the stress of a heavy debt, a madam may "ride a submarine" (run away), sometimes to another country, but most of the time her escape is not successful.

As a protection against this danger, the waiter stands surety for the madam. When a madam signs a contract, therefore, her partner-waiter also signs it, as a financial affidavit. They work as a team, with a division of labor: The madam handles patrons and the waiter handles money. The waiter calculates and decides how much money his madam can take for a certain month. Security is also the waiter's responsibility, as well as visiting the patron's office to collect money or to deliver the madam's presents. A dishonest waiter sometimes pockets the money. Waiters are paid a basic monthy wage, which is supplemented with 20 percent of the tips of his partner-madam's hostesses.

The waiter also serves as a channel of communication between the madam and other establishments, as the managers of the room-salons are usually men, even when the owner is a woman. If the madam is someone with a good substance, meaning that she makes large sales and settles accounts well, her waiter will receive many offers from managers of other room-salons. If the team has a good relationship, they usually move to a new job together. The waiter may also induce a hostess to take another job or to be a baby-madam, an intermediate stage between being a hostess and a madam. Thus, a waiter is a manager; he is more than just an employee who waits the customers' table.

Until 1970, men, who were called "members," carried out much of the work that the madam now does. As hostesses learned the business, they moved into the managing position of madam and displaced male members. In most room-salons, hostesses are no longer managed by members but by madams.

Each madam uses a different approach to increase sales. Besides giving gifts, the method most widely used is to make telephone contacts and, if the patron has some free time, meet him over a cup of coffee. Because most of the room-salon patrons are married, the phone calls are made to their workplace. One madam said she called her patron the next day every time he used her room-salon to ask if he felt all right (after the night's drinking). A phone call is "effective for about a week—if the patron has another occasion for drinks, he will recall my face first."

Each madam usually manages from five to fifteen hostesses, who live entirely on tips from the patrons and charges for occasional sleep-outs with customers. A sleep-out, which is a euphemism for sex between a hostess and her customer, is also called the "second," because a hostess offers her "first" service to her customer at the establishment. In a 1989 survey, tips ranged from 20,000 won to 50,000 won (about $27 to $68) per customer, with the average hostess attending three or four rooms per night between 8 P.M. and 3 A.M. (Seoul YMCA 1989c). Since January 1990, however, with the new government regulation of no-business-after-midnight in effect, sales have dropped. Hostesses attend only one or two rooms per night, but tips are up so that their incomes remain the same. At the time of the 1990 interviews, the average tip was 50,000 won. If the patron is rich and is pleased, he might tip as much as 100,000 won. If the patron is satisfied, he may pay more. The waiter takes 20 percent, and the hostess takes the rest. The usual fee for a sleep-out is 100,000 won. Hostesses in South Korea do not charge per hour or per sexual act, unlike sex workers in Europe and America (Delacoste and Alexander 1987).

According to madams, hostesses are what attracts business in the entertainment industry; hostesses draw patrons and increase sales. An owner-madam of a cafe with hostesses said that it was her patrons who advised her to hire hostesses because "drinking places are all the same and the liquor they serve is the same." Another madam said that "without hostesses, there would be no business. The customers would just keep on talking (without placing more orders) even when they run out of liquor and hors d'oeuvres." Clearly then, hostesses are critical to the business of any room-salon. When asked how they recruit hostesses, madams say that they usually don't have to worry because hostesses bring friends, who bring other friends, or they walk in asking for a job on their own. Other surveys with large samples confirm this observation. In Kim and Won's study (1984, 88), 56.6 percent of the hostesses surveyed found their job through a friend and 22.7 percent found it by themselves; Choi (1982, 144) reported 40 percent and 23 percent for the corresponding routes. If these conventional ways of tapping the pool do not satisfy demand, madams go to places such as nightclubs in Itaewon, a district that is located near the U.S. 8th Army base in Seoul and is famous as a shopping place for foreign tourists and for a cluster of some 200 entertainment establishments. Or they may go to the beauty salons near Young-dong Apartments, a complex of hundreds of apartments located in southern Seoul, where many entertainment establishments are concentrated. People in the entertainment industry say that about 98 percent of the residents of Young-dong Apartments are hostesses. In addition, if a madam is financially able, she can secure hostesses from other establishments or from a secret information agency by lending them money.

There are no strict rules for a hostess's work. Because the hostess earns tips on a daily basis, she is not structurally bound to anyone. If she doesn't feel well or simply does not want to go to work, she can skip the day. One madam, however, who had a strong professionalism, was very strict: if hostesses were absent or late for work without notice, she forced them to resign. But this madam was also able to guarantee her hostesses a high income because she had many patrons. To discourage absenteeism and encourage continued work, some madams set a small fine for being late or absent. With this money, the madam might buy a present, such as a gold ring, as a bonus for a hostess who had a good attendance record. At some room-salons, hostesses pay an attendance fee of

1,000 to 2,000 won each day they work, and the money is used for seasonal group picnics.

Hostesses do not know exactly how much they earn each month because they bring home a different amount each day and do not keep records. The approximate amounts they reported ranged from a minimum of 1 million won (which is equal to a starting assistant professor's salary) up to 3 million won (equal to a corporate general manager's salary). All the madams who were once hostesses said that a hostess can make more money than a madam, although one madam thought that a baby-madam with many patrons could make the most money.

In the course of their work, hostesses and their madam develop a symbiotic relationship: When a hostess works under an able madam, she can make more money and can "grow up," that is she can prepare to become a madam. The hostesses interviewed felt that they had a high degree of autonomy, possibly because madams depend upon a stable supply of pretty, reliable hostesses. Unless the patron asks for a specific hostess, it is the madam who makes the selection and decides which hostess sits next to which patron. The madam knows each patron's personality as well as his financial status, which is reflected in his tips to the hostess and determines his future relationship with her. Madams favor hostesses with good looks who follow their instructions closely.

Each madam has her own style of business. Some want to create an intellectual atmosphere with hostesses who look like students, whereas others demand that hostesses wear expensive clothing and heavy make-up. In some room-cafes, the madam does not allow hostesses to sleep out, reasoning that this policy keeps regular patrons, who are presumed to lose interest in hostesses once they sleep with them. Some madams do just the opposite—they force the hostess to sleep out. Because of the cooperative and conflict-ridden relationship between the hostess and the madam, it is quite common for a madam to take her favorite hostesses to her new job, but just as frequently a hostess will move to another place after quarreling with her madam.

When a madam does not have enough hostesses of her own, she either makes her hostesses "run the double," that is tend two rooms at the same time, or she borrows hostesses from another madam. Or, as a last resort, she calls a secret information agency, but madams do not like the hostesses supplied by the agency. According to one madam, these women are not sophisticated enough "to behave properly according to the atmosphere" or they are just simply "ugly and strange." Because it is a one-time service, the information agency hostesses often break their sleep-out dates with the patrons.

When a madam's own hostesses run the double, it is to the patron's disadvantage because the hostesses are constantly in and out of their room. Patrons usually complain, and some of them do not pay the full tip. Although they can make more money in a limited time, some hostesses do not like running the double and are even ashamed of it, especially when patrons complain and ridicule them. In one extreme case, the double was the reason for a fight between two groups of patrons, which resulted in bloodshed.[6]

The real tension between a madam and her hostesses is usually about the sleep-out: The madam demands that the hostess sleep with the patron even when she doesn't want to. The madam yells at the hostess and curses in abusive language in front of all the other hostesses and madams. One hostess working at a night club said that she worked at a room-salon for only a week because "I had to drink a lot, the patrons were annoying and sleeping out was forced on us." A room-salon madam in her fifties said that hostesses who work through secret information agencies prefer to work as hostess-servers and collect tips but not to work as hostess-prostitutes, because most of them had lovers.

Hostesses can be also pressured by the management to increase sales. They do so by initiating the placement of orders for liquor and hors d'oeuvres for their own as well as their patron's consumption. Sometimes the patron asks for a hostess who is a heavy drinker. The president of a small company in the food industry, a light drinker, said in an interview that for his business entertainment in room-salons, he requests "a hostess who drinks well" in his place. In order not to drink too much, however, hostesses learn a trick: they do not swallow the liquor but hold it in their mouths for a moment and empty it back into their glasses, which the waiter keeps changing. The entire process is supposed to go unnoticed by the patrons.

As a hostess gains experience in the sex industry, she ages, gets to know more patrons, and grows up. In the process she may pass through a stage of baby-madam, when she is half-hostess and half-madam. A baby-madam is someone who cannot make big sales: She has some of her own patrons, but not enough. She is still hostess to her madam's patrons, but she acts as a madam to her own patrons, from whom she usually receives 20 percent of her sales.

Because of the absence of structural restraints and the symbiotic relationship with the madam, hostesses move frequently within the same kind of entertainment establishment as well as between different kinds—usually between room-salons and room-cafes. Madams also move frequently, primarily due to the short contract period. Frequent changes in the ownership of entertainment establishments also contribute to the high mobility of madams. Madam Park has worked in as many as nine different establishments in six years, sometimes staying for only two months at one place. Some establishments went out of business; others were sold to new owners. When a madam is forced to quit, her only compensation is that she does not have to repay the PR expenses even if she has not yet sold the amount specified in her contract.

Although a madam's work (attracting customers and controlling hostesses) is the most important aspect of the room-salon business, her position is extremely vulnerable. She is responsible for any financial loss caused by her patrons, and she has no fringe benefits or job protection. At the same time, her ability to move to other establishments is controlled by men in the industry.

HOSTESSES AND MADAMS: PRESENT AND FUTURE ASPIRATIONS

High incomes for a seemingly easy job, more than anything else, induce women to enter the entertainment industry. College student-cum-hostess Lee, who initially served in an open dining hall, was persuaded by a madam to start hostessing in one of the rooms. "I sat for about three hours and the tip was 50,000 won [about $70]. If you worked at Lotteria [a fast food chain], you were paid 450 won an hour. I don't know how much I cried over the 45,000 won I received [after a 10 percent deduction]." Even Madam Ahn, whose salary as a kindergarten teacher in the mid–1970s was a decent 120,000 won, and who now runs a room-salon as well as two other ordinary restaurants, said she earned more than one million won as a baby-madam:

I didn't know where I should spend all the money I was making. I even didn't know the exact amount—I never calculated how much I was making and I still don't. I paid back all my debts, which were more than two million won, including the interest, within three months, and brought home the living expenses, and I could still save a lot of money.

Madam Cho talks about the same experience: "I was making so much money, to the extent that I couldn't handle it."

Once these women earn enough money to be economically independent, their family can no longer exercise any control over their lives. Initially, they all tried to hide the fact that they were working as a hostess at a drinking place; they lied and said that they were cashiers or plain waitresses at the restaurant.[7] Some parents of the women interviewed still don't know what their daughter's real job is, although they might be suspicious. Hostess Noh's relatives wonder why she has to go somewhere else every time there is a family gathering. Hostess Yoo's mother found out because of Yoo's frequent drinking and money-spending. She cried, saying she wished she could see her daughter have a wedding. Madam Lee's older brother concealed himself and caught her in front of her workplace and brought her home. Her eldest brother tried to make her quit, saying that "they won't consider her as their sister if she keeps working in such a place." Unlike before, she talked back, "You can think so," and secretly left the family house the next morning. "Financially incapable parents," the hostesses and madams say, "cannot interfere with your life."

Not all women entered the hostess world because they badly wanted the money. Some wanted to have a free life, away from the control of their family. Hostess Noh, a college student, left home as a revolt against her rich father, who was "too conservative and oppressive." He imposed a 9 P.M. curfew on her and objected to her wearing make-up, nail polish, and fancy clothes, while he lived a "ragged life," battering her mother and flirting with many women. "This life is more comfortable, more fun, and I make money also. I don't have to do what I don't want to. If I put my mind in the right place, I can have a better life." Hostess Kang worked at her former job as an inspector at a down-jacket manufacturing company for six months. She was more attracted to the seemingly "easy and free life" of the hostesses she saw in the cafe where her live-in boyfriend was working as a chef. She did not know how much money the hostesses made. She took the recommendation of the "sister president" of the cafe and started working as a hostess one day a week in another room-cafe without the knowledge of her boyfriend. After two weeks, her boyfriend found out and they broke up. In the beginning she thought her new job was "fun and autonomous, without any restraints." After a while, she acquired a taste for the money and learned about the restrictions of the job, and she began to have doubts. However, she feels that "even with doubts, this job is still better than other jobs."

The women's sense of independence and autonomy along with the curiosity and even fun in the beginning are soon eroded by doubts and conflicts as they continue to work as hostesses. Their doubts and conflicts come mainly from three sources: the unruly and abusive patrons, the controlling madams, and the uncertain future. The more they work because of financial necessity, the bigger and stronger their doubts and conflicts become. Whereas hostesses with stable finances can exercise control over an undesirable situation, for example, by refusing to serve a really annoying patron (although she loses the tip), or can get away from a controlling madam by moving to another establishment, hostesses who have debts do not have such choices.

Hostesses have to deal with all kinds of patrons. There are "weird patrons with strange personalities, who are vicious drinkers, throwing glasses and heaping abuses." Hostess Kim considers drunk patrons to be "dogs." One of the patrons' most common annoying behaviors is fondling the hostess; the underlying assumption is that a hostess is a plaything bought by the man's tip and hence not to be treated as a human being. In fact, not being treated as a human being was listed by 48.1 percent of female employees as the top difficulty at drinking places, and one-third experienced physical assault, sexual harassment, and forced drinking (Kwon 1988, 144–145). Several years ago, a hostess was killed by too many "bomb drinks"—a shot of whisky inside a glass of beer. She chose bomb drinks instead of taking her clothes off as a punishment every time she lost a game. Hostess Kang once had a big fight with three other hostesses who were under the control of another madam because

one day I happened to serve with them in the same room, and they volunteered to strip off. I said I couldn't do it, and the patrons demanded that instead I should have five bomb drinks. I gathered my guts, drank them, and the film in my head was cut off [she lost consciousness]. When the patrons were gone, I said to the hostesses, "why are you behaving like ragpickers?" One of them hit my head with a metal ashtray and I had to have five stitches on my head. The hostess who hit me was wearing a tank top, and her madam stripped it off her and beat her. Her madam paid my hospital bill and also gave me 200,000 won. That hostess got fired and her madam also quit. I rested up for about two weeks.

Rather than see the problem as one of sexist exploitation by customers, however, she blamed the hostesses for their lack of pride. She also considered the hiring policy problematic: "When the establishments need hostesses, they just accept anybody. There should be some kind of standard, as to level of education, beauty, culture, and so on. Some hostesses think that they just fill the seats and that's all."

Having the second or sleep-out with the patron is an unavoidable aspect of the hostess job, although nobody can physically force a hostess to do it. Except in the rare room-cafes whose madams do not let hostesses have the seconds for business reasons, hostesses are sooner or later faced with the problem. Especially when a patron brings guests for business entertainment, the hostess is expected to sleep with any of the guests who like her.

Many women in the entertainment business eventually develop a mistress relationship with a patron. Such patrons are usually rich Korean residents of Japan or Japanese. Often the relationship develops in the following way: If a patron does not dislike the first hostess assigned to him, the madam will assign the same hostess the next time he visits. In this way, a hostess acquires "appointed partners" in the course of working. Hostess Kang has four or five appointed partners. Rather than go out for the second with the patron from the salon or cafe, she prefers to meet her appointed partner outside during the day. This arrangement can be interpreted as her way of trying to avoid the feeling that she is prostituting herself. Instead, she can feel romantic. The men give her pocket money or things she needs. When interviewed at her rented apartment, Kang pointed out that almost everything in her place—the bed, washing machine, audio-system as well as the television set and her watch—is from her patrons. Sometimes she is surprised with a gift of a large sum of money, even 1 million won. She earns on average 2 or 3 million won a month, and she goes out for seconds only when she needs money or when the patron is okay. Twenty-one-year-old Hostess Noh does not like sex at all, but she goes out with the patron if her madam asks, because she wants to "help her madam out." She was in a steady relationship for more than two years with a fifty-seven-year-old Korean resident of Japan. Her madam informed me in a jealous voice that Noh recently met a "biggie"—a rich man—and was showered with expensive jewelry. To "catch a biggie" is every hostess's dream.

To some hostesses, a controlling madam is a problem. Hostess Kim shows her anger toward her madam:

My madam is picky. She pays attention to every detail—the clothes I wear, my make-up and my hair style—and wants to make them in her style. I came out here to make money, so I don't want to spend a lot on clothes. But she teases me, saying, "You always wear cheap clothes, don't you?" So I have to buy new clothes every month, about two dresses. I can't buy just any clothes, because she will then say something. So I have to buy name-brand clothes. There were no restrictions of this kind in the other place I worked before. She also forces me into the "second." I have a lover, so I don't want to sleep with the patrons. But if I say no, the madam says (with a sarcastic twist), "Why, do you have a date with your lover?"

Her lover, by the way, is married and has a daughter in the eighth grade. He demands that she not go out for seconds with the patrons. He caught her going out with customers two or three times, and she showed the bruises he made the night before the interview.

The madam tries to control her hostesses in order not to lose face with her patrons. Dealing with patrons and hostesses is a source of stress over and above the problems of attracting customers and collecting money. A patron might not be satisfied with his assigned hostess and demand another. A hostess whose feelings were hurt by a nasty patron can just leave the scene, putting her madam in a difficult position. When a hostess refuses to go out with the patron who requested her, her madam loses face and potentially future business with the patron.

The hostess's self-acclaimed autonomy from her own family is eroded by abusive and unruly patrons, domineering madams, and hostess coworkers with no self-respect. In fact, the high income for working in the entertainment industry is in a sense a compensation for loss of respect (Won, 1985, 25). Many women said they cried a lot in the beginning. Baby-Madam Yoo was in tears during her interview. That is why patrons seem to treat a novice hostess differently, especially when she is a student. The former-teacher Madam Ahn mentioned above was treated very nicely and even protected by her patrons because she was considered to be a woman "not supposed to be in such a place." Student hostess Noh distinguishes herself from other hostesses. At her workplace, she circles around madams and does not mix with hostesses in the hostess's waiting room. According to Madam Ahn, patrons want "pretty, submissive and naive hostesses who are beginners and do not reject a patron's fondling as well as the sleep-out." Knowing this, a hostess may deceive her patrons, lying that she is in the business for only ten days or one month, when actually it is much longer, for example, three years. In the process of turning into a professional entertainer, she learns the technique of "handling the moment of patron's breast-fondling without making a big fuss about it." A hostess has to choose "between high tips and her pride"— it is not possible to have both at the same time.

Due to the loss of respect from society, realistic hostesses do not see marriage as a viable option. Most of the patrons they meet are already married and they rarely have a chance to meet "normal men," that is single men who are not in the entertainment industry. A marriage between a former hostess and a normal man can happen, however, and in such a case, her friends all help in concealing her former identity. The madam's assessment is that one or two out of ten hostesses marry and leave the entertainment business completely. There seem to be more live-in situations with a waiter or a bandsman that dissolve after a while. Two of the hostesses interviewed are living in this situation. More frequently, though, they become mistresses of rich men, off and on.

Another one or two out of ten hostesses become madams. Before the 1970s, when the job of hostess was not popular among young women, there were only a limited number of madams and the job of controlling hostesses was left to the male members. When a hostess was controlled by a member, she had to pay him monthly bribe money so that he would not overlook her when allocating hostesses to customers. As more hostesses went into the industry and learned how it worked, they advanced into the new job of madam. Waiters also tempt hostesses with many regular patrons to become madams. Some women become the owner of an entertainment establishment on their own or with the financial support of their rich lover, usually a small cafe which needs less capital.[8] Men own most of the big establishments, and more waiters than madams become owners.

Baby-Madam Yoo, aged twenty-eight, had a *seon*, or a prearranged meeting with prospective husbands, three or four times. She felt guilty about her lie that she previously held an office job and was now staying at home to help with the household. What she is most scared of in an arranged marriage is that her husband might find out about her past. Because of this guilty feeling and fear, she gave up any more *seons*. Her plan is to grow up more under her madam and to be a successful madam herself. She wants to continue making money in this industry until she is thirty-five or thirty-six, and then start her own business, either a clothes shop, goods store, or beauty salon.

Baby-Madam Kim sees only a 10 percent possibility of her ever marrying. Her future plans are in a state of flux between becoming a madam or quitting her job. If she had money, she would want to open her own business. While being a hostess, she was spotted by a Japanese real estate broker, who wanted her to quit her job the next day. He bought her an apartment, but he was imprisoned because of his real estate speculation in Hawaii. She rented her apartment to someone else and with the money started a noodle business. After eight months, however, she closed it because "the working hours were too long." When she returned to the entertainment industry, she was "getting old—twenty-eight years of age—for a hostess" and became a baby-madam. She now stays in the entertainment business because "there is no other appropriate business to do." She is "just killing time, without any meaning in life." Her present work does not cause her any big inconvenience, and she has to earn her living.

Most hostesses and madams interviewed had doubts about their present jobs as well as a sense of instability and anxiety about their future. Even the seemingly successful and self-confident cafe-owner Yoon expressed anxiety about her life. She initially thought that she would quit after making money for several months from hostessing, but during this time she beame a professional before she realized it. Now as the owner, she regrets that she is too old (forty-two years) to go back to the position of madam, at which she was so successful. She wishes she could live with a man she loves.

Hostesses gain economic independence at the cost of society's respect, and the feelings of freedom and autonomy are only temporary, as long as their youth lasts. In the long run, hostesses do not have many options for their future and are faced with uncertainty. Within the entertainment industry, the contract works against the madam, leaving her in a constant state of debt, and her movement to other jobs is controlled by men. In Korean society, the patriarchal tradition of the double standard is strong; once a hostess, a woman is not accepted as a proper marriage partner. Whatever limited autonomy an entertainment woman has, it is subject to patriarchal control within the industry as well as in society.

CONCLUDING REMARKS

The field of women and development has not recognized or given proper weight to the contributions of women in the sex industry to economic development, except in the area of sex tourism. The contribution of the female sexual worker to South Korean economic development has been considerable. Although the "nimble hands" of female factory workers contributed a great deal directly to the production of cheap commodities for export, the sexy smiles and bodies of female service workers certainly helped with other aspects of economic activities, such as obtaining credits and securing favors, as well as contributing to the sales of commodities in domestic and world markets. By providing sexual services in business entertainment, women in the entertainment industry have contributed considerably in bridging business deals and bringing in much-needed foreign currency, especially Japanese yen and American dollars.

It should be emphasized that the women subjects in this study were a specific group of sex workers, who have relatively high autonomy. A much higher income than that of most other employed women, though unstable and short-lived, is the main factor that makes women stay in the industry. Although this study clearly shows the sexual exploitation of women in the entertainment industry, their exploitation is made invisible. Their luxurious, albeit often superficial lifestyle, combined with the still-strong ideology of chastity in South Korean society, casily allows the public to pass moral judgment on them.

If development were pursued simply to attain a higher standard of living, a certain number of women entertainers in South Korea, such as the room-salon hostesses in this study, could be said to be enjoying the fruits of successful economic development. They are doing much better economically than their sisters in service occupations in South Korea or in other developing countries, which enables them to lead independent lives away from the control of their families.

Any question about the relationship between women and development, however, should ultimately focus on the liberation of women. In this regard, the question of the effect of development on women in the sex industry requires a somewhat complicated answer. In view of the economic independence and the autonomy gained by that independence, they seem to have achieved economic liberation as long as they earn good money. With a high income, they have considerable control over how often they sleep with their patrons, and they can avoid exploitative customers. Their independence and autonomy, however, are precarious and temporary, remaining only as long as they are attractive. At the same time, the sex industry reinforces patriarchal and heterosexist notions of sexuality. The temporary economic independence or autonomy, therefore, is gained only by becoming and remaining the sexual objects of men, and it is ultimately dependent on men.

Concerning the liberation of women as a whole, the expansion of the entertainment industry certainly brought negative effects. Increased violence against women, especially trafficking in women in the industry and rape, is a visible consequence of the expansion of the industry. Another negative effect is the greater commercialization of women's sexuality. The hostess's life is the theme of movies, plays, and video tapes, and the subject of soap operas. These shows are produced mostly for commercial purposes and are more interested in depicting women as sex objects than in challenging the existing ideology or social structure.

The increasing commercialization of women's sexuality is not a phenomenon confined to South Korea or Asia, but is becoming more and more of a worldwide phenomenon. Recently added to the sex tour circuit are countries in other regions: Kenya, Senegal, and Brazil (Cincone 1988, 53). In Eastern European countries that recently experienced rapid political and economic changes, prostitution is increasingly becoming a means of livelihood for women. In Czechoslovakia, for example, the hidden prostitution of the past has now become an open activity. In the past, women who wanted to be rich engaged in prostitution. Now, more women are openly prostituting themselves out of economic need.[9]

Women's sexual services have not only increased globally but have also developed into a hierarchical division of labor between the First World and the Third World. Just as the international division of labor in manufacturing has developed to exploit the cheap labor of Third World women, the new international division of sexual labor has developed a system of exploitation. A German or Japanese man can fly to Asian and other Third World countries to enjoy sex tourism in an exotic setting, or he can enjoy the cheap sexual services of migrant women in his own country.

The expansion of women's sexual services in various forms requires new directions for future research work. In academia, researchers in the field of women and development should pay attention to this subject. Although the debate on prostitution in the West has produced a large body of thought, Third World social scientists have by and large neglected the subject (Truong 1990). In addition, the international division of sexual labor requires cooperation between researchers in the developed and developing countries.

At the same time, activism against the sexual exploitation of women is needed at both local and global levels. Although some Western sex workers organize themselves and demand their right to work legitimately (Pheterson 1989), Third

World sex workers are much less visible, and they take a different position. What is needed is to understand the differences and diversity in the realities of women's lives and to build cooperative networks among feminists in developed and developing countries toward the common struggle for the liberation of women.

8

Planning for Prostitution: An Analysis of Thailand's Sex Industry

Catherine Hill

In the past two decades, a new international form of prostitution has developed in some countries in Southeast Asia and the Caribbean. Prostitution in these countries is an international matter, often beginning with a foreign military's "rest and recreation" and expanding to serve wealthy male businessmen and tourists who are managers and consumers of our increasingly global economy. These businessmen constitute a new class of transitory men who, like the soldiers before them, often travel without wives and create a demand for prostitution. On the supply side, developing nations find the foreign currency prostitution generates economically beneficial and many seem willing to tolerate the social costs.

Thailand is a useful case study not because it is unique, but owing to the availability of data compiled by scholars (see in particular Truong 1990; Richter 1989). As an American, I am particularly concerned with the role of the U.S. military and industry in developing international prostitution in Thailand. As a planner, I am interested in whether tourism and/or militarization in a region causes prostitution. Finally, as a feminist, I am concerned with how prostitution affects the women and girls involved and the status of women generally.

In this chapter, I examine the factors contributing to the development of Thailand's international sex trade, distinguishing supply factors, such as Thai government policies and the status of Thai women, and demand factors, such as American militarization and international tourism. Although not generally cast as women's issues, both military "rest and relaxation" policies and tourism have profound effects on women. I conclude that the presence of foreign soldiers

The author is grateful for the comments and suggestions of Siriporn Skrobanek and Meredeth Turshen.

and businessmen in developing nations is both an economic opportunity and a hazard for women and girls, as well as for the host nations as a whole.

THE DEMAND FOR PROSTITUTION: THE MILITARY PRESENCE

The scale and character of Thai prostitution dramatically altered with the U.S. military presence in the 1960s and 1970s. Skrobanek (1983a, 33–38) cites a 1957 UN report which estimated that at the time there were 20,000 prostitutes in Thailand (total population of 22 million); by 1964, she cites police estimates of 400,000 prostitutes (total population of 27 million). In 1981, estimates of the number of prostitutes in Thailand ranged from 500,000 to 700,000; assuming prostitutes are between the ages of fifteen and thirty-four, then 6.2 to 8.7 percent of all Thai women between these ages work as prostitutes (Truong 1990, 181). All analysts agree that prostitution has grown dramatically since the 1960s.

It is well documented that Thailand served American interests during the Vietnam War. Thitsa (1980, 5) notes that not only did Thailand permit American forces to base their war against Vietnam on Thai soil, but they also provided mercenaries to fight in Vietnam and neighboring Laos. In his book on CIA history, William Blum (1986, 140) reiterates Thitsa's observation:

To the men who walked the corridors of power in Washington, to the military men in the field, Indochina—nay, South-East Asia—was a single large battlefield. Troops of South Vietnam were used in Laos and Cambodia. Troops of Thailand were used in Laos, Cambodia and South Vietnam. Thailand and the Philippines were used as bases from which to bomb the three countries of Indochina.

Blum points out that the CIA Southeast Asia headquarters was also located in Thailand (ibid., 155).

Thailand's main role, however, was as a rest and recreation area for American military men. In addition to the 50,000 U.S. soldiers stationed in Thailand, some 70,000 were flown to Bangkok each year to recover from the stress of daily warfare (Holden et al. 1983, 15). In 1967, a formal treaty between the United States and Thailand permitted the U.S. military to send its men to Thailand for "R & R"—rest and recreation (Truong 1990, 161). Skrobanek (1983a, 35–37) estimates that an average of 700,000 American GIs took their R & R in Thailand between 1962–76; their expenditures at restaurants, bars, and brothels exceeded 40 percent of Thailand's export earnings at the time. The American soldiers wielded significant influence on their hosts. Their practice of buying girls to clean their apartments and provide sexual services, for example, introduced a new word into the Thai language *mia chao* or "rented wife" (Barry, Bunch, and Castley 1984, 39).

The extensive literature on the Vietnam War is curiously silent on the recreational practices of American GIs.[1] However, military experts believe that rest and recreation are essential for troop morale and indeed for the very functioning of military units. Sociologist Larry Ingraham claims that soldiers' abusive behavior toward women can be understood as a need for affiliation and a chain of command among each other. Ingraham attributes their extensive drinking, drug use, and their trips to prostitutes and topless bars to this need for connection with one another (Ingraham 1984, 91–129). As well as bringing them together, these escapades establish informal hierarchies that are a necessary supplement to the army's official, but often inaccurate, power structure.

Many of the escapades Ingraham and others document—purchasing sex, violence against one another and women, drinking, and drugs—can be found in any place in which groups of young men congregate, including fraternities and street corner gangs. The need for cohesion within the army, however, differs from normal male bonding in its intensity and perceived importance. In the army, men count on each other in life and death situations; they kill together and risk their own death. Therefore cohesion and rest and recreation provisions to facilitate this bonding are instrumental. S.L.A. Marshall (1964), the army's premier historian, noted the need for cohesion:

I hold it to be one of the simple truths of war that the thing which enables an infantry soldier to keep going with his weapon is the near presence or the presumed presence of a comrade. . . . Should he lack this feeling for any reason, . . . he would become a castaway in the middle of a battle and as incapable of effective offensive action as if he were stranded somewhere without weapons.

Rest and recreation, then, are important to the military to the extent that the experience binds soldiers together emotionally. The importance of social cohesion in the military helps us explain the "boys will be boys" attitude of the Pentagon toward prostitution. The cultural belief that men need sex also contributes to the official sanction of prostitution.

Since the United States's withdrawal from Vietnam, the Philippines rather than Thailand has become the major outpost of U.S. military and military-related prostitution. American servicemen, particularly the navy, do continue to visit Thailand to purchase sex. Following the recent U.S. war against Iraq, for example, the military sent soldiers to Thailand for R & R. Soldiers, however, are no longer the only international customers for Thailand's prostitution industry. Since the 1970s, businessmen and tourists have become a second important market.

THE DEMAND FOR PROSTITUTION: TOURISM

Thailand is one of many countries now employing tourism as a growth strategy. Indeed, tourism has become a major international economic activity. By the mid–1980s, the global tourist business employed more people than the oil industry (Enloe 1989, 20). In 1989, there were 200 million international tourists a year and the UN World Tourism Organization forecasts that by the year 2000 tourism will be the single most important global economic activity. This development began in the 1950s, when air travel and tourism grew at spectacular rates. Aircraft manufacturers were the leaders in the development of international tourism. After World War II, U.S. military aircraft manufacturers faced enormous overcapacity problems. Industry leaders promoted tourism to create demand for their planes. Together with hotel entrepreneurs, tour operators, and travel agents, the U.S. airlines industry pressured governments and world organizations to promote tourism. The businessmen who promote tourism considered their industry to be of great significance to the world's economy. In the 1950s, the founder of the Hilton chain boasted, "No new nation has got it going until it has a seat in the United Nations, a national airline and a Hilton hotel" (quoted in Truong 1990, 109). The leaders of these industries shared resources, and in some cases, airlines or hotel owners were also owners of travel agencies (Matthews 1978, 51).

International agencies heralded tourism as a growth strategy for developing nations. In 1963, the United Nations hosted a conference on international travel and tourism and adopted the recommendations of the U.S.–funded Checchi Report entitled *The Future of Tourism in the Far East and Pacific*. The report stated that "governments should be recommended to adopt special measures (financial, fiscal, customs, bylaws) in favor of that industry [tourism] . . . the conference recommends that governments should, whenever possible avoid any kind of activity hostile to tourism and based on arguments of religious, racial or political nature" (quoted in Truong 1990, 108). The UN declared 1967 the Year of the Tourist and pledged to promote this clean industry throughout the world. In 1974, the World Tourism Organization was established as an intergovernmental agency at the global level. By the end of the 1970s, there were eighty-one corporations active in the world hotel industry associated with over one thousand hotels outside their home countries. More recently, involvement is shifting from ownership to management contracts (Truong 1990, 121).

Enloe (1989, 31) describes tourism as "a powerful motor for global integration." In fact, this was the explicit goal of many of the proponents of world tourism. Industry leaders claimed that tourism was good not only for generating foreign currency, but also had positive cultural effects. Industry and government leaders came together to promote this new clean industry, dismissing any reservations as "conservative."

Thailand's efforts to attract tourists have been very successful. Since the 1960s, the number of tourists to Thailand has grown significantly. In 1960, 81,340 foreigners visited Thailand, in 1986, over 2.8 million arrived (Truong 1990, 164). In the next three years, the number of tourists almost doubled to 4.2 million in 1989 (Richter 1989, 20). This burgeoning industry contributes substantially to the nation's economy. Since 1982, Thailand has earned more foreign currency from tourism ($1.5 billion in 1982) than it did from any other economic activity, including its traditional export leader, rice (ibid., 84). By 1988, the annual revenue from tourism had risen to $3 billion (ibid., 20). As a shortage of foreign exchange is a continuing constraint on development efforts by nonoil exporting developing countries, tourism's capacity to generate foreign currency is a strong incentive to encourage this industry (Jenkins and Henry 1982). The Thai government also extracted revenue directly from the tourist industry by imposing special hotel room and restaurant taxes (Richter 1989, 84).

It is difficult to gauge the precise role of prostitution in tourism due to its illegality. The export or import of girls and women for the purpose of prostitution was made illegal in Thailand in 1928. A 1979 Immigration Act provides additional punitive measures against persons entering Thailand for this purpose. The 1960 Prostitution Suppression Act made it illegal to be a prostitute, and a 1990 Decree of the Ministry of Interior prevents employers from hiring children (under eighteen) in entertainment businesses that provide women for services (Skrobanek 1990, 16). The government has neglected to enforce these laws, and in spite of formal illegality, prostitution businessmen continue to advertise audaciously. A 1990 survey of foreign tourists found that 63 percent had experienced Thai night life (for example, patronized bars, clubs, or massage parlors) and 40 percent of the men said they had or were planning to have sex with a Thai person (Muecke 1990, 3).

Many travel advertisements promise sex, but few with the candor and practicality that accompany guidebooks to Thailand. A popular American travel guide to Thailand states the obvious:

World famous for licentious nightlife, Bangkok offers red-hot, buffet style entertainment. Appetizers range from family-type Thai classic dancing and boxing to "the other" which is what most tourists want to see. After dark the Thai capital assumes its official name . . . —in short, Krun Thep, "the City of Angels," though not perhaps what the ancients had in mind. Beautiful girls, usually from poor northeast villages, are skilled in all sorts of feats. A "Light Show" means topless dancing and nothing more. Other acts take place upstairs, with peep-holes to warn of police raids. Customers are not arrested. . . . Massage parlors and Bangkok go together like gin and tonic. . . . A "Body Massage" means sex. There is a basic hourly rate and the amount to tip depends on "extra services" (Osborne 1990).

The Thai government is also becoming increasingly candid about the nature of its tourist trade. In 1980, which Thailand declared the Year of the Tourist, the government attempted to bring the tourist industry under regulation and taxation. In that year, then Deputy Prime Minister Boonchu Rojanasathian advised governors "to contribute to the national tourism effort by developing scenic spots in their provinces while encouraging certain entertainment activities which some of you may find disgusting and embarrassing because they are related to sexual pleasure" (quoted in Holden et al. 1983).

The Thai government's efforts to promote tourism have been successful. As expected, the tourists are disproportionately male; in 1982, for example, 71.4 percent of Thailand's tourists were men. By region, this statistic is even more striking; for instance, 86.4 percent of the visitors to Pattaya, an outlying town of greater Bangkok which is known for its prostitutes, are men (Holden et al. 1983). Bangkok offers 119 massage parlors, 119 teahouses which provide sexual services, 97 nightclubs, 248 brothels, and 394 restaurants which have added sex to their menu (Enloe 1989, 36). Although it is impossible to extract the actual fees paid for sexual services from the tourism profits generally, the prominence of sexual services in the tourism industry is announced by the presence of a large number of prostitutes and brothels, by the disproportionate number of male tourists, and by advertisements.

Soldiers and businessmen primarily from First World countries have created a demand for prostitution internationally. As the world economy becomes increasingly integrated, this demand will probably grow. Yet many countries have not responded to this demand. In Germany, for example, the presence of American soldiers has not generated prostitution on the scale found in Thailand. Why do some countries serve as hosts for prostitution, while others do not? Although demand tells us part of the story, there are also significant supply factors involved.

SUPPLY SIDE: THAILAND'S ECONOMIC INTERESTS

Tourism played a significant role in Thailand's strong economic growth, particularly in the 1980s. Between 1981 and 1986, tourism was the country's top foreign exchange earner, helping balance a high level of imports (LePoer 1989, 134). Thailand is an oil importer without a stable source of foreign exchange. The government maintains a high rate of foreign debt, primarily in yen and dollars, which creates a need for foreign exchange to pay the interest on the deficit, if not the principal. The proportion of Thailand's foreign debt to gross national product (GNP) increased from 11 percent in 1970 to 36 percent in 1985 (ibid., 138). This large deficit has not slowed the country's economic growth. Between 1965 and 1988, the gross domestic product (GDP) grew from $4,390 million to $57,950 million and exports shifted from primarily agricultural to primarily manufactured goods (ibid., 134). The people of Thailand have enjoyed some benefits of industrialization. Since the 1960s, real incomes have risen at an annual average of 4.7 percent, one of the highest among developing countries (Kharas and Shishido 1985, 59).

The Thai government achieved this level of growth by vigorously promoting foreign investment and export-oriented industry (Thorbek 1987, 9). Tourism has played an important role as a primarily earner of foreign currency. Thailand's prominence in tourism may also improve its name recognition among businessmen and encourage foreign investors to locate their capital in the country.

The economic advantages of tourism for Thailand are clearly significant. For individual women, the incentives to work as prostitutes are also considerable. In her book *From Peasant Girls to Bangkok Masseuses*, Pasuk Phongpaichit (1982, 8) presents a comprehensive discussion of the incentives prostitution offers Thai women, including wages up to twenty-five times those offered to women in other industries. Phongpaichit notes that some women and girls are able to purchase houses for their families with their earnings.

SUPPLY SIDE: STATUS OF WOMEN

Religious practices in Thailand help us understand the seemingly contradictory role of women. Theravada Buddhism is the major religion and permeates all aspects of daily life. Buddhist monks are held in the highest esteem, and over 40 percent of all Thai men spend some portion of their life as a monk. By entering the religious order, men accumulate merit. In Buddhism, the goal of every individual is to accumulate merit and to be reborn into a higher life. According to many Buddhists, birth as a woman is the result of insufficient merit owing to shortcomings in a past life. Like the other major world religions, Buddhism considers women less spiritual than men.

In *Providence and Prostitution: Images and Reality for Women in Buddhist Thailand*, Khin Thitsa (1980, 20) relates a parable that indicates a Buddhist attitude toward gender and work:

The parable of the Buddha's second last incarnation (a Thai version) is as follows: he is born a prince, Vessantara, who gives up his wealth and glory and retires to the forest, accompanied by his faithful wife and two young children. Everyday while he meditates, she goes in search of food for the family, leaving the boy and girl under his care. One day while she was away, a beggar comes and asks Vessantara for his children, as servants for the beggar's wife. . . . Vessantara, of course, in order to free himself further from his earthly ties, gives his children away. . . . This story of Vessantara and his remarkable renunciation is recited by men upon their ordination into the monastic order.

His wife, caught in the material struggle for food, did not participate in the renunciation and did not earn merit. Many Buddhists believe that men are more spiritual and that women are more materialistic. One important outcome of this tradition is that women are encouraged to participate in production and public life. In fact, Thai men prefer to have women providing for them so that they can serve as monks and earn merit. Thus a contradictory situation develops in which women are encouraged to work and yet their work does not translate into higher social status.

FEMINISTS FIGHT BACK

Given the existing class of tourists, it is clear that prostitution will accompany international tourism, particularly when the government takes no action against it as has been the case in Thailand. Thus far, international tourists have demonstrated a greater interest in sexual exploitation than cultural exchange and international understanding. Indeed, tourists often seek out destinations where they can "let themselves go." In an article entitled "Americans in Thailand,"

Rolling Stone magazine advises its readers: "Used to be a man could get a blow job while taking a dump in any barn in Bangkok, or so they say. . . . Here is where you drink till your face goes numb, here is where you find your darkeyed orb for the evening, here is your frat house, your locker room, and your Elks club" (Sager and Nichols 1984, 28). The article goes on to celebrate the lack of any restrictions on men's sexual behavior in Thailand. The anonymity of a foreign land enables men to behave in socially unacceptable ways. The presence of these kinds of tourists has had a significant impact on sexual relations, specifically by expanding prostitution.

Prostitution has consequences for all women as well as those involved in the business. The popular myth that prostitution acts as a release for male sexual aggression is refuted by evidence in Thailand. In fact, the presence of sexually aggressive tourists and soldiers may place Thai women and girls at even greater risk of rape or assault. Bangkok is a dangerous city, particularly for its female residents. A UN study found that 67 percent of women in Bangkok were afraid of being raped in the streets at night (Buendia 1989, 46). Moreover, the authors found this fear justified, citing hospital evidence of high numbers of rape victims (ibid., 33).

The Tourism Agency of Thailand (TAT) has responded to the general problem of violence in its tourist regions by expanding the number of police officers assigned to the tourism police. In 1984, TAT tripled the tourism police force from 255 to 850 men; officers received part of their pay from TAT but worked closely with the rest of the Thai police force (Richter 1989, 91).

Tourism security forces are designed to ensure the customers' safety, but do little to help women. Thai feminists have begun to organize against the violence sustained by women in prostitution. A Rape Crisis Center was established in 1982 under the auspices of the Population and Community Development Association. Unfortunately, services are limited by financial constraints and reliance primarily on volunteer help (Buendia 1989). Independent feminist groups such as Friends of Women, Empower, Emergency Home, and Foundation for Women also provide assistance to women who are victims of violence.

As well as helping individuals, Thai feminists have also spoken out against prostitution in their society. Siriporn Skrobanek, who is the director of the Women's Information Center, a service provider for prostitutes and other women in Bangkok, takes the following positions:

Prostitution can be broadly divided into two categories: forced and free. It is mostly innocent, ignorant, young girls from rural areas who are lured into forced prostitution. The conditions of work are extremely exploitative. For this type of prostitution, legal measures that exist already should be enforced to help those young girls out of their deplorable situation, but penalize only procurers and other agents. Legal protection is also required for free prostitution. According to interviews with women in this category, none of them wants to stay long in this "profession." They see prostitution as a short-term means for their survival. Therefore, solutions like registration of prostitutes would stigmatize them and make it more difficult for them to leave this institution (Skrobanek 1983b, 214).

Skrobanek later argues that prostitution reflects an inequality between men and women and ultimately should be abolished. Her knowledge of the immediate problems of Thai prostitutes informs this position, and she does not argue for police action, further regulation, or rehabilitation programs. Rather, her work centers on immediate aid to prostitutes, ending forced prostitution, and education of the public on the issue.

This is more or less the position of the Thai Women's Information Center which along with other Thai feminist groups, such Empower, Women's Lawyers Association, Friends of Women, and the Association for the Promotion of the Status of Women lead the fight for women's rights in Thailand. Religious organizations, such as the Ecumenical Coalition on Third World Tourism, based in Bangkok, are also fighting against child sexploitation. Academic groups, such as the Women in Development Consortium in Thailand, a joint project of universities in Thailand and Canada, are studying alternative development strategies to empower women.

Phongpaichit (1982) notes that since the 1970s, "Thailand has kept the channels of international trade as open as possible, and counted on private enterprise to achieve economic growth by pursuing the comparative advantages which Thailand enjoys." One of the industries that has grown with this strategy is prostitution. There is little doubt that prostitution has had a major impact on Thai culture. Whether prostitution is good or bad for Thai women, or for any women, is a more difficult question. Thai women's experience with the prostitution industry provides evidence on both sides.

On the one hand, Thai women do receive substantial amounts of money for their work as prostitutes, particularly when compared with other women's occupations. Information about the income derived from prostitution is scanty; some estimates are that prostitutes get about 90 baht out of the client's fee of 450 baht (Holden et al. 1983, 48). Given that a baht is worth about 4 cents, the women or girls' fee equals $3.60 in American currency. With this fraction of the profits, however, women can build homes for their families and support many dependents, and a prostitute's income may reach approximately 25 times what women can earn in other jobs, such as factory work, waitressing, or clerical jobs (Phongpaichit 1982, 8). Although the financial rewards for prostitutes far outweigh the wages offered by other jobs, a prostitute can only sell herself for a limited period of her lifetime, usually up to twenty-five years of age. Moreover, a pretty girl commands a higher rate of pay than a plain one, which suggests that prostitution may be more lucrative for some than others (ibid., 9). Nevertheless, compared with other economic opportunities available to women and girls, prostitution must be described as lucrative.

On the other hand, there are health and emotional risks associated with prostitution. Venereal disease is a problem for many prostitutes. Gonorrhea is rampant, infecting over 70 percent of Thai prostitutes with an increasingly antibiotic-resistant strain (Richter 1989, 91). AIDS is a looming deadly issue. In the past three years, the cumulative number of AIDS cases in Thailand has shot up from 171 HIV cases, 13 ARC cases, and 7 AIDS cases in 1987 to a total of 23,279 known HIV cases, 200 ARC cases, and 69 cases of active AIDS (Muecke 1990, 4). Government officials and other observers estimate that the actual number of AIDS cases is closer to 200,000 (ibid., 5). The virus is most prevalent among intravenous drug users and lower status prostitutes. The infection rate among prostitutes in the Chiang Mai Province in 1990, for example, was 23.2 percent in "undisguised female prostitutes," 8.4 percent among "hidden" prostitutes (those working in bars, nightclubs, escort services) and 14 percent among male prostitutes (ibid., 6). The government has been experimenting with certifications for prostitutes, which will verify that they are free of AIDS (*Economist* 1990c, 44). Of course, customers will not be required to be tested, leaving the women and girls potential recipients of the deadly virus. A few brothels are experimenting with "condom only" policies and report fewer venereal infections among their prostitutes. Mechai Viravaidya, secretary general of the Population and Community Development Association, who has been instrumental in distributing birth control throughout Thailand, has launched a vigorous campaign for safer sex practices, including condom use (*Economist* 1990b, 40). Given the government's reluctance to regulate the lucrative sex industry, however, the fight against AIDS faces an uphill battle.

Health concerns are not the only problem with the sex industry. Thailand's experience suggests that an expanding free prostitution industry encourages the practice of forced prostitution to cut costs. It is simply cheaper to purchase young, rural girls than to pay independent adult women a wage; moreover, girls fetch a higher price from customers. Yayori Matsui, a Japanese journalist, describes the youth of the prostitutes, many of whom were sold by their parents:

Particularly disturbing is the fact that age of the prostitutes is getting lower and lower. Professor Mattani says that ten percent are now under fourteen years of age. In Spring 1984, around one hundred prostitutes were taken into "protective custody" by Bangkok police. Nearly all of them were thirteen- and fourteen-year-olds. To force a young girl into prostitution is to practice slavery, and a violation of human rights. Child prostitution is increasing in every Asian country, and since it is profitable, competition is high among those involved in it. Therefore, the young, fresh, easy-to-control, early teenage girls become a much sought-after commodity (Matsui 1987, 63).

Conservative news magazines such as the *Economist* (1990a, 38) also note a growth of child sexual slavery in Thailand. A majority of the child prostitutes are brought to the brothels by their own parents (Skrobanek 1990, 13). A recent study by the Foundation of Women of the attitudes of teachers and girls on the sex trade reveals an important difference of opinion. Although 78 percent of the girls interviewed believed that girls were forced into prostitution, only 50 percent of the teachers believed that girls did not enter prostitution of their own free will (Skrobanek 1990, 14).

A less tangible but no less important problem with the institution of prostitution is its contribution to sexist ideas. In prostitution, the qualities women are credited with revolving around beauty and sexiness. A younger or more beautiful prostitute will be more successful than an older or less attractive one. Women's experience and wisdom are of only secondary importance in this trade. Prostitution reinforces sexist ideas about women's worth and has a negative impact on all women's self-esteem.

CONCLUSION

Bolstered by the Thai government, by the airline and hotel industries, by cultural practices, and used by millions of middle-class and wealthy men annually, Thai prostitution seems here to stay. There are efforts underway to curb its worst abuses, and a few feminists are challenging the institution itself. As a result of international feminist pressure, the United Nations has again undertaken a study of the prostitution problem. Jean Fernard Laurent who led the research concluded the following:

Like slavery in the usual sense, prostitution has an economic aspect. While being a cultural phenomenon rooted in the masculine and feminine images given currency by society, it is a market and indeed a very lucrative one. The merchandise involved is men's pleasure, or their image of pleasure. This merchandise is unfortunately supplied by physical intimacy with women or children. Thus, the alienation of the person is here more far reaching than in slavery in its usual sense, where what is alienated is working strength, not intimacy (cited in Barry, Bunch, and Castley 1984, 24).

Research and human rights organizations have begun to accept the similarity of prostitution to slavery, although generally these organizations focus on child prostitution. In *International Feminism: Networking Against Female Sexual Slavery*, Barry, Bunch, and Castley (1984, 30) caution against dividing the issue of child and adult prostitution: "Our patriarchal but benevolent organizations enter into some dangerous inconsistencies when they assume that it is a crime for men to buy sexual perversion and to employ sadistic behavior on children, but that it is a form of work and an expression of sex for adult women." Barry's criticism raises a number of difficult theoretical questions around the issue of consent. Barry, Bunch, and Castley define sexual slavery to include women who must go into prostitution for economic reasons; where this line is drawn is a matter of some debate. Moreover, although the International Women's Tribune and other feminists fighting against the international sex trade make a careful distinction between forced and free prostitution, their position on free prostitution is not unanimous.

American feminist Catherine McKinnon (1987, 16) recognized a paradoxical aspect of feminist struggle when she wrote the following: "One genius of the system we live under is that the strategies it requires to survive it from day to day are exactly the opposite of what is required to change it." Although prostitution can be seen as an excellent means for surviving from day to day for individual women, it is the opposite of the kind of behavior women need to engage in to change the system. Selling men their sexual fantasies produces a short-term profit for individual women, but it further entrenches those fantasies in the minds of men. Although this can be interpreted as the free speech of individual women, McKinnon (ibid., 15) notes that "anyone with an ounce of political analysis should know that freedom before equality, freedom before justice, will only further liberate the power of the powerful and will never free what is most in need of expression."

A sexual practice that men pay for is defined by men. The freedom to engage in prostitution before achieving the equality of men and women only tips the power scales further in men's favor. The Thai case demonstrates other, more specific problems associated with prostitution, such as female slavery and deadly health risks. Although there is no reason, theoretically, why tourism or a foreign military presence should always result in prostitution, it is clear that in the case of Thailand these institutions were directly related to the growth of prostitution. Planners and others involved in the development process must be conscious of the connection between tourism and prostitution. International prostitution may seem overwhelmingly well established, with its cadre of related international and local industries and hundreds of thousands of wealthy male customers. Nevertheless, as citizens of an increasingly integrated world, we have the obligation to fight against this exploitative industry.

9

Dowry Murders in India: A Preliminary Examination of the Historical Evidence

Veena Talwar Oldenburg

Seldom has there been so firm a consensus on a social issue in India as exists today among its scholars, journalists, feminists, politicians, legislators, and the police on the subject of dowry and its causal relationship to the prejudice and violence against women. The most dramatic form that violence against women has taken is what the Indian media labeled "bride-burning" until, in 1978 or so, feminists cut out the alliterative fuzz by redesignating it quite baldly as "dowry murder."

THE BURNING OF WIVES

During the 1980s, urban north India has seen a growing number of murders of married women, variously called dowry murders or bride burnings. Although accurate figures are difficult to compile because all such tragedies are not reported, it is probably conservative to estimate that between 1979–89 approximately 5,000 women burned to death in Delhi alone. These deaths are variously alleged to be murders, suicides, or accidents, and their number, greater by far than anywhere else in the country, is on the increase.

A clarification is essential at the outset: The burning of wives is neither an extension of nor culturally related to the notorious practice of *sati* (or *suttee*), the voluntary immolation of Bengali widows on the funeral pyres of their husbands. The resonances are startling—the burning of women, the thin line between suicide and murder—but the differences are significant because they point to a serious further devaluation of women in present-day India in spite of a century of progressive legislation on women's rights. *Sati* was socially countenanced suicide because the widow was perceived as having failed in her ritual duties to ensure the longevity of her husband by using her special female power or *shakti*; bride burning, however, is murder and equally culpable by social and legal standards. The method of dying or killing, that is, the immolation of women in both cases, is also a false parallel. The rituals that are prescribed for *sati* are adequately described elsewhere; suffice it to say that it was a public act that generated social awe, status, religious merit, and even material gain for the woman's kin and affines and made her *sati*, or the virtuous wife in death.

Burning a wife, a ritually auspicious person, is perhaps more appalling than the less sensational ways of doing her in (poisoning, drowning, strangling, shooting, or bludgeoning, among others) but is chosen chiefly for the forensic advantage it has over the others. It virtually destroys the evidence of murder along with the victim and can easily be made to look like an accident. It is also relatively simple to commit. It occurs in the kitchen, where the lower middle-class housewife spends a large amount of time each day. Pressurized kerosene stoves are in common use in such homes; a tin of fuel is always kept in reserve. This can be quickly poured over the intended victim and a lighted match will do the rest. It is easy to pass off the event as an accident because these stoves are prone to explode (consumer reports confirmed this), and the now ubiquitous but highly inflammable nylon sari easily catches fire and engulfs the wearer in flames. Signs of a struggle simply do not show up on bodies with 90 or more percent third-degree burns. The bereaved widower, who has equipped himself with a cast-iron alibi, is soon in the marriage market again looking for a new bride with perhaps a more handsome dowry. Often it is the mother-in-law, with or without her son as accomplice, who will obligingly commit the murder.

DOWRY AND CULTURE

Dowry serves as the foundation on which explanations for discrimination against women have been built; it has the conceptual richness to satisfy a variety of analytical tastes over time. The colonialists stressed its cultural roots in a benighted Hinduism; Marxists see it as an economic institution, feminists view it as gender discrimination for daughters did not traditionally inherit land. Today, the dowry system is seen as the prime motive for two other crimes akin to infanticide widely prevalent in the subcontinent: Female infant neglect reflected in the worst adverse female to male sex ratios in the world today, and the abortion of female fetuses made possible by the abuse of recent advances in fetal diagnostic technology. Until recently, billboard advertisements in Bombay, for instance, made an unabashed appeal to pregnant women to take the expensive and somewhat risky amniocentesis test. It importuned them to spend 500 rupees now on the test in order to save 50,000 rupees in the future on a daughter's dowry. As a prochoice feminist living in the United States, I am loath to condemn these abortions or approve their ban by the government; as a historian I can only brood darkly over the difference in the meanings of the word *choice* for postcolonial First and Third World women. Ironically, this difference reaffirms the "fact" that culture is the culprit. This fact has attained the status of an axiom, or at least that of the most-favored explanation for a variety of crimes against women that endanger not just their health but their lives.

So, when I began my research on dowry in the archives and in the field and began to formulate the direction my investigations would take for the book I would write on the subject, I thought I had grasped at least one indisputable fact: that the cause of bride-burnings or dowry deaths in India was, indeed, dowry, and indubitably a cultural problem.[1] This alleged fact has found wide support expressed in both detailed historical and anthropological analyses of female infanticide, the oldest and most widespread form of murder believed to be related, even in other cultures, to the practice of dowry.[2] Dowry, an integral part of Hindu high caste culture, appeared to be a timeless and pernicious custom that constructs women as a financial liability to their natal families and therefore as the inevitable victims of violence or neglect in their natal homes as infants and in their marital homes as brides. Its ban, by an act of the Indian Parliament in 1961, seems only to have entrenched the custom deeper.

However, I found the analyses of contemporary dowry murders ahistorical and the treatments of female infanticide unsatisfactory. There were glaring contradictions in the explanations I read. Culture was blamed on the one hand, but so were Westernization, which brought in gross materialism, greed, and a desire for consumer goods and modernization, which put a cash value on everything and commercialized human relationships. Here was the puzzle: Was this violence against women related to the ancient custom of dowry or was it a product of acculturation to Western and modern culture? But why then in the West, where dowries were once common, had the practice all but disappeared? Clearly culture does change; what made the culture of dowry gradually disappear in the West and change for the worse in India? I decided to embark on a systematic exploration of the changing meanings of dowry and the various types of dowry deaths over time to answer this puzzle.

When examining the evidence, particularly the colonial evidence on infanticide, the explanation that I had hoped only to deepen and endorse began to unravel. Statistical evidence on sex ratios in the subcontinent point to a serious anomaly in the logic that underpinned the colonial verdict on the dowry system and made their figures suspect. On close inspection a startling fact emerged: Several families from Hindu lower castes and religions, such as Islam and Sikhism, which did not follow the practice of dowry and even received bride price (bride price is paid in cash and/or goods to the bride's family by the groom's family), were found guilty of committing infanticide, so it was awkward to insist on either dowry or upper caste pride (as pronounced in the case of Rajputs [powerful landowning and ruling castes in North India]) to be the cultural justification of so heinous a crime. The convenient lie of branding dowry as the motivating culprit, or finding barbaric practices particularly among the upper caste Hindus, was begun by colonial bureaucrats in the mid-nineteenth century for sound political reasons. Continued colonial rule in India by the officials of the East India Company chartered only to trade needed compelling justification to pacify an increasingly critical Parliament in Britain. Parliamentary inquiries about the impoverishment of the India peasantry had to be answered satisfactorily. It was expedient to lay the blame on culturally sanctioned "improvidence" and wasteful ceremonies and rituals, chiefly marriage celebrations and dowry, than to reverse the colonial land revenue policies that had uprooted the old system and transformed the basic relationship between peasants and their land.

These official documents generated by colonial bureaucrats are laced with information that flatly contradicts their own assertions, and the net result was that the one clear fact about the nature of this timeless custom of dowry dissolved into a murky half-truth. The politics of the process of describing and attributing meaning to the cultures of the colonized became more important to understand than their unhappy social consequences. Dowry in its menacing form for some women, as we know it today, was patently the artifact not of an organically unchangeable and permanently constituted Hindu or Sikh culture but of ac-culturation in colonial time and space. This change, fortunately, did not occur evenly across castes and classes, and today, the majority of Hindu families practice what might be seen as a precolonial form of dowry. It is this process of change—sporadic, uneven, and regrettably irreversible—that this study endeavors to re-construct from the very documents that claim otherwise.

DOWRY AND ITS MEANING

In this chapter, I wish to propose and rigorously defend a diametrically opposite view. After a careful rereading of colonial sources, dowry could be called one of the few indigenous feminist institutions in an overwhelmingly patriarchal and agrarian society (since the term *feminist* is hotly contested, I do not insist on it). In the late nineteenth and early twentieth century, dowry was not the enemy but rather an ally of women, acting as an economic safety net in a setting where women always married outside their natal villages (village exogamy is still almost mandatory) and where they did not normally inherit land. This institution was invented by women for women and the resources that were given to women were substantially under their direct control. Items for a daughter's dowry were accumulated gradually for each daughter not just by her immediate family, but by the entire village, which shared in an intricate web of reciprocal obligations; very few items were purchased, since most of them were produced at home, bartered, or received as part of the reciprocal gift exchange among village families. Nor were daughters perceived as an economic burden. The dowry was the only independent material resource over which women had partial, if not total, con-trol. It was viewed by a woman's natal family not only as a matter of pride but also as a means of securing for her the best possible match, while providing her with recourse in an emergency. Dowry can be reckoned not only as the index of the appreciation bestowed upon daughters in their natal villages and the measure of their status in their conjugal villages, but the practical concern of families to ensure for their daughters a husband from a comparable family in which her children would be raised. How then did such a strongly spun safety net twist into a deadly noose?

The time span studied covers the mid-nineteenth century to the present. The place is the Punjab, in the northwestern part of the subcontinent, a varying and often partitioned space. By focusing on the eastern Punjab, I hope to study the most culpable community for both allegedly dowry-related crimes—female infanticide and dowry murder—in a region that had practiced dowry and bride price.

In 1851, the Sikh Bedis were found guilty of female infanticide. This discovery became political capital for the British and justified their two unsanctioned bitter and bloody wars against the Sikh ruler of the Punjab, Maharaja Ranjit Singh, that led to the annexation of the Punjab only two years earlier. The righteousness of British aggression was further underscored, in their own estimation, by the fact that Guru Nanak, the founder of the Sikh religion in the fifteenth century, was of the Bedi caste. The present-day Indian states of Punjab and Haryana (which was part of the Indian Punjab until 1966) continue to have the most adverse female to male ratios, or 879 and 870 per 1,000 males respectively in the 1981 census. Female infanticide is treated as an aberration of the past because the British government set up a department to deal with it in 1870 and closed the department in 1906, claiming total success in their campaign to suppress the practice and make the Punjabis less improvident about dowries. They were wrong on both counts: Sex ratios have steadily worsened nationwide in the twentieth century. In 1901, there were 972 females for every 1,000 males, while in 1971 and 1991, the ratios have declined to 930 and 920 females per 1,000 males respectively. The practice of killing female infants may have become less prevalent, but it was substituted by the less detectable practice of medical or nutritional neglect that achieved the same end more slowly.

It was the current sex ratios in India and comparable ratios in Pakistan and Bangladesh that aroused my suspicion that female child mortality has little to do with dowry or Hindu culture, since the partition of the subcontinent had been on religious lines and removed Hindus from west Punjab and east Bengal in 1947. Since dowries do not figure prominently in Muslim culture, why were the sex ratios not all that much better in these two Muslim nations? This suspicion began the quest for a new culprit and the reappraisal of this intriguing cultural whodunit. The result of the investigation was not startling: Female infanticide was found among all castes and classes of people and the rationale for it was to have a planned family with the right number of children of the two sexes, in a convenient birth order. The bias in favor of boys was also universal, whether Hindu or Muslim or Sikh, and whether urban or rural. The British did not exactly manipulate the numbers to build the case against hypergamous, landowning castes; they merely ignored the numbers that contradicted that clean-cut explanation, which seemed to strike at the roots of the culture of the Hindu ruling classes, while their own policies strengthened the bias against women. What I am not sure they realized, but which I argue here, was that their presence and "civilizing mission" had enormous social costs and reinvented dowry as the incubus that they purported only to describe and ultimately abolish.

By a careful rereading of colonial records not only on infanticide but also on a variety of seemingly unrelated matters, such as land revenue, peasant indebtedness, and foreclosures of agricultural property, it is possible to establish that the meaning of dowry changed drastically in the colonial period in qualitative and quantitative terms and that it skewed gender inequalities further. The records that indict the custom of dowry as the cause for killing female infants are littered with clues that lead to the history of a changing custom rather than the characterization of it as a practice frozen in time and supported by the ruinous extravagance and the tradition-bound behavior of a caste society. This gradual but radical transformation in the meaning, practice, and effects of the dowry system in the Punjab, and by implication elsewhere, was triggered by the changes in the colonial political economy and the extension of political and social control in areas where the practice existed.

When the British encountered the practice of dowry in the Punjab, they collected opinions on the nature of the custom. None of the reports describe dowry as gifts that could be demanded by the groom's family. They found it to be a collection of voluntary gifts of clothes, jewelry, household goods, and cash bestowed on the bride by family and friends at the time of the wedding. In forty-nine separate volumes of customary law of an equal number of districts in the vast territory that constituted colonial Punjab—present-day Pakistan and Indian Punjab, Haryana, Jammu, Delhi, and Himachal Pradesh—this definition of dowry has been reiterated as many times.[3] Nowhere was it treated as the prerogative of the groom and his family to demand specific consumer goods and large sums of cash for the groom's business, education, or mobility; it was voluntary and depended on the pecuniary circumstances of the bride's parents. The British charge of "improvidence" was not based on the expense for dowry but on wedding celebrations. These latter costs were strictly itemized and evaluated in cash for three economic tiers in society and became part of the bureaucrats' handbook for enforcement. Wedding expenses did not mean only a daughter's wedding expenses; many cases cited as evidence of profligacy in the handbooks refer to the weddings of sons.

CHANGES IN DOWRY SYSTEM

Yet the concerns about the escalating pressures of enhanced dowry in the late nineteenth and the twentieth centuries suggest that changes in this period affected the nature of this institution. The upward spiral in costs continued; cash and an ever-increasing range of consumer goods that became available in the Punjab as imports from Europe made the increase especially steep. The "right" to demand a specific amount of cash or expensive consumer goods did not end with dowry or the wedding ceremony. It slowly encompassed other traditional gift-giving occasions observed by parents and their married daughters. Demands for cash at the time of betrothal, lavish feasting and entertainment of the wedding guests, gifts for the family of the groom, expenses for the celebration of annual fasts and festivals, and the birth of children and their naming and tonsure ceremonies changed in time the nature of the daughter-parent bond. This trend has steadily aggravated in the postcolonial period and in its extreme form it has been the cause for violence against women and, more recently, the burning to death of wives who brought inadequate dowries.

What we are dealing with is not just a dowry problem but a pathology or a syndrome rooted in history and gender inequality in a patriarchal society. Colonialism and patriarchal values became meshed in an alliance against women, even when the avowed purpose of legislative reform in this period was to uplift the status of women in Indian society. Because the issue of violence against women is not merely an academic puzzle, but a matter of life and death, a re-examination of contemporary evidence in the light that history and feminist theory shed, is urgently warranted. In other words although dowry is the centerpiece of this study, it cannot help but illumine the pervasive commercialization of social relations in general and the central event in women's lives—marriage—in particular. This will help in assessing the loss of women's economic power and social appreciation even as they gained in legal and political rights through the process of changes unleashed in this period. This complex interaction of local customs, such as dowry, and colonialism has hardly been suspected to exist, let alone been adequately analyzed.

The widely accepted denunciation of dowry undergirds a host of corollaries that have blurred the thinking on the triangular relationship among marriage, gender, and property, which needs to be discussed in some detail. It also pushes to the fore other, perhaps, bigger questions. Did colonial policies often create, or aggravate, the very problems they sought to ameliorate? "Social evils" was the common designation for Indian customs such as *sati* and *thugee* (the practice of thugs, a criminal caste), "discovered" by the East India Company collectors and magistrates and described as part of the exotic and "barbaric" culture they encountered. Systematic legal and police measures were taken to eradicate these practices. It was in this context that Indian women and their status in Hindu society became a central preoccupation of the colonial powers. Were the social evils, such as accelerating chronic indebtedness, increasing drunkenness, and improvidence in the Punjabi countryside, the unwitting consequence of rules and regulations of the new regime rather than the consequences of Hindu or Muslim culture? What influence did the colonial codification of customary law (*rivaj-i-am*) and its implementation in the new colonial courts in the Punjab have on various customs, particularly on the definition of the rights of women and the notions of *dahej* (dowry) and *stridhan* (women's wealth)? These questions are explored in detail in the larger study to plumb the depths of social change and disruption under British rule; we will see here how that slice of Punjab history constructed the current meaning of dowry.

CULTURE AND COLONIALISM

Before I can present an abridged version of my arguments (foregoing scholarly footnotes and caution), I have to explain the politics of two key terms, *culture* and *colonialism* and their interrelationship on which the arguments rest. Neither represents a permanently constituted entity; both are continually contested and negotiated sets of power relations, and history has constructed their meanings. Moreover, native culture and British colonialism were in a dynamic relationship with each other and not without mutual, albeit unequal, effect on each other. In other words, it would be as narrow-minded to construe Hindu culture or tradition as a timeless, frozen entity as it would to think of the more than 250 years of British rule in India as a fully imagined and executed vision that can be called British colonialism. Both continually changed in the process of inter-action and acculturation.

Colonialism in mid–nineteenth-century Punjab could not be mistaken for the colonialism that Bengal experienced when it was first overtaken in 1757; differing strategies produced different results in the two places. Colonial investment in the Punjab, although accomplished at little cost to the British, greatly expanded agriculture production. By building canals, communications, and railway lines, this ultrafertile grain-producing region was linked to a thriving international market. The British extracted wealth from the countryside through heavy taxation and exports of wheat and other raw materials to Europe. Although this development was self-interested, it brought prosperity to this region along with enormous changes in the peasant's way of life.

There was also an intensified colonial interest in understanding, describing, and ultimately reforming the varieties of cultures encountered among the subjugated people; this interest was not academic or philanthropic but political. The stubborn tendency to interpret indigenous culture as an organic entity with immutable values, symbols, and belief systems was plainly self-serving. That the culture of the colonialists was dynamic and ever-changing and Indian culture was static, timeless, and inflexible were representations that bestowed legitimacy on the project of colonialism. These representations enabled bureaucrats to devise means of social control in addition to political and economic domination. It was colonialism's professed mission to improve, civilize, and regenerate Indian society, but this could be done only after the serious flaws in the culture were located. The abominable status of women became the ground on which this legitimacy was founded. Anthropology was invented to study the unchanging structures (kinship patterns, marriage rules) for societies without history.

When Bengal was the locus of the colonialists' concern, vivid accounts of *sati* fulfilled this role admirably and fattened the volumes of the Parliamentary Papers in the late eighteenth and early nineteenth centuries. Descriptions of female infanticide made horrifying reading in subsequent years from the provinces annexed later. The discovery of, and operations to control and abolish, female infanticide in the North-West Provinces, Punjab, and Oudh caught international attention through the same media. It goes without saying that their horror was genuine, as is ours, even while we endeavor to explain the political purposes the suffering of others often serves. What is extremely interesting is the construction of the crime as a cultural artifact, and how a colonial agenda was served by social reform.

REVIEW OF LITERATURE

Miller (1981) and Panigrahi (1972) accept the cultural construction unquestioningly. Miller (1981, 44) goes further and says that

culture provides the motivations for infanticide, whether they are seen by the people involved as ritualistic, . . . economic, . . . or ecological. . . . It is culture that "invents" the reasons for which some children who are born are not desired. Second, it is culture that sketches the outlines of the group that is to be the target of infanticide: whether it is to be only boys, only girls, first sons, daughters beyond the first, children born on Thursday, children born with teeth, or children with crippling deformities.

This argument involves a sleight of hand that conflates material and ecological reasons under the rubric of culture and is therefore difficult to refute. Miller, in an uncritical application of the classic "work equals worth" argument, shows how the masculine sex ratios of the north and the balanced sex ratios of the south of India can be explained. Swidden and wet rice cultivation, with a high demand for female labor in the south, leads to inclusion of females in property-holding and land being given as dowry, giving women the social advantage of being in the work force, which leads to an (emotional?) appreciation of daughters and balanced juvenile sex ratios. The opposite is true, in her view, in dry-field plow cultivation areas in the north, where women are excluded from production (which is patently inaccurate) and given dowries of movable property only. The high cost of raising and marrying daughters leads to discrimination against them, which explains the masculine juvenile sex ratios (Miller 1981, 28).

This thesis, although elegantly argued and well intentioned, has its limitations in a status-based preindustrial society. It is predicated mainly on census figures and data from postcolonial ethnographies, which have descriptions of marriage costs that my research shows have grown in response to the forces at work in the nineteenth and early twentieth centuries. In the Punjab, for example, bride price and dowry simply coexist, and it is therefore untenable to argue that women's work in the fields alone determines the mode of marriage payments. The thesis is ahistorical and mistakenly takes culture as a given that constantly reproduces the same power and economic relationships over time. Miller dismisses the case for infanticide being a means of birth control for a wide range of castes and classes, and she, like the sources on which she depends, does not make an effort to explain Muslim juvenile ratios, or the case of Bengal (a rice-growing region with high masculine ratios), which disrupts the entire flow chart.

COLONIAL ECONOMIC CHANGES

My rereading of a greater range of historical evidence for unfavorable female sex ratios and dowries changes the story critically. Briefly, what happened under colonial rule to the Punjab countryside is recorded in a succession of revenue settlement reports. The British had pioneered the permanent settlement in Bengal presidency in 1793; its revolutionary feature was that it transformed land, in which all classes and castes of people had varying rights and shared unequally in its produce, into private property that could be bought, sold, or mortgaged. This created (very crudely and quickly) a class of *zamindars* with immense holdings on the one hand and landless peasants on the other. This is because the revenue payments were fixed in perpetuity and due on a certain fixed date every quarter. These amounts and dates had little sensitivity to seasonal variations in the quantity of produce or to delayed harvest times, both of which depended on the caprice of the weather. In a bad year, there would be no recourse but to mortgage or sell the land to meet government demand, which was set at a higher, more "efficient" level than the past rulers had deemed fair. This created absentee landlords, for traders and money lenders from Calcutta could now buy this land in government-sponsored auctions or foreclosures of mortgaged land. An army of landless peasants roamed the countryside for food, shelter, and wage labor. The economic and social havoc this caused in Bengal has been adequately dealt with in the works of a large number of historians and economists.[4]

In the Punjab, which was conquered after two aggressive wars between 1840 and 1849, the British tried to find a less disastrous revenue policy than the one they had pursued in once-rich Bengal. They settled on a *ryotwari* settlement by giving titles to the land directly to the peasants (*ryots*) who tilled it. This method might have been less disastrous except for two components: the fixed amounts and dates for payment of land revenue and the newly created ability of peasant proprietors, who were in this case more numerous with small holdings, to alienate their land through mortgage or sale. These components proved as disastrous as any attempt to "rationalize" customary man/land relations that the British had hitherto undertaken. Money lenders in the past had advanced small loans, and the object was never to let a debt be paid off entirely, keeping the debtor as a permanent customer. The new breed of truly avaricious money lenders, with a new appetite for appropriating the debtor's land rather than the repayment of the debt was also a creation of colonialism.

With land as collateral and with prices of land rising, the peasant was able to borrow far more than he could ever before: up to 70 percent of the value of his land. He borrowed either in a bad year or in a year when the harvest was late, chiefly to pay his taxes on time. Chronic indebtedness became the other side of the coin of prosperity for the vast majority of these small peasant proprietors. The figures on foreclosures on the lands of the people who were not seen as the best cultivators, namely Rajputs, and of the self-exploiting jat, tell a painful story. Interest rates went up from an already high level around 18 to 24 percent to an exorbitant 24 to 40 percent range, with various other tricks and deceits built into the loans secured with land titles to hoodwink the illiterate peasant. Prices of land went up too, particularly as monetization of the economy moved along apace with the building of canals, roads, railways, and market facilities, and the price of grain increased as exports rose. Apart from the colonial government, the grain merchant and the money lender, not the peasant, were the most direct beneficiaries of this trend. They no longer wanted to sustain the traditional symbiotic relationship with their peasant debtors; they now wanted as quickly as possible to foreclose on the mortgaged property and hire the former proprietor as an ill-paid day laborer. The corresponding increase in holdings of *bania* and *khatri* (commercial castes) who were the moneylenders and merchants was a dramatic overall 40 percent loss for the traditional peasantry within the first twenty years of the *ryotwari* settlement.

Canals were not entirely beneficial either and brought two tragic consequences that were difficult to deal with—malaria epidemics and infertility to irrigated lowlands due to an increase in the salinity of the soil. The opening of the Western Jumna Canal in 1840–41, for example, raised the water table and made some of the contiguous eastern districts, such as Panipat and Karnal, a barren waste of water-logged, saline land that looked like "snow-covered fields." For thirty years, there was no resurvey or reassessment of land revenue, and appeals from the distressed peasants were not heeded. Acts of last resort—desertions, vagrancy, immigrating to a fertile district, and serving as bonded labor—became routine. This, I suggest, eliminated the difference between the security of rights in land that sons inherited and the "movable property" that daughters inherited as dowry. The dowry became a prize for men as much as their inherited rights in land had been. If anything, dowry was the more versatile in a situation where land was barren. The other unfortunate effect of the canal was the spread of water- and vermin-borne diseases, such as malaria and typhoid, that claimed the lives of thousands of peasants. These were not the expected outcomes of a dark colonial plot—just tragic and unintended ecological and etiological disasters that undermined the ability of the peasants to pay their fixed dues. So, indebtedness and poverty grew in the midst of the new prosperity.

A sample statement from the dozens of reports from revenue officials gives us a flavor of the peasant's lot in 1872–80, after three decades of British rule in the Punjab. A Mr. Sharer was dispatched to examine the complaints of the peasants in Karnal district. His investigations showed that the water table had risen sixty feet, barely two or three feet below the surface, causing the tract of land to become totally barren.

The possible resources of the *biswadars* [peasant owners] of several estates are now exhausted. They have borrowed money at extravagant interest; they have become farm slaves of some *Bania* [money lender] residing in their village; they have sold their trees on their estates; they have sold their daughters; they have sold silver ornaments and brass utensils [presumably the dowries brought by their wives or daughters-in-law] and as many of their cattle as was possible to spare; and no conceivable source of income is any longer available. . . . No remissions [in revenue payments] have ever been made, so far as I can discover, on account of general deterioration [of the soil]. . . . [Dr. Taylor shows that 60 to 80 percent of the inhabitants in *banjar* villages had fevers, enlarged spleens,] langour and depression of manner, and stunted and shrivelled forms of the inhabitants of the villages in close proximity to the swamps [created by the West Jumna Canal.][5]

One report put the area of land in Karnal district rendered uncultivable because of increased salinity at 507,974 acres in 1878, up from 1,255 acres in 1820.

EFFECTS OF CHANGE

These few sentences and a few figures tell the tale of a great deal of eastern Punjab and how it affected social exchange. This quiet desperation built pressure to exploit customary ways of obtaining cash or gold or silver to buy land elsewhere, or to replenish a herd—and dowry was a logical place to look. The will to obtain larger dowries from the families of daughters-in-law, to demand more in cash, gold, and other liquid assets, becomes vivid after leafing through pages of official reports that dutifully record the effects of indebtedness, foreclosures, barren plots, and cattle dying for lack of fodder. The voluntary aspects of dowry, its meaning as a mark of love for the daughter, gradually evaporates. Dowry becomes dreaded payments on demand that accompany and follow the marriage of a daughter. Women appear to have resisted giving up their ornaments to the very last, when the situation became utterly dire. Jewelry would be the last thing a peasant had to offer when in arrears over revenue and had to save his land from the auctioneer's block. The social effects of this indebtedness were enormous. It made the raising of daughters into a kind of economic burden that never existed before the new revenue settlements. Wedding expenses of both males and females could be curtailed and so could funeral expenses, but dowry became the lever that a woman's affines grasped with tenacity.

The ritual calendar and the harvest calendar in peasant society are intimately linked: betrothals, marriages, tonsure ceremonies, sacred thread initiation ceremonies occurred at "auspicious times" and were celebrated on the small profits of the harvest. British revenue policies never permitted capital accumulation, but kept the peasant at his wonted subsistence level. Inflexible British revenue payment timetables proved often not to synchronize with nature—a late monsoon would mean a late harvest and that would drive the marginal cultivators to deplete their savings or to the moneylender's door to meet their payment schedules. These short-term loans frequently became life-long debts because land as collateral gave the money lender the incentive to make his conditions of repayment as difficult as possible. The next thing the peasant would need was a further loan to marry off his pubescent daughter because the profits of the harvest were now pledged to the money lender. Those with whom he had reciprocal social obligations would also find it difficult to honor them in late or poor seasons.

What this spiral of events boils down to is that a daughter's marriage, which customarily could not wait too long past her puberty, became the last straw that broke the camel's back. A son's wedding cost as much as a daughter's wedding (and this is true even today in Punjabi urban and rural families), but a son's wedding could be postponed. While funeral expenses could be trimmed, wedding expenses that could be borne by the bride's family steadily climbed because of reasons that will emerge presently. The crucial fact, however, was that neither daughters' weddings nor funerals could wait; other ritual events could be postponed, particularly the son's bethrothal or wedding day. So it was not the cost of the wedding but the constraints of time that made a daughter's wedding an exploitable condition in early colonial times. A daughter's wedding, therefore, necessitated a loan more often than a son's; and a possible demand for a bigger dowry from her in-laws would occasion an even bigger loan. In disaggregating a farmer's debt, the amounts that pertained to a daughter's dowry were seen as inexcusable improvidence. This kind of circumstantial evidence against dowry finally indicted it as the killer. The British increasingly understood the devastating ramifications of their own revenue policies but they preferred to blame the culturally based dowry system, rather than their own rational reconstruction of the land holding and revenue system. The notoriety about dowries quickly gained currency, and women were the losers in both natal and affinal families.

It can be asserted with confidence, because a plethora of evidence dots the journals, reports, and other accounts of British officers, that in the colonial period the cost of a daughter's wedding went up as a result not just of higher tax levels but of other policy decisions as well. The chief among these was the policy to reduce drastically the allowance that villages had customarily received for social expenses for the community. Although these were still collected as common charges for the village, several Settlement Reports describe a 90 percent reduction in what the village elders or the headman received because this common fund customarily defrayed expenses on ritual occasions the colonial authorities deemed unnecessary or "improvident." This common fund sustained certain aspects of the social life of the village; it had formerly paid for the upkeep of the *chaupal* or guest house in which villagers offered hospitality to visitors, passersby, and, most important, for events such as the wedding of a daughter of the village. The groom's party (the *baraat*, the groom's friends and relatives), which customarily came to the bride's village for the wedding ceremonies, was accommodated in the *chaupal*. These monies also took care of other expenses, such as water, lamps, illumination, temple ornamentation, and the fees to the *bhands* and *mirasis* (musicians).

In the attempt to reduce customary waste in the village, muscle was mistaken for flab, and this improvident fund quickly became a casualty. Once this money was no longer available, the *chaupal* fell into disrepair. When the time came for a daughter's wedding, these formerly community costs and responsibilities fell increasingly on individual families to bear. The finely spun web of communal, filial, and reciprocal obligations was swept away with the new broom of tidy-minded colonial officers, which in turn transformed the structure of gender relations. The custom of *dahej* or dowry slowly attained the status of the key indicator of the subjugation of north Indian women.

SUMMARY

Arguably then, economic and social trends unleashed in this period transformed dowry payments into an incubus of debt and blackmail in the average household, with fatal consequences for a growing number of females. There are obviously many more pieces to this argument but it is not possible to present them all here. A gender-targeted family was achieved, in those medically primitive days, by female infanticide.[6] In a remarkable paradox, the social prejudice against women was strengthened and made more pervasive even as their legal rights were enlarged in the colonial and postcolonial periods. Patriarchal values were simultaneously contested and reinforced; contested by the movement for women's rights and reinforced by the attempt to run an efficient colonial empire.

10

Paying the Price of Change: Women, Modernization, and Arranged Marriages in India

Uma Narayan

INTRODUCTION

This chapter analyzes changes in the structure of arranged marriages that resulted from the modernization of India. I argue that many of the problems caused by the traditional forms, roles, and expectations underlying arranged marriages continue to affect the lives of women and that women face new burdens as a result of modernization. Broadly speaking, many Indian women may be experiencing the worst of the old and the new—the loss of old traditional structures of support and protection and the new problems imposed by modernization. I shall consider what might be done to alleviate some of these problems.

THE NATURE AND IMPORTANCE OF CASTE

Traditionally, parents arranged marriages within a particular caste. Before examining the role that arranged marriages play in the perpetuation of caste, it is necessary to elaborate on how the term *caste* is to be understood. One needs to distinguish between two Hindi terms, *jati* and *varna*. The traditional schema of *varnas* best corresponds to the hierarchy of estates in the sense in which the term was used in revolutionary France. Four categories of *varnas* are distinguished in hierarchical order: at the top are the Brahmins or priests, next the Kshatriyas or warriors, then the Vaishyas or merchants, and last the Shudras or laborers. The Untouchables, who are regarded as falling outside this classification, nevertheless form a fifth category (Dumont 1966).

The term *jati* refers to a hereditary group that was more or less confined to a limited geographical area. The *jatis* were distinguished from and connected to each other by separation in matters of marriage, social contact, and division of labor. Traditionally, each group had a profession or range of professions and was ranked hierarchically with the groups classified as relatively superior or inferior to it. The *jatis* in a given territory were also sorted so that each fell into one of the five *varnas* (Dumont 1966). The term *caste* is used here narrowly to refer to the endogamous group within which caste members are expected to marry. This use follows Ghurye (1950), who argues that these endogamous groups, which are often called subcastes, should be recognized as full castes, because one marries not just anywhere within one's caste broadly construed, but within one's subcaste. Karve (1961) also refers to the endogamous group as the caste and suggests the term *caste-cluster* for the larger caste group, which she believes results from an aggregation of castes. The word *caste* is of Portuguese origin, and it is often used indiscriminately to refer to *varna*, caste-cluster, or the endogamous group.

Castes functioned as indicators of occupation and social status and as endogamous groups. Although modernization has reduced the importance of caste as a determinant of occupation and social interaction, it still affects the role of caste in arranged marriages to a certain degree. Today, though marriage within one's caste is still regarded as an ideal, it is often sufficient to marry within a different caste in one's caste-cluster (Beteille 1969). This extension of the limits of endogamy is most conspicuous among professional higher-income groups in urban areas, which often tolerate even intercaste marriages outside the caste-cluster, provided the castes are not too distant in the traditional scale (ibid.).

How can one explain this tolerance? It seems that, with increasing avenues of occupational mobility open, castes are no longer fairly homogenous in their occupational composition and economic rank; also, new considerations based on occupation, education, and income are responsible for the weakening of the tradition that one marry within one's endogamous group. Although such considerations of class seem to be weakening those of caste in arranged marriages, they seem to do so only to a degree. Similarities of class background between families do not cause marriages to be arranged between castes having markedly different statuses on the traditional caste scale (Beteille 1969).

In former times, marriages outside the caste were widely regarded as deviant and could result in social hostility and ostracism. With modernization, attitudes toward intercaste marriages have changed in that substantial numbers of people are no longer morally outraged by the idea of intercaste marriage. But marriage within one's caste is still widely regarded as ideal, and marriage across caste lines, when the castes have widely differing statuses, would still be regarded as "deviant." Data on intercaste marriages suggests that caste continues to be an important consideration, despite the effects of modernization.

Intercaste marriages are, nevertheless, on the increase, growing from 0.32 percent of all marriages in 1964 to 12 percent in 1978 to roughly 16 percent in 1988 (Banerjee and Chowdhuri 1988). Over two-thirds of these intercaste marriages are chosen by the couple themselves and so are not arranged marriages. It is highly likely, though not explored by this study, that the bulk of the arranged intercaste marriages are contracted within the same caste-cluster. However, 84 percent of marriages continue to occur within the same caste (ibid.).

THE CONTINUING IMPORTANCE OF CASTE IN ARRANGED MARRIAGES

Siddiqui and Reeves (1987) found that more women (73 percent) than men (62 percent) place great emphasis on caste in the selection of a mate. Their explanation for this preference is that more women than men hold traditional values. This finding suggests that the continuing importance of caste in arranged marriages is a symptom of the persistence of traditional values and that gender difference in the emphasis on caste is merely a symbol of women's greater commitment to those values.

There is an alternative explanation for the continuing importance of caste in arranged marriages and for women's greater emphasis on caste in this context. In arranged marriages, women are transplanted to live among comparative strangers, and they have an advance idea of the difficult accommodations and adjustments awaiting them. The traditional process of arranged marriage was never easy on the bride. Married young, women had to face life in a family that had no prior ties to her; her status as an outsider meant that she ranked at the bottom of the family hierarchy and had to defer not only to her husband but to his entire family. Various forms of physical and mental harassment from her husband and her in-laws were fairly routine, sometimes as a result of dissatisfaction with the amount of dowry she had brought, but often as a way of "breaking her in" and teaching her place.

Customs, dialects, food, and dress often differ across caste lines. Beteille (1969) suggests that the higher castes in particular jealously preserved these differences to foster a sense of caste status and community. Intercaste marriages add to the burdens of adjustment in an already difficult transition to life in a new family. Despite the fact that modernization has reduced the importance of caste, so long as marriages continue to be arranged and traditional roles dictate that women bear the burdens of adjustment, women have a pragmatic incentive to marry within their own caste. Families also have a pragmatic incentive to arrange marriages for their daughters within their caste, as they too believe it may ease their transition to a new life.

The groom's family, especially the prospective mother-in-law, also has a pragmatic reason to arrange marriages within the caste. Mothers-in-law have authority in the domestic sphere of the joint family and are chiefly responsible for the direction and distribution of domestic tasks. It is primarily their function to "break in" the daughter-in-law and direct her in fulfilling the tasks expected of her in her conjugal family. Traditionally, girls were often married before puberty, when they were more amendable to their mother-in-law's advice and admonition. As the average age of marriage increases, especially among the urban middle class, mothers-in-law face a more difficult prospect in obtaining conformity from an older daughter-in-law. The task is easier if the bride has been brought up with the same traditions and routines and is already trained to conform to them (Gore 1968).

In light of recent outbreaks of caste and communal violence in many parts of India, it is important to realize the role arranged marriages play in perpetuating caste and communal identity. Opposed as we might be to prejudices and privileges based on caste and to the perpetuation of the caste system, it is important for Indian feminists to realize that individual women may have high stakes in arranging marriages within a caste. Cultural similarities that exist within a caste may make the transition to a new home less alienating for many young women. Conjugal families may prefer same-caste marriages because they make it easier to incorporate their daughter-in-law into the routines of family life. People tend to arrange marriages within their own caste for these sorts of reasons and not merely out of respect for traditional social practice.

CASTE DISPERSAL AND ITS EFFECTS ON WOMEN

Although families still arrange same-caste marriages for the reasons suggested above, modernization has complicated the process of finding suitable partners within one's caste. One such complication is caste dispersal. As a result of more people moving out of their original communities in search of jobs and education, many castes that were once relatively confined to a geographical region are now more widely dispersed across the country. Education and employment opportunities are often greater in urban centers, causing people to migrate from adjoining and distant rural areas (Gore 1968). Increasing urbanization results in many people living far away from their communities of origin, in the hybrid and heterogeneous environments of towns and cities. Employment opportunities for middle-class professionals, in both public and private sectors, are relatively scarce and are likely to require their resettlement at a distance from their states of origin.

In these ways, modernization has made it more difficult for many people to find suitable same-caste marriage partners near their new locations. The total number of caste members in the area is likely to be far smaller than it was when caste was geographically more concentrated. Acquaintance with, and access to, caste members who are located nearby is harder in urban environments and caste-based institutions are likely to be rare. In short, caste plays a declining role in urban social life.

In traditional communities, marriages were often arranged through the mediation of kin, or by people in the community who knew both families. In towns and cities, traditional go-betweens are no longer readily available. Urban families have taken to extensive use of matrimonial columns in newspapers as a means of finding same-caste partners for their children. A look at the matrimonial columns in any Indian newspaper will confirm that caste is almost always mentioned.

Whereas same-caste arranged marriages once meant that women were likely to remain relatively near their family and community of origin, caste dispersal means that women increasingly enter marriages that locate them far away. More and more often, parents entrust the lives and safety of their daughters to families they know very little about; they can gain no information or assurance from common acquaintances, and they will not be close by to look out for their daughters' welfare. Parents experience the marriage of their daughter as "losing" her to another family because they know that access to her will be restricted both by the demands of her new status and by social norms that make it shameful for parents to accept a married daughter's hospitality in any extended form. Natal kin are expected to meet transportation costs, and they are less likely to be willing or able to pay for a daughter's visits home if she lives far away. Returning to the natal home for holidays, festivals, marriages, and other events provides a space of warm, supportive relationships and a respite from deference and surveillance. Living at a distance from the natal family severely curtails this sort of emotional support. Urbanization and the problems that arise with living in cramped urban dwellings make it increasingly difficult for families to have several children and grandchildren visit at the same time. This tends to reduce severely the contact between siblings after marriage. The adverse effects of this change on women's well-being should not be underestimated.

Geographical proximity to her natal family was a great advantage to a woman in an arranged marriage. If she were badly treated, the news was likely to reach her natal family quickly. If the situation became unbearable, she could seek shelter with her family. Elders of her natal family could try to mediate with her conjugal family to procure kinder treatment (Jeffrey, Jeffrey, and Lyon 1988). The latter recognize that access to her natal family gives a daughter-in-law certain powers of resistance, and they often use their authority to limit those contacts. Recognition of these powers is evident in men's negative comments on the topic of marrying women whose families live nearby. They say that frequent contacts between a woman and her kin inhibit them from beating her and that a distant son-in-law is more likely to be treated like a prince and not as someone commonplace (ibid.). It is clear that men and women have reasons to differ in the value they place on the woman remaining near her family after marriage. Modernization is making it easier for men to satisfy their preferences on this issue and more difficult for women.

Proximity to the family of origin is important to the well-being of Indian women in other ways as well. A woman's primary emotional ties continue to be with members of her natal family. This is not surprising because the transition into the life of her conjugal family is difficult and alienating and because she continues to be regarded as an outsider for a long time. It is usually not until their children are grown that women acquire any significant status or power in the families into which they marry.

Caste dispersal and the weakening of community and kinship links have also resulted in a reduced number of marriages arranged between kin. In many Indian communities, marriage rules permitted alliances with relatives, especially maternal kin (Agarwal 1988). Marriage to a mother's brother or to his son was allowed and often sought by a girl's parents in the hope that marrying one's daughter to a kinsman would make the shift to a new role easier. The daughter's prior familiarity with the family into which she was marrying would make her feel less of a stranger in their midst. The previous affection of the mother-in-law for her grand-daughter or niece was calculated to result in kinder treatment when she became a daughter-in-law and to create fewer dowry-related problems.

When a daughter marries a nonrelative, her parents' visits to her conjugal home are expected to be brief and infrequent. Marrying one's daughter to kin increases a mother's access to her daughter because she is visiting her own relatives. In castes with such patterns of kin intermarriage, a woman from one's daughter's conjugal family was often, in turn, married into one's own family. Thus, each family had a woman who served as a hostage against ill-treatment by the other family. As kinship networks weaken, such marriages are less common, leaving more women isolated and at the mercy of strangers. The practice of arranging marriages between relatives may also be declining because of a growing awareness that Westerners and some Indian communities consider such marriages incestuous (Caplan 1985).

Modernization and its attendant caste dispersal have made it extremely difficult for women to continue to enjoy the psychological benefits and protection once conferred by arranged marriages that kept them in relative proximity to their natal families. In addition to the costs imposed by distance, modernization has made life in the conjugal family liable to be dangerous to the welfare of women in some new ways.

NEW COSTS AND NEW RISKS FOR WOMEN

Nuclear Families

As more people migrate to cities in search of jobs, the nuclear family becomes more common. Many families prefer to arrange for their daughter's marriage into a family that has a son who owns or rents his own home so that the daughter can start her own home rather than live in a joint family. The reason for this preference is the belief that living in a nuclear family will reduce the extent of interference and harassment from the in-laws and give the woman a greater measure of autonomy. On the other hand, arranged marriages in which the woman lives in a nuclear family are a mixed blessing.

Life in a nuclear family may be more isolating than life in a joint family, especially for women who are used to living in a complex web of family relationships. Social norms of respectability that curtail women's movements and interactions are reinforced by living in a community of strangers, in an unfamiliar terrain. Extended visits to her natal home become more difficult because there are no other women in the household to take over her domestic tasks while she is away. Marriage into a nuclear family setting may also contribute to escalated demands for consumer goods as part of the dowry, on the grounds that the girl's family is, after all, merely helping to set up their own daughter in comfort. The nuclear family situation may also increase a wife's risk of abuse by the husband, who might otherwise feel restrained by the presence of elders, at least in some joint family contexts.

Dowries

Dowry deaths and the even more prevalent problem of dowry-related harassment are heinous phenomena associated with the contemporary practice of arranged marriage in India. They are important concerns of Indian feminists. Dowry has been illegal for many years, but the law has not been at all successful in curbing the practice.

Modernization has contributed to the increased importance of dowry and the growth of dowry-related harassment in several ways. One way concerns the transformation of women's work into paid labor and the declining number of jobs for women in India. Although male labor force participation has been more or less uniform, the percentage of women workers in the total labor force, as well as their percentage in the total female population has been declining (De Souza 1975). Work for female agricultural labor has not been increasing relative to supply. Male labor appears to be substituting for female labor and accounts for more than 60 percent of the total shrinkage in female labor force participation in many districts (Desai and Krishnaraj 1987). Women's labor force participation is even lower in urban than in rural areas. Decreased labor force participation leads to women being seen as economic liabilities and results in increased expectations of dowry to compensate for marrying this liability.

Another way modernization affects dowry concerns the changed form of the exchange. Whereas the traditional form of dowry consisted mostly of jewelry and cooking vessels that remained the bride's property, modern dowries often include gifts of cash and expensive consumer goods that are given outright to the groom and his family (Caplan 1985). Thus, dowries increasingly function as economic assets that the conjugal family can use as a modern economy necessitates, for example to secure credit or repay loans (Agarwal 1988). This economic potential provides a reason for conjugal families to harass brides in order to secure more dowry from the bride's family. It also provides an incentive to kill daughters-in-law (usually by setting them ablaze and passing this off as a kitchen accident), so that the family can acquire yet another dowry when the son remarries. Government figures presented in Parliament in 1987 showed recorded dowry deaths to have risen from 999 in 1985 to 1,319 in 1986 and to 1,786 in 1987 (Bumiller 1990). These are undoubtedly only a fraction of actual dowry deaths. As incentives for dowry-related harassment and murder increase, women face unprecedented dowry-related risks when they enter an arranged marriage. The increasing distance from and lack of access to the natal families become even more menacing, given these new risks.

The Missing Women

Dowry may also be linked to India's remarkably imbalanced sex ratios. There is a considerable and growing deficit of women in the Indian population. The ratio of women to men has fallen steadily from 97 women per 100 men in 1901 to 93 women per 100 men in 1971. The deficit of women is not evenly distributed throughout India. Punjab and Haryana, which are the wealthiest and most economically advanced states, have the worst ratios—86 women per 100 men (Sen 1990). Agarwal (1988) links this deficit to the low involvement of women in economically productive activities and to the relatively high costs of dowry. These factors encourage families in the fatal neglect of their female children by discriminating against them in the areas of nutrition and health care. There is substantial evidence for the much lower levels of caloric and protein intakes of girls and women, higher levels of malnutrition, and greater neglect during illness (ibid.).

The data on fatal neglect of female children, plus evidence of the recent emergence of dowry-linked female infanticide in parts of South India, and the growing use of sex determination tests to abort female fetuses do not bode well for the treatment daughters can hope to receive in their natal families (Bumiller 1990). Natal families, which were once a source of protection and assistance in the lives of their married daughters, are becoming threats to their own female children. Fatal neglect of daughters, female infanticide, and feticide simply remove the problem of exorbitant dowries that impoverish families.

It is important not to overlook the consequences of modernization and how they intersect with persisting traditional values in creating a deficit of women. If tradition did not deem it shameful for a family to fail to marry off its daughters fairly young and did not stigmatize families with single daughters, parents might be less inclined to let dowry become a motive for neglecting daughters fatally. If tradition did not deem it shameful for families to depend economically on daughters, more families might be motivated to educate girls and help them to be economically productive, instead of concentrating on the welfare of sons on whom they expect to depend in old age.

STRATEGIES FOR CHANGE

What might be done to improve the position of women? For a start, there are alternatives to same-caste arranged marriages, namely marriages based on "romantic love" or personal choice; there are also attempts to arrange mass marriages outside traditional caste boundaries.

Despite the continued prevalence of arranged marriage, the process of modernization has involved the wide dissemination of the idea of romantic love and marriage based on personal choice. Indian movies, which have a wide audience in rural and urban areas, are full of such themes. Their popularity suggests that many people view romantic love as an intriguing and positive possibility. Apart from increasing congeniality and personal intimacy between partners, such marriages may have great pragmatic utility for women.

First, such marriages may not require a dowry, making the occasion less burdensome to families. Second, in case of harassment by in-laws, the husband is potentially a source of psychological support for the wife. Third, the husband is less likely to harass his wife because emotional power is more evenly distributed between them, and the wife is at less of a disadvantage because the transition to her new role is less alienating. However, despite the prevalence of the idea and its potential advantages, self-arranged marriages tend to be rare, even though they are on the increase. What are some of the factors that deter such marriages and outweigh their attraction and utility?

Marriages of choice often meet with intense opposition from both families because people rarely tend to fall in love with persons from the same caste or linguistic community. Data suggest that 64 percent of intercaste marriages are self-arranged, compared to only 11.5 percent of same-caste marriages (Banerjee and Chowdhuri 1988). Violations of traditionally important boundaries such as caste are likely to cause distress in families that take these determinants of identity seriously. But family opposition is also common when self-arranged marriages do not cross caste or community lines. This suggests that family opposition may be based not only on the fact that self-arranged marriages run counter to tradition but also on the perception that they challenge the power and authority of the family.

Parents have a great stake in keeping a strong emotional hold on their sons. Most Indian parents face the prospect of partial or total economic dependence on their sons in old age. Data indicate that roughly 90 percent of elderly men and 82 percent of elderly women in rural areas live with their sons (Biswas and Tripathi 1990). Elderly women tend to be more completely dependent on their sons than elderly men. Although 84 percent of elderly rural men continue to work, 95 percent of elderly rural women and 97 percent of elderly urban women are nonworking (ibid.). Sons who marry without the mediation of their parents are often seen as bad risks for security in old age because their primary emotional loyalties are likely to shift to their wives, making their ties to their parents more precarious. Gore (1968) argues that the joint family traditionally sees the conjugal relationship as a threat to its stability and therefore tends to minimize the emotional significance of the husband-wife relationship. Sons who have strong emotional attachments to their wives are perceived as less likely to take on the burden of caring for their parents in old age.

Women, who are likely to outlive their husbands and face the near certainty of dependence on their sons, have an even greater stake in ensuring their son's marriage to a woman they have chosen and can dominate. It is their way of keeping the son's attachment to his wife from interfering with their emotional control over him. Women's dependence on their sons in old age is reinforced by the low rates at which widows remarry. Although only 18 percent of respondents in Gore's study (1968) declared themselves against widow remarriage, many of those who approve of it do so only when the widow is young and childless; in these cases, remarriage forestalls economic destitution and the moral danger of her engaging in illicit sexual activity.

Marriages of choice are also opposed by families who consider it improper for young men and women to mix together freely. The fact that a couple got to know each other well enough to wish to marry each other is regarded as evidence of their lack of circumspection. A daughter's breach of propriety in associating with a man without the knowledge of her family is taken seriously because any ensuing scandal could adversely affect not only her own marriage prospects, but also those of her siblings (Caplan 1985). Indian youth often find family opposition to attempts to marry out of personal choice hard to accept. Personal identity is often more closely tied to family, and family attachments seem to carry greater weight than they do in the West. Besides, many men and women are at least partially economically dependent on their families when starting out in life, sharing domestic quarters and household expenses with them. There is often a serious economic price to pay for marrying without family consent. In the face of family opposition and in the absence of financial help, marriages of choice may founder, confirming the dire view that marriages of choice do not work (ibid.).

Thus, parents have an incentive to prefer arranged marriages for their children, and children have an incentive not to oppose their parents. It is also possible that many young men and women do not oppose the norm of arranged marriages because they find it useful. They do not have to deal with the anxiety of finding partners or deal with the pressures of trying to be "successful" with the opposite sex (Caplan 1985).

Especially in the urban middle class, there are interesting attempts to compromise between youths' attraction to the idea of romantic love and their parents' desire to arrange their marriages. The couple is often given time to go out on dates and get to know each other after the marriage is negotiated but before the ceremony is performed. This gives the couple a chance to engage in courtship and "fall in love" with the safety of knowing they have their parents' blessing (Bumiller 1990). Many college students see their years in college, when they have relative freedom from parental surveillance and more access to the opposite sex, as a chance to engage in a romance. These romances usually do not survive college, and many people afterwards conform to marriages arranged by their parents.

Other options to traditional arranged marriages include mass intercaste and even interreligious marriages, such as those organized by the Working Women's Forum (Arunachalam 1988). These marriages provide chances for people to marry across caste and communal lines, without dowries and expensive ceremonies. The large-scale nature of such functions gives them social visibility and helps foster the sense that individuals can indeed contribute to bringing about social change. There have also been movements aimed at having young men and women and their families pledge not to give or take dowries and to boycott marriages that involve dowries. If moral opposition to dowry were to become widespread, the moral opposition of family members and friends is more likely to deter the practice than its illegality. I would also advocate efforts to make people rethink their stigmatization of women who remain single, whether out of choice or necessity.

CONCLUSION

If, as I have argued, the intersection of traditional ways of life with changes caused by modernization has contributed to the increased difficulty and danger of arranged marriage, then the problem deserves widespread recognition. Parents who learn of the dangers might try to take more precautions in choosing partners for their daughters and perhaps be less coercive in insisting on arranged marriage as the only appropriate choice for their children. They might begin to see that marriages of choice would not only relieve them of the burdens of providing dowries for their daughters, but help to weaken the importance of dowry as an institution. If parental opposition to marriages of choice decreases, more young people might be emboldened to pursue them as a preferred option. A marriage of choice may be more advantageous to women and therefore may be a better option than an arranged marriage. Marriages of choice are also more likely to work against the perpetuation of the caste system.

Parental opposition to marriages of choice is sometimes based on a desire to see children respect and perpetuate cultural and social traditions. Parents should realize that their vision of their children carrying on an unchanging tradition and way of life is problematic. They need to understand the ways in which the traditional institution of arranged marriage in its modern context poses risks for their daughters that its older forms did not. Although public awareness of the dangers of dowry deaths and dowry-related harassment is growing, there is a tendency to see these phenomena as resulting from the special viciousness of a few individuals. Refusal to acknowledge the systemic nature of these problems leads to the view that one can preserve one's daughters from such fates by marrying them into good or respectable families. Education and consciousness-raising are necessary to counteract idealizing and worshipful visions of traditional institutions and ways of life and to make the public aware that these are systemic problems that threaten the general welfare of Indian women.

It is not just options to traditional arranged marriages that have to be explored. Tremendous efforts are needed to counteract the many factors that cause the current devaluation of women. Education for women, greater chances for their gainful employment, securing property rights and access to credit, providing easier access to health care, improving social security provisions so that people do not feel they need sons to provide for them in old age would help to ameliorate the position of women. Attempts to create a national awareness of the ways in which women are mistreated and deprived, as well as education and participatory political action to create changes, are clearly necessary. Such awareness must include the role played by complex modern economic and social change, as well as the role played by customary and traditional views of women's place and worth in making it dangerous to be an Indian women. Solutions must address not just improving women's economic and social lot, but challenge the traditional culture at the points at which it is detrimental to the status of women.

In exploring women's reality in order to change it, we need to be sensitive to social data, as well as to women's life experiences, and avoid some of the preconceptions that often detract from our ability to understand with clarity. We must refuse to subscribe to the dogmatic vision of modernization as necessarily entailing progress, as compared to oppressive traditional ways of life, or to the equally simplistic vision of a pristine and wonderful traditional way of life being destroyed by the evil forces of modernization. We need to be open and sensitive to the empirical patterns and consequences of social change as they affect the lives of women and recognize the often cruel results that the interplay between tradition and modernity has on the lives of women.

Epilogue: Representations of Urban Life in African Women's Literature

Carole Boyce Davies

African women writers examine urban life within the context of changing societal patterns, oppressive economic systems, and traditional expectations of women's place and role in society as they interface with contemporary, liberatory attitudes concerning womanhood. So in the literature by women, urban life is difficult but challenging. And, importantly, rural life for women is rarely romanticized as it is in the literature by male writers. Women writers do recognize a certain defined order and predictability in the rural community, which make for less tension. In many cases, they describe the rural community as the site of clearly defined gender roles, but also as the place where there is more space for physical movement and the possibility of distancing oneself from bourgeois expectations.

The urban space, by contrast, is a site of contradictions. It allows a degree of freedom from restrictive patterns, but it imports sometimes more repressive Western patterns of social organization. For many writers, the urban center is a site of vitality and alternative modes of being for some of the characters. For others, the contemporary urban situation is recognized as the site of decadence and Western bourgeois social standards and moralities, the locus of a certain destruction of some important African cultural values.

HISTORICIZING URBANIZATION IN AFRICAN CONTEXTS

In any examination of urbanization in African contexts, one must begin with the fact that urbanization is not new to Africa. What we are responding to, instead, is the particular, recent historical reality of colonialism and the importation of Western, urban patterns and systems. Africa has a long and well-documented precolonial history of cities and urban centers. Any contemporary discussions of African social systems must start with its ancient systems of political and social organization. A number of scholars have addressed this history, including Cheikh Anta Diop in *Precolonial Black Africa* (1987), Walter Rodney in *How Europe Underdeveloped Africa* (1974), Martin Bernal in *Black Athena* (1987), and Richard Hull in *African Cities and Towns Before the European Conquest* (1976).

Rodney, for example, posits that African development was comparable to Europe's in the fifteenth century. He cites one account of the Dutch visiting the city of Benin and describing it as having paved streets "seven or eight times broader than the Warmoes street in Amsterdam" with a king's palace occupying "as much space as the town of Harlem" with "fine galleries, most of which are as big as those on the Exchange at Amsterdam." Further, in terms of physical layout,

the town [was] composed of thirty main streets, very straight and 120 feet wide, apart from an infinity of small intersecting streets. The houses are close to one another and arranged in good order. These people are in no way inferior to the Dutch as regards cleanliness: they wash and scrub their houses so well that they are polished and shining like a looking glass (Rodney 1974, 69).

Diop (1987) explores the social and political evolution of the ancient cities and shows how "preconceived ideas of African societies" militate against our understanding of commercial, intellectual, and organizational structures of traditional African kingdoms.

The position of women in these precolonial African societies is less well documented. It is clear from a number of sources that women's status varied across cultures and nations and was not determined mainly by biology but by economics, social status, class, and political and other power relationships. The consensus is that women's traditional and historical bases of influence and authority were eroded, reduced, obliterated, or destroyed during the colonial and postcolonial periods.

Much more information is becoming available on the role and status of women in the colonial period. Steady (1981) argues for African women's advanced status relative to European women, as have a number of other scholars of African women's history and culture. Morrow (1986, 290–375) provides an annotated bibliography of sources for studying this issue. Similarly, Robertson and Berger (1986) address the colonial and modern periods.

We must consider studies of representations of urban life in African women's literature within these contexts and this history because they lead us to a different understanding of how urban life and "development" are represented by African women writers.

Because the urban center is usually the location of Western patterns and systems and is often the site of the primary encounter with the West, the women of the city, in particular, begin to function as symbols for all that is negative in Westernization and urbanization. Many African women scholars find this a problematic positioning of the woman, since she is often made the traditional representative of the culture, and her behavior and personal choices become linked to the maintenance or erosion of traditional patterns. Ama Ata Aidoo (1984, 265) makes this point forcefully in her closing statement of *To Be a Woman*: "And don't be shocked if—when the victory is won—they return you to the veil as part of the process of consolidating the gains of the revolution." This problematic positioning of women is clearly revealed in any examination of literature by male writers.

URBAN AND RURAL LIFE IN AFRICAN MALE LITERATURE

In order to understand how African women writers represent urban life, it is important to address, briefly, the characterization of urban and rural women in male literature, since these representations of African women are the dominant ones. Mutiso (1974) approached some of these issues in his chapters on "The Role of Women" and "The Rural-Urban Contradiction."

In male literature, man is the primary political actor and agent in the colonial period; woman becomes the symbol of all that is traditional and wholesome and paradoxically all that is Western, urban, and evil. Gaidzanwa (1985, 67) shows that "the portrayal of [Zimbabwean] women in literature is closely tied to the conceptions the writers have about rural and urban life." As such, he finds "there is a marked association between women's virtue and a rural, peasant lifestyle." Further, "rural women are portrayed as simple, innocent and honest unless they have been influenced by urban people and their values. Those rural women who are not ideal mothers or wives are shown to be motivated by urban values that do not conform with rural ones" (ibid., 70). Most of the urban professional and waged women in the literature are prostitutes. "Urban women are used to make moral points and to illustrate the virtues of living and acting in ways conventionally defined for women. They seldom get away with mischief and they get punished most of the time" (ibid., 74). It is necessary to question the motivations behind this criminalization of urban women.

This negative characterization has to be placed in historical perspective. According to Gaidzanwa, again, the historical and social basis for this negative representation in Southern Africa resides in the social realities of urbanization. In particular, the migratory patterns of young adult males to work in towns, farms, and mines create a demographic imbalance between sexes with the following result:

There were few women in towns then. These were mostly women who had been marginalized by widowhood, childlessness or orphanhood. In towns there were very few jobs for women. Even domestic work such as cleaning and child-minding was done by males, mostly of foreign origin. This state of affairs in the economy left the few urban women without many options if they wanted to survive. Some of the women married foreign labourers, went into consensual unions with labour migrants most of whom had wives in the rural areas. Others simply prostituted themselves if they could not marry or attach themselves to men on any basis. The casual nature of town-based liaisons generated a negative perception of town-based women. Those women who had jobs or professions ran the risk of being labelled as prostitutes especially if they were not married. . . . Rural women resented urban women for siphoning money off labour migrants (1985, 70–71).

Although women's professional lives have changed in the urban centers, Gaidzanwa continues, "The image of women in towns has not kept pace with the social reality of the towns. Urban women who are prostitutes are a minority in towns and yet they are the majority of female characters in literature of Zimbabwe" (1985, 71). In all of the literature of the city written by African male writers, from Cyprian Ekwensi to Ngugi wa Thiong'o, this portrayal of the woman is consistent.

DEROMANTICIZING RURAL LIFE AND THE MYTH OF THE VILLAGE WOMAN

For these reasons, among others, African women's writing seems to have as a major concern more developed representations of African women. I would argue further that literature is perhaps the most legitimate source for women's representations of gender, development, and urban life.

Extremely important in this exploration is the deliberate way in which rural life is deromanticized. In fact, the rural is often represented as the site of traditional, binding expectations for women and of difficult life and drudgery. Tsitsi Dangarembga's *Nervous Conditions* (1989) is a graphic deromanticization of the rural landscape with poverty, colonialism, incompetent men, and inadequate resources all critically linked. Marina Gashe (1963), in her poem "The Village," writes of "old women dark and bent/young wives like donkeys" and men who "ride away at dawn" leaving the women to "fend for the bony goats and crying children." Clearly, there is no romanticization of the village in such a portrait.

One of the most dramatic representations of this demystification of village life can be seen in Aidoo's *Anowa*, when the title character leaves the stifling confines of her village saying that "I shall walk so well that I will not find my feet back here again" (1970, 19). Similarly, in Rebeka Njau's *Ripples in the Pool* (1975), the protagonist Selina who is a vibrant, attractive nurse in great demand by men, well liked and admired in the urban center, becomes an abused, crazed woman when she marries and follows her husband to the village. In the city, Selina is described this way: "She seems so full of life, so free. Self-sufficient. And she had money. Every man knew that. She could afford to buy the most expensive dresses and jewelry in town but she never spent a single cent of her own money to do so. There was always a man somewhere to foot her bills. No wonder so many girls envied her" (ibid., 2). But Selina's life is transformed after she marries Gikere and runs into conflict with her rural mother-in-law who laments her son's marriage, without her consent, to a city girl. She says to him, "You have chosen a woman of the city and I have lost you. You have chosen a conceited woman and I know she will bring you nothing but misery" (ibid., 9). The situation deteriorates after Selina moves to the village and her ways and those of the village and her mother-in-law do not coincide. This culminates in her being physically chastised by Gikere. The vibrant Selina of the city, described above, is reduced to the following:

You selfish and mad woman! he cried as he caught hold of his wife and gave her two hard blows with his fists. She threw herself down on the floor but he continued striking her without care where the blows fell. Then he seized her head and banged it against the walls, the floor and anything that came his way. She screamed wildly but he went on slapping her hard on the face and did not stop beating her even when he noticed blood coming out of her nostrils (ibid., 44).

Although the narrator is critical, to a certain degree, of Selina and her inability to become a "village woman," she allows Selina space to explore a lesbian relationship with her sister-in-law. With the inclusion of this lesbian scene, often overlooked by most critics, Njau becomes the only African woman writer in this group who attempts to provide even a small glimpse at the lives of women whose sexuality and life-style do not center only on men.

The accepted options in the village as presented are motherhood and small trading or petty gardening and/or the option of becoming a priestess. Many texts—for example Flora Nwapa's *Efuru* (1966)—make this point. Efuru struggles against a number of traditional and rural restrictions to become a successful businesswoman; eventually she makes peace by becoming a devotee of the woman of the lake. Selina, in *Ripples in the Pool*, wants to open a factory to make African dolls and other toys but this effort is marred by her own inability to resolve her personal situation. Njau seems to suggest that all the characters in the text need to re-engage with the spirituality that comes from the "pool," the traditional source of healing in their community.

Several authors deal with the rural/urban transition and contrasts. Anowa, in Aidoo's play (1985), is freest "On the Highway," a borderland space of sorts where she is not constrained by any societal structures. Mariama Ba in *So Long a Letter* (1981) shows the rural as the source of the traditional male/female patterns that negatively affect her characters' lives. And Buchi Emecheta in *The Joys of Motherhood* (1979) deals at a fundamental level with the theme of rural-urban migration and shows the difficulty in both spaces.

It is important to say here that it is not the village by itself that generates these problems. Rather it is the immersion into international economic systems that transform traditional, negotiated bases of labor and devalue local agricultural systems. South African life-story collections paint the rural as a site of desolation and barrenness, as the men migrate to the towns and the women wait or are consigned to the worst land under the restrictive apartheid policies.

Many African women writers try to dismantle the myth of the rural as a site of all bounty and freedom. Professional life and personal advancement, obtainable in the urban center, are missing in the rural, as revealed in *Ripples in the Pool*, in *Anowa*, and in *Nervous Conditions*. In many cases, the rural is also the site of struggle and change. According to Ogundipe-Leslie (1990), there is a tendency to portray the rural as a flat, unchanging, traditional space that women enjoy. This picture is at variance with countless interviews and discussions with rural women who want changed relationships and better economic situations wherever they may live.

PROBLEMATIC URBAN COMMUNITIES AND THE CHALLENGE OF CHANGE

The urban environment and the change it represents open new possibilities for women. Yet there are regional variations on this theme. Among South African women writers, in particular, Johannesburg is the site of the intense barbarism that comes from apartheid. In *Working Women* (Lawson 1985), women are presented doing primarily service jobs: cleaning, cooking, waitressing, hairdressing or domestic service, factory jobs. Professional, clerical, and sales jobs are the smallest categories of work for women. Rural women are agricultural workers or farm laborers. In all of these contexts, urban women are overworked, maintaining the double or triple shift of home and workplace responsibilities.

Lauretta Ngcobo's *Cross of Gold* (1981), Miriam Tlali's *Muriel at Metropolitan* (1979), and *Mihloti* (1984), Ellen Kuzwayo's *Call Me Woman* (1985), and Zoe Wicomb *You Can't Get Lost in Capetown* (1987) all reveal an intense struggle with the urban environment and a distaste for the city as it exists. The appropriation of land, prolonged oppression, and the destruction of African social and cultural patterns are all revealed and struggled with. Concomitantly, the rural home is seen as a site of desolation, barrenness, deathly quietness. These questions are linked to the lack of space or the inability to control one's space.

Gcina Mhlope in "The Toilet" (1988) describes, autobiographically, coming to the city and having to stay clandestinely in her sister's accommodations in the servant's quarters. The only place that she can call her own to read, think, or write in is a public toilet which eventually gets padlocked, leaving her with no space of her own except the open or wild space. I described this absence of space in a previous article, which explores how gender and race combine to dislocate and disenfranchise African women in the context of apartheid in South Africa (Boyce Davies 1986–87). When contrasted with the rural desolation of the bantustan, there is a resolution; the rural area seems to take on the characteristics of the urban environment with all its difficulties.

Wicomb in *You Can't Get Lost in Capetown* (1987) writes in "A Trip to Gifberge" of the difficulties of returning to the rural home community after living in the city and studying in England. Part of her journey home is to come to terms with the rural landscape and the meaning of her relationships with her mother and her deceased father. She travels with her mother to a mountaintop that was off limits while her father was alive.

Another angle on this issue is revealed in the writings of northern Africans such as Nawal el Saadawi and others. Again, the rural environment is a space of a certain type of freedom for the girl-child and for the peasant woman but it also means abuse, an absence of opportunities for personal development, or professional choices. The urban environment means entrapment in bourgeois values, devalued women's work, constriction of space, veiling, and sexual oppression. Paradoxically, it offers the possibility of education but forecloses opportunity by allowing sexual harassment and limited possibilities for advancement. African women's texts are very clear on this issue of putting the rural environment in context in these changing societies.

TRANSPORTING RURAL GENDER RELATIONSHIPS TO THE URBAN CENTER

Difficulties for women often reside in the traditional and rural patterns that subordinate women and are then transported to the urban center. The urban space becomes contested space because women are seeing a tendency "to give a liberation of sorts with one hand and take it back with the other." This trend is, of course, identical with what has happened in the West as far as women's rights are concerned. As Gwendoline Konie (1984, 74) of Zambia has expressed it, "The struggle for equal rights between the sexes is going to prove even more difficult than that of decolonization."

"The Political Education of Women," a pamphlet by the Nigerian Department of Family and Social Relations, identifies the tendency of men to speak patronizingly to all women, regardless of their status. In the workplace, this patronizing attitude is a primary indicator of social patterns of domination imported into the urban professional space.

African women writers identify marital patterns like polygymy as tolerable when practiced in the rural environment, but as posing grave problems in the urban context. In the rural environment, each woman has her own defined space. In the cramped urban environment with its poverty of relationships, man-sharing is intolerable.

One of the most graphic explorations of this issue is Emecheta's *The Joys of Motherhood* in which the character Nnaife inherits his brother's wives, and the youngest comes to live with them in their tiny city quarters. The women find themselves in conflict over his attentions, his meager resources, competitive childbearing, and limited space.

As the months passed, Nnu Ego began to act in this way. She did everything she could to make Adaku jealous of her sons. She looked for every opportunity to call the names of her children in full, telling herself she was having her own back. Minor quarrels started between the two women, and Ubani, Nwakusor and their other friends were usually called in to settle disputes (1979, 162).

This novel details a difficult situation when disputes were settled in Nnu Ego's favor because she was the senior wife and also the mother of sons, while Adaku had only girls. Adaku eventually resolves to leave "this stinking room," become successful, and educate her daughters, whatever it takes, even if it means prostituting herself.

Motherhood and maternal responsibility in the urban center are presented as burdensome because the rural patterns of family support or communal caretaking of children and elders are often absent. Childcare becomes, as in the West, women's primary responsibility. South African stories in *Working Women* (Lawson 1985) reveal the difficulties of mothering as a single parent and the demands of childbearing and nurturing; Emecheta echoes these themes in *The Joys of Motherhood* (1979) and Aidoo in "The Message" (1972).

The status of women and the selective application of traditional patterns are overarching issues in most African women's representations of urban life. The construction of woman as wife/girlfriend or mother, as Gaidzanwa (1985) reveals, militates against any other constructions of women. For this reason, it seems to me, these prescribed heterosexual roles are necessarily dismantled in many African women's texts.

WESTERN MODELS OF URBANIZATION AND WOMEN'S LIVES

Western models of urban development and the role of the woman as they relate to housing arrangements, capitalist economic systems, colonialism, and neocolonialism are issues in African women's representation of urban life. In "African Woman, Culture and Another Development," Ogundipe-Leslie (1984, 77–92) outlines what she calls the mountains on African women's backs as they relate to the development issue. These mountains are layered in terms of external oppression, tradition, colonization, neocolonialism, male domination, gender, and racial positioning vis-à-vis the international economic order and woman's own internalized oppression. These issues populate the works of African women writers.

A fair number of texts challenge corruption in political and economic circles. Aminata Sow Fall in *The Beggars' Strike* (1981) deals with a politician who tries to clear the city of beggars in a violent way to secure his own political ambitions. He subsequently tries to bring them back and offer them food to meet the requirements of ritual sacrifice that is meant to assure him the advancement he craves. The whole endeavor ends unsuccessfully and leads to his demise.

Emecheta writes in *Naira Power* (1982) about political corruption, and in *Double Yoke* (1983), she links the oppression of women to corrupt professors. Ifeoma Okoye in *Men Without Ears* (1984) also challenges political corruption. Nwapa, in an interesting twist in *One Is Enough* (1981), shows a woman manipulating the system in the urban context to her advantage and becoming a successful entrepreneur through a combination of business acumen and feminine wiles. In *Our Sister Killjoy* (1979), Aidoo shows her protagonist, Sissie, taking on a range of issues that relate to political, economic, and social development in Africa. And in *Anowa* (Aidoo 1985), traditional corrupt practices and male dominance are interrogated simultaneously.

African women seem to be challenging both traditional and Western patterns of social organization that have caught women between two systems and make for degenerative social interactions. In Dangarembga's *Nervous Conditions* (1989), for example, both the rural and urban are difficult. In the urban context, colonial patterns dominate in the home and create an intolerable combination of relationships for women. The educated wife of Babamukuru has no power in the home. Her daughter, Nyasha, has a nervous breakdown because she is unable to accommodate allowed patterns of domination. At the close of the novel, Tambu, the protagonist, goes to a school in which we know she will be devalued and lose much of her Shona cultural identity.

FREEING REPRESENTATIONS IN WOMEN'S LITERATURE: PROSTITUTION, ENTREPRENEURSHIP, EXILE

Responses to women's situation are varied: Writers portray women as prostitutes, entrepreneurs, and exiles. One questionable possibility of liberation is prostitution. Unlike the male writers who either glamorize prostitution or make the prostitute the symbol of the city's ills, a number of women writers link prostitution to women's attempts to find a route to self-sufficiency.

One of the most graphic of these representations is in *Woman at Point Zero* (1983) in which Nawal el Saadawi attributes the constricted definition, emotional limitations, and physical abuse of the title character Firdaus to male-dominated social patterns. The narrative begins and ends with Firdaus, incarcerated but mentally liberated. She left her rural community as a young girl, attended school in town, and was finally married off to a repulsive old man. She leaves his abusive household and eventually becomes a successful prostitute. Subsequently she decided to do conventional women's office work, only to find herself subject to the manipulations of men and with no money to show for her labors. She returns to prostitution and ends by killing the pimp who tried to exploit her and return her to a dependent situation.

In African contexts, the term *prostitute* is not as specific as it is in the West; it is often used loosely to refer to a wide range of women who are not under the protection of patriarchy. One illustration of the multiple meanings of the term *prostitute* occurs in Emecheta's *The Joys of Motherhood* (1979, 168) when Adaku, the second wife, leaves saying, "I am leaving this stuffy room tomorrow, senior wife . . . I am going to be a prostitute." Adaku claims she is going to work with the women who are entertaining men and when we next see her she is a successful woman, but we never get the sense that she did become a prostitute.

In some places, college students, actresses, women out alone, professional women, and other educated women, are referred to as prostitutes. As Beverly

Mack shows in "Songs from Silence" (1986, 181–190), some oral, itinerant poets in Hausaland are also referred to as prostitutes. The prostitute figure is contradictory, complex, and problematic in African women's literature. Prostitution is a freeing representation, but one still limited by larger social definitions of women in patriarchal societies.

The entrepreneur is another representation of the liberated woman in African women's writing. Efuru is one example (Nwapa 1966). She remains childless and bereft of two husbands, but she gains respect for her business acumen. Nwapa goes even further in *One Is Enough* (1981) to have her character, Amaka, achieve rapid business success through manipulating the Lagos capitalist machinery for contracts. Amaka uses her body, friendships, and other negotiating techniques to acquire business. In the process, she conceives twins for her priest boyfriend, but she turns down his request for marriage. A range of entrepreneurial women appear in African women's literature but in all cases, their success is still regulated by larger social constraints.

Exile is posed as one other mode of escaping specific cultural regulations. Ba (1981) presents this option in her character, Aissatou, who abandons the society and her family relations to live abroad after her mother-in-law brings a new wife from the village for her husband. Bessie Head deals with marginality and exile in *A Question of Power* (1974), as does Aidoo in *Anowa* (1985). Exile may be achieved through physical migration from the village, town, nation, or continent, or, ultimately, through mental exile. The latter is the case for Elizabeth, in Head's novel; she leaves South Africa and lives in a village in Botswana. But even here all sorts of issues intrude. For Anowa there seems to be no escape. She is understandably unable to deal with the idea that there is nowhere else to go; she left her village swearing never to return, only to find her husband less than a true partner and with questionable business ethics in their growing business and in personal relationships. Selina, in *Ripples in the Pool* (Njau 1975), seeks to develop a woman-identified (lesbian) relationship with her sister-in-law as she finds her life with Gikere no longer tenable. At the same time, she tries to build a business, but both are unsuccessful in the particular context.

Wicomb, in *You Can't Get Lost in Capetown* (1987), flirts with exile as a possibility, but her character admits that she has to yet make peace with home. Emecheta, in *Second Class Citizen* (1975), shows that exile into the European centers means being relegated to the lowest rungs of those societies, layered as the experience is with class, race, and gender prejudices.

The ultimate freeing representation, pessimistic though it is, is death. It is the resolution of *The Joys of Motherhood* (Emecheta 1979) and of *Woman at Point Zero* (el Saadawi 1983). But one has to admit that in many ways, death and exile still represent an abandonment of struggle.

REVOLUTIONARY WOMEN STRUGGLING FOR SOCIAL CHANGE

There are fewer representations of women struggling for social change in an overt and political way. One of the most definite of these occurs in Ngcobo's

Cross of Gold (1981) in which the character, Sindisiwe, is engaged in liberation struggles in South Africa and later dies trying to cross the border with her sons. The more typical representations are those of negotiated relationships and social change at home and in society. Nafissatou Diallo's autobiographical novel, *A Dakar Childhood* (1982), is one of these as it shows the protagonist, Safi, negotiating domestic and public spaces through education, a supportive grandmother, and her own assertiveness as a young girl and woman. In *So Long a Letter* (Ba 1981), the daughter Daba is a modern woman in an urban context, educated, negotiating the relationships between her husband and herself, demanding more of her mother.

Education, learning, the dismantling of patterns of self-imposed and socially imposed dominance and voicing these are primary in the social reconstruction that is demanded by these writings. Efua Sutherland's "New Life at Kyrefaso" (1983) is the story of a young woman who rejects the terms of traditional definitions of womanhood and traditional prescriptions for marriage and works to rebuild her rural community. When she finds a man who shares her political positions and is ready to rebuild this community, she develops a relationship. In these cases, the urban environment is paradoxically a site of possibility. In these contexts as well, writing is a central tool in the dismantling of negative and oppressive patterns. The vision is to reconstitute more equitable patterns of social organization in both rural and urban systems.

Women freedom fighters in South Africa, Eritrea, and Ethiopia are making room for radical and revolutionary transformations of their societies. Although we have a growing body of literature by South African women, the literature from Eritrean women is less available in the West. Some women are making films and writing poetry and short, easily circulated pieces of literature. Hammond and Druce (1990), in their collection of testimonies of Tigrayan women, assert that women, in the context of revolutionary struggle, empower and liberate themselves. One woman says, "Even though I have two children, even though I have no income, even though I have many problems, still I support the TPLF. But these problems are temporary; I will not kneel down under them. I have mental satisfactions, mental resistance. There could not be anything more than this" (ibid., 158).

Finally, it is important to reiterate that urban-rural dichotomies are helpful only to the extent that they allow us to see how representations change according to social and economic organizational structures. In urban and rural settings, it seems, writers reveal a need for different patterns; both rural and urban environments are sites of contradiction depending on gender relations and who has the power to transform them. Representations of urban life by African women seem to be hinged to the rural and to an understanding that women's status in contemporary neocolonial or postcolonial systems is still subject to a range of dominating relationships.

Notes

CHAPTER 1

1. Jelin's edited collection, *Women and Social Change in Latin America* (1990), provides an important contribution to this subject.

2. It is worth noting that, according to Young (1985, 62), the active involvement of Scottish women in forms of popular protest has tended to be invisible to historians because of the powerful myth of the Scottish working class, and Scottish women in particular, as compliant and docile. Young suggests that "because it is often argued that Scottish plebeian women did not have any consciousness, it is not considered necessary to look at the struggles they waged," and yet, as he points out, "Scottish women not only participated in strikes, riots and demonstrations, they led and spoke at them, too, and they did so in the Lowlands as well as in the Highlands" (ibid., 62, 64).

CHAPTER 2

1. In Latin America there is a weak correlation between material well-being and literacy, on the one hand, and women's suffrage, on the other hand. Ecuador enfranchised women in 1929, whereas the suffrage movement in Argentina and Chile was not successful until after the Second World War. See Leahy (1986) and Chuchryk (1989) for a comparative review.

2. The testimonies noted in this section are taken from a video produced by the author and designed for classroom instruction. Copies are available through the University of Iowa. See Joseph L. Scarpaci, 1989, *Testimonies of the Urban Poor: Sewing and Housing Cooperatives in Santiago Shantytown*. University of Iowa (Tape G671), Department of Video, Seashore Hall, Iowa City, IA 52242.

3. All interviews were in Spanish, and the author has translated the excerpts reproduced here.

CHAPTER 4

1. In 1981, the average physician/population ratio for low-income economies was one per 6,050; the average nurse/population ratio was one per 3,890 (World Bank 1988, 278).

2. See Miyan (1984, 15). Staffing problems are also reported in World Bank (1987b).

3. See other articles in *Social Science and Medicine* 26 (9) (1988), for a further critique of selective primary care.

CHAPTER 5

1. All quotes from French secondary sources are translated by Meredeth Turshen.

CHAPTER 7

1. Cabarets differ from other businesses in that they employ male dancers who teach social dancing to women customers. Many women, including housewives, are hooked by these "dance teachers" into sexual relationships, blackmailed into paying large amounts of money, and eventually end up divorced from their husband who finds out about the extra-marital relationships.

2. Woo Jin Kim, security manager of the National Police Headquarters, "Discussion on Current Affairs: Regulation of Late Night Business", MBC-TV, 19 January 1990.

3. The number of women drafted is estimated at over 200,000. Many of these war prostitutes were massacred by the retreating Japanese army. (The Japanese government formally admitted that tens of thousands of Korean women were forced to serve as "comfort girls" during World War II and offered an apology [*New York Times*, 14 January 1992] editors' note.)

4. For the relationship between the military and prostitution, see chapter 2, "The Militarization of Prostitution," in Cynthia Enloe, *Does Khaki Become You?* (Boston: South End Press, 1983).

5. Sex tourism is widespread in Asia and is especially notorious in Thailand (see chapter 8 by Catherine Hill, this volume), the Philippines, and South Korea, where the state allows an institutionalized sex tourism.

6. This happened in the Limousine Room–salon located on the 8th floor of Family Tourist Hotel in Taechon City on 12 January 1990. A leader of organized crime and his subordinate were treating a Korean congressman and two high military CIA personnel. The hostesses often left their table to serve the boss of a rival group who was drinking with a judge and a prosecutor in the next room. A fight broke out between the two groups of criminals, and later the owner of the Limousine Room–salon, who is the boss of a third organized crime group, was attacked. This incident shocked the public because of the close relationships between congressman, prosecutor, judge and criminals (*Sae Gae Times*, 3 December 1990).

7. This finding corresponds to an earlier study of hostesses. In a survey of 396 hostesses, only 10.9 percent answered that they would tell a person sitting next to them on a train or an express bus that they were hostesses, while the rest would either name some other occupation (23.0 percent) or not tell at all (66.2 percent) (Won, 1985, 27).

8. Madam Im, the owner of a small room-cafe with four tables and two rooms, invested

55 million won (about $78,000) in 1985. Her monthly expenditure is around 2.5 million won, including the rent (650,000 won).

9. From the presentation of a Czech participant in the First Women's Leadership Institute on "Women, Violence, and Human Rights" (3–14 June 1991, Center for Women's Global Leadership, Rutgers University, New Brunswick, NJ).

CHAPTER 8

1. For example, Stanley Karnow's *Vietnam: A History. The First Complete Account of Vietnam at War* (1983), on which the Public Broadcasting System miniseries was based, makes no reference to the use of Thailand as a recreation area. Leftist literature on the subject shares this silence; for example, Howard Zinn's *Vietnam: The Logic of Withdrawal* (1967) does not include any discussion of prostitution or rape among his reasons why the United States should leave Vietnam.

CHAPTER 9

1. The author is writing a book-length history of the political economy of dowry in colonial Punjab in India. This chapter is a brief report of some of the arguments and conclusions, which emerged from five years of research and analysis. The author wishes to thank the American Institute for Indian Studies and the American Council of Learned Societies-Social Science Research Council Joint Committee on South Asia for their generous support for the research done in India and Great Britain respectively and is grateful for the supplementary grants from the American Philosophical Society, Baruch College and The Research Foundation of the City University of New York. As a Rock-efeller Humanist-in-Residence at Rutgers University in 1987–88, the author was able to undertake the analysis of the data gathered in the field and in the archives.

2. There is extensive work done on China, Greece, Sicily, Brazil, and Florence in different historical periods. Here, a historical work by Lalita Panigrahi is referred to, *British Social Policy and Female Infanticide in India* (1972), as well as a more up-to-date and anthropological work by Barbara D. Miller, *The Endangered Sex* (1981). The latter work has been particularly influential and will be reviewed in detail in this chapter. The recent explosion of media analyses of female infanticide offer no new explanations.

3. See C. L. Tupper (1881). There are, in addition, forty-nine volumes of customary law, one per district of the Punjab province, with a section in each devoted to defining dowry and the goods given at the time. These volumes were compiled by questioning the head male of each household; the males invariably state that the control of dowry is left with the bride except when the family suffers a financial crisis.

4. The definitive work on this subject is by Ranajit Guha, *A Rule of Property for Bengal: An Essay on the Idea of the Permanent Settlement* (1963).

5. D.C.J. Ibbetson (1883).

6. A fine study of contemporary conditions that sustains this view is Monica Das Gupta, "Selective Discrimination Against Female Children in Rural Punjab, India" (1987).

References

Abrahamian, E. 1968. The crowd in Iranian politics, 1905–1953. *Past and Present* 41:184–210.

Achurra, X. and J. Salinas. 1989. *Salud y promocion social: Catastro de instituciones de Santiago*. Santiago, Chile: INFOCAP.

Afshar, Haleh, ed. 1985. *Women, work and ideology in the Third World*. London: Tavistock.

Agarwal, Bina. 1988a. Neither sustenance nor sustainability: Agricultural strategies, ecological degradation and Indian women in poverty. In *Structures of patriarchy: State, community and household in modernising Asia*, ed. Bina Agarwal, pp. 83–120. London: Zed Books.

————, ed. 1988b. *Structures of patriarchy: State, community and household in modernising Asia*. London: Zed Books.

Agosin, Marjorie. 1988. *Scraps of life*. Toronto: Williams Wallace Publishers.

Aidoo, Ama Ata. 1972. The message. In *No sweetness here*, pp. 38–46. London: Longman.

————. 1979. *Our sister Killjoy. Or reflections from a black-eyed squint*. New York: Nok Publishers International.

————. 1984. To be a woman. In *Sisterhood is global*, ed. Robin Morgan, pp. 255–265. New York: Anchor Press/Doubleday.

————. 1985. *The dilemma of a ghost and Anowa*. London: Longman.

Akhter, Farida. 1984a. On population control policies and practices in Bangladesh. Dhaka, Bangladesh: UBINIG, March.

————. 1984b. Depopulating Bangladesh: A brief history of external intervention into the reproductive behavior of a society. Paper delivered to the Women's International Tribunal on Reproductive Rights, Amsterdam, July.

Alexander, M. 1990. ERP hits women hardest. *Nsamankow* 2:8–9.

Alvarez, S. E. 1989. Women's movements and gender politics in the Brazilian transition. In *The women's movement in Latin America*, ed. J. S. Jaquette, pp. 18–71. Boston: Unwin Hyman.

Ameen, F. 1990. Breaking our bondage: Ending violence against women. *MATCH News*, January–March.

Anker, Richard and Catherine Hein. 1986. *Sex inequalities in urban employment in the Third World*. London: Macmillan.

Armstrong, Alice, ed. 1987. *Women and law in Southern Africa*. Harare, Zimbabwe: Zimbabwe Publishing House.

Armstrong, Warwick and T. G. McGee. 1985. Women workers or working women? A case study of female workers in Malaysia. In *Theatres of accumulation: Studies in Asian and Latin American urbanization*. London: Methuen.

Arunachalam, Jaya. 1988. *Decade of the Forum*. Madras, India: Working Women's Forum.

Ashworth, G. 1986. *Of violence and violation: Women and human rights*. London: Change.

Asian Development Bank. 1986. *Key indicators of developing member countries of ADB*. Vol. 17. Manila: Asian Development Bank.

Austin, J. E. 1980. *Confronting urban malnutrition: The design of nutrition programs*. Baltimore, MD: Johns Hopkins University Press for the World Bank.

Australian National Committee on Violence. 1990. *Violence: Directions for Australia*. Australian Institute of Criminology.

AWRAN. 1985. Report of the Asian Women's Research and Action Network.

Azad, Naudini. 1986. *Empowering women workers: The W.W.F. experiment in Indian cities*. New Delhi: UNICEF.

Ba, Mariama. 1981. *So long a letter*. London: Heinemann.

Babb, F. 1990. Women and work in Latin America. *Latin American Research Review* 25: 236–247.

Banerjee. A. R. and Lipi Chowdhuri. 1988. Caste exogamy and Clan/Gotra exogamy in contemporary Bengalee society. *Man in India* (June): 200–218.

The Bank of Korea. 1987. *Financial statements analysis for 1987*. Seoul: The Bank of Korea.

Barry, Kathleen, Charlotte Bunch, and Shirley Castley, eds. 1984. *International feminism: Networking against female sexual slavery*. New York: International Women's Tribune Center.

Basler, Barbara. 1990. Underpaid, overworked and from the Philippines. *New York Times*, 28 August, p. A3.

Bello, Walden and Stephanie Rosenfield. 1990. *Dragons in distress: Asia's miracle economies in crisis*. San Francisco: The Institute for Food and Development Policy.

Benería, Lourdes. 1981. Conceptualizing the labor force: The underestimation of women's economic activities. *Journal of Development Studies* 17: 10–28.

Benería, Lourdes and Martha Roldan. 1987. *The crossroads of class and gender: Industrial homework, subcontracting and household dynamics in Mexico City*. Chicago: University of Chicago Press.

Berlin, Margalit. 1983. The formation of an ethnic group: Colombian female workers in Venezuela. In *Women, men and the international division of labor*, ed. J. Nash and M. P. Fernandez Kelly, pp. 257–270. Albany: State University of New York Press.

———. 1986. Migrant female labor in the Venezuelan garment industry. In *Women and change in Latin America*, ed. June Nash and Helen Safa, pp. 260–272. South Hadley, MA: Bergin & Garvey.

Bernal, Martin. 1987. *Black Athena*. New Brunswick, NJ: Rutgers University Press.

Bernard, Chantal. 1990. Les femmes salariées et non salariées au Maghreb, des travailleuses à plein temps et "hors du temps." In *Femmes due Maghreb au présent* sous la direction de Monique Gadant et Michèle Kasriel, pp. 89–139. Paris: Editions du Center National de la Recherche Scientifique.

Beteille, Andre. 1969. *Castes: Old and new, essays in social structure and social stratification*. Bombay: Asia Publishing House.

Bhatt, Ela. 1989. Toward empowerment. *World Development* 17: 1059–1065.

Biswas, K. and T. P. Tripathi. 1990. A comparative study of the employment situation of the aged. *Man in India* (March): 30–41.

Bjorkman, James Warner. 1986. *The changing division of labor in South Asia: Women and men in India's society, economy, and politics*. Riverdale, MD: Riverdale.

Blaikie, Piers M., John Cameron, and David Seddon. 1979. *The struggle for basic needs in Nepal*. Paris: OECD Development Center.

Blum, William. 1986. *The CIA: A forgotten history*. London: Zed Books.

Bohstedt, J. 1983. *Riots and community politics in England and Wales, 1790–1810*. Cambridge, MA: Harvard University Press.

Bolles, A. L. 1983. Kitchens hit by priorities: Employed working-class Jamaican women confront the IMF. In *Women, men and the international division of labour*, ed. J. Nash and M. P. Fernandez-Kelly, pp. 138–159. Albany: State University of New York Press.

———. 1986. Economic crisis and female-headed households in Latin America. In *Women and change in Latin America*, ed. June Nash and Helen Safa, pp. 65–83. South Hadley, MA: Bergin & Garvey.

Bongaarts, John. 1987. Does family planning reduce infant mortality rates? *Population and Development Review* 13(2): 323–334.

Boserup, Ester. 1970. *Woman's role in economic development*. New York: St. Martin's Press.

———. 1990. Economic change and the roles of women. In *Persistent inequalities: Women and world development*, ed. Irene Tinker, pp. 14–24. New York: Oxford University Press.

Boyce Davies, Carole. 1986–87. Finding some space: South African women writers. A *Current Bibliography of African Affairs* 19: 31–45.

Bradley, C. 1988. Wife beating in PNG: Is it a problem? *Papua New Guinea Medical Journal*, September.

Bretin, H., et al. 1991. Women, physicians and injectable contraception: The experience of family planning centers in Ile-de France. *European Journal of Public Health* 1(2).

Brettell, Caroline and Rita James Simon, eds. 1986. *International migration: The female experience*. Totowa, NJ: Rowman & Allanheld.

Brown, Barbara B. 1989. Women in Botswana. In *Women and development in Africa: Comparative Perspectives*, ed. Jane L. Parpart, pp. 257–278. Lanham, MD: University Press of America.

Bruce, Judith. 1989. Homes divided. *World Development* 17: 979–991.

Brucker, G. 1989. Les migrants. In *Santé publique* sous la direction de G. Brucker et D. Fassin, pp. 781–812. Paris: Edition Marketing.

Brydon, Lynne and Sylvia Chant. 1989. *Women in the Third World: Gender issues in rural and urban areas*. New Brunswick, NJ: Rutgers University Press.

Buendia, Hernando Gomez, ed. 1989. *Urban crime: Global trends and policies.* Tokyo: UN University.

Bumiller, Elisabeth. 1990. *May you be the mother of a hundred sons.* New York: Random House.

Bunch, Charlotte. 1990. Women's rights as human rights: Toward a re-vision of human rights. *Human Rights Quarterly* 12(4): 486.

Bunch, Charlotte and Roxanna Carrillo. 1991. Feminist perspectives on women in development. In *Persistent inequalities: Women and world development,* ed. Irene Tinker, pp. 70–82. New York: Oxford University Press.

Butterworth, Douglas and John Chance. 1981. *Latin American Urbanization.* Cambridge: Cambridge University Press.

Buvinić, Mayra. 1984. *Projects for women in the Third World: Explaining their misbehavior.* Washington, DC: International Center for Research on Women.

———. 1986. Projects for women in the Third World: Explaining their misbehavior. *World Development* 14: 653–664.

———. 1989. Investing in poor women: The psychology of donor support. *World Development* 17: 1045–1057.

Buvinić, Mayra, Margaret A. Lycette, and William Paul McGreevey, eds. 1983. *Women and poverty in the Third World.* Baltimore, MD: Johns Hopkins University Press.

Buvinić, Mayra and Nadia H. Youssef, with Barbara Von Elm. 1987. *Women-headed households: The ignored factor in development planning.* Washington, DC: Office of Women in Development, Agency for International Development.

Buvinić, M. and S. W. Yudelman. 1989. *Women, poverty and progress in the Third World.* New York: Foreign Policy Association.

Campero, G. 1985. *Movimentos sindicales en Chile.* Santiago, Chile: ILET.

Caplan, Patricia. 1985. *Class and gender in India: Women and their organizations in a South Indian city.* London: Tavistock.

Carloni, A. S. 1984. *The impact of maternal employment and income on the nutritional status of children in rural areas of developing countries.* Rome: UN Subcommittee on Nutrition.

Carroll, B. A. 1989. "Women take action!" Women's direct action and social change. *Women's Studies International Forum* 12: 3–24.

Castells, M. 1983. *The city and the grassroots.* Berkeley: University of California Press.

CGRS (Coordinating Group for Religion in Society). 1981. *Human rights in Thailand report.* Bangkok: CGRS.

Chant, Sylvia. 1987. Family structure and female labour in Querétaro, Mexico. In *Geography of gender in the Third World,* ed. Janet H. Momsen and Janet Townsend, pp. 277–293. London: Hutchinson.

Charlton, Sue Ellen M. 1984. *Women in Third World development.* Boulder, CO: Westview Press.

Chikhi, S. 1990. The working class, the social nexus and democracy in Algeria. Paper presented to the CODESRIA Seminar on Social Movements, Social Transformation and the Struggle for Democracy in Africa, Tunis, 21–23 May 1990. Dakar, Senegal: Council for the Development of Economic and Social Research in Africa (CODESRIA).

Chuchryk, P. 1989. Feminist anti-authoritarian politics: The role of women's organizations in the Chilean transition to democracy. In *The women's movement in*

Latin America: Feminism and the transition to democracy, ed. J. Jaquette, pp. 149–184. Boston: Unwin Hyman.

Cincone, Lillian. 1988. The role of development in the exploitation of Southeast Asian women: Sex tourism in Thailand. Master's thesis, Dept. of Social Sciences, San Jose State University, San Jose, California.

Cleary, S. 1989. Structural adjustment in Africa. *Trocaire Development Review:* 41–58.

Clement, J. F. 1985. Strategies repressives et techniques du maintien de l'ordre: les revoltes urbaines de janvier 1984 au Maroc. Unpublished paper, September 1985.

———. 1986. Les révoltes urbaines de janvier 1984 au Maroc. *Réseau Scientifique et Documentaire Etats Villes: Rapports sociaux et mouvements urbains dans le monde arabe, Bulletin* no. 5 (November): 3–46.

Cohen, R. 1982. Resistance and hidden forms of consciousness among African workers. In *Third World lives of struggle,* ed. H. Johnson and H. Bernstein, pp. 244–257. London: Heinemann and the Open University.

Columbia Human Rights Law Review, ed. 1977. *Law and the status of women: An international symposium.* New York: UN Center for Social Development and Humanitarian Affairs.

Commission Nationale Consultative des Droits de l'Homme. 1991. *1990. La lutte contre le racisme et la xenophobie.* Paris: La Documentation Française.

Commonwealth Secretariat. 1987. Women and development program. Confronting violence: A manual for commonwealth action. Prepared by J. F. Connors, 1987.

———. 1989. *Engendering adjustment for the 1990s.* London: Commonwealth Secretariat.

Concertación. 1989. Bases para un programa de salud. Santiago, Chile: Concertacion (mimeo).

Connell, R. W. 1987. *Gender and power.* Stanford, CA: Stanford University Press.

Cornia, G. 1984. A survey of cross-sectional and time-series literature on factors affecting child welfare. In *Impact of the world recession on children,* ed. R. Jolly and G. Cornia, pp. 17–32. Oxford: Pergamon Press.

———. 1987a. Adjustment at the household level: Potentials and limitations of survival strategies. In *Adjustment with a human face,* ed. G. Cornia, R. Jolly, and F. Stewart, pp. 90–104. Oxford: Clarendon Press.

———. 1987b. Adjustment policies 1980–1985: Effects on child welfare. In *Adjustment with a human face,* ed. G. Cornia, R. Jolly, and F. Stewart, pp. 48–72. Oxford: Clarendon Press.

Cornia. G. 1987c. Economic decline and human welfare in the first half of the 1980s. In *Adjustment with a human face,* ed. G. Cornia, R. Jolly, and F. Stewart, pp. 11–47. Oxford: Clarendon Press.

Cornia, G., R. Jolly, and F. Stewart, eds. 1987. *Adjustment with a human face,* 2 vols. Oxford: Clarendon Press.

Correspondencia. 1990. De mujer a mujer. August.

Cousins, W. J. and G. Goydre. 1979. *Changing slum communities.* New Delhi: Manohar.

Covarrubias, P. and R. Franco. 1978. *Chile: Mujer y sociedad.* Santiago, Chile: Fondo de las Naciones Unidas para la Infancia.

Daines, V. and D. Seddon. 1991. Survival struggles, protest and resistance: Women's responses to "austerity" and "structural adjustment." *Gender Analysis in Development Sub-Series* no. 4 (February). Norwich, UK: University of East Anglia.

Dangarembga, Tsitsi. 1989. *Nervous conditions*. London: Women's Press and Seattle, WA: Seal Press.

Das Gupta, Monica. 1987. Selective discrimination against female children in rural Punjab, India. *Population and Development Review* 13(1): 77–100.

Davies, Miranda, ed. 1983. *Third World: Second sex*. Vol. 2. London: Zed Books.

Decade of the Forum. 1988. Madras, India : Working Women's Forum.

DeGraff, D. S., J. F. Phillips, R. Simmons, and J. Chakraborty. 1986. Integrating health services into an MCH-FP program in Matlab, Bangladesh: An analytical update. *Studies in Family Planning* 17(5): 228–234.

de Groot, J. 1989. The formation and reformation of popular political movements in Iran. In *Urban Crisis and Social Movements in the Middle East/Etat, Ville et Mouvements Sociaux au Maghreb et au Moyen-Orient*, ed. K. Brown et al., pp. 214–234. Paris: L'Harmattan Villes et Enterprises.

Delacoste, Frederique and Priscilla Alexander, eds. 1987. *Sex work: Writings by women in the sex industry*. Pittsburgh, PA: Cleis Press.

Desai, Neera and Maithreyi Krishnaraj. 1987. *Women and society in India*. Delhi: Ajanta Publications.

De Souza, Alfred. 1975. *Women in contemporary India: Traditional images and changing roles*. New Delhi: Manohar Press, 1975.

Diallo, Nafissatou. 1982. *A Dakar childhood*. London: Longman.

Diop, Cheikh Anta. 1987. *Precolonial black Africa*. Westport, CT: Lawrence Hill and Co.

Dobash, R. P. and R. E. Dobash. 1976. The importance of historical and contemporary contexts in understanding marital violence. Paper presented at the Annual Meeting of the American Sociological Association. New York, August.

The Dong A-Ilbo. 1990. Company expense accounts under stricter surveillance by tax office. 18 November, p. 1.

Duley, Margot I. and Mary I. Edwards. 1986. *The cross-cultural study of women: A comprehensive guide*. New York: The Feminist Press.

Dumont, Louis. 1966. *Homo hierarchicus: The caste system and its implications*. London: Weidenfeld and Nicolson.

Dwyer, Daisy and Judith Bruce, ed. 1988. *A home divided: Women and income in the Third World*. Stanford, CA: Stanford University Press.

Ebole, O., M. Mitjavila, and D. Alsonso. 1986. *Salud, condiciones de vida, y participacion communitaria*. Montevideo, Uruguay: Centro Latinamericano de Economica Humana (CLAEH).

Economic Planning Board. 1980. *Population and housing census*.

———. 1986, 1987. *A survey of economically active population*.

The Economist. 1989. Protecting the taste of Thailand. 25 February, p. 30.

———. 1990a. By any other name. 6 January, p. 38.

———. 1990b. Cops and rubbers. 10 November, p. 40.

———. 1990c. The new lepers. 15 September, p. 44.

Eckstein, S. 1989a. Power and popular protest. In *Power and popular protest, Latin American social movements*, ed. S. Eckstein, pp. 1–57. Berkeley: University of California Press.

———, ed. 1989b. *Power and popular protest: Latin American social movements*. Berkeley: University of California Press.

————. 1990. Urbanization revisited: Inner city slums of hope and squatter settlements of despair. *World Development* 18 (2): 165–181.

el Saadawi, Nawal. 1983. *Woman at point zero.* London: Zed Books.

Elson, D. 1989. The impact of structural adjustment on women. In *The IMF, the World Bank and the African debt: The social and political impact,* ed. B. Onimode, pp. 56–74. London: Zed Books.

Emecheta, Buchi. 1975. *Second class citizen.* New York: George Braziller.

————. 1979. *The joys of motherhood.* New York: George Braziller.

————. 1982. *Naira power.* London: Macmillan.

————. 1983. *Double yoke.* New York: George Braziller.

Enloe, Cynthia. 1989. *Bananas, beaches and bases: Making feminist sense of international politics.* Berkeley: University of California Press.

Fainzang, Sylvie and Odile Journet. 1988. *La Femme de Mon Mari: Anthropologie du mariage polygamique en Afrique et en France.* Paris: L'Harmattan.

Fox-Genovese, E. 1982. Placing women's history in history. *New Left Review* 133: 5–29.

Ffrench-Davis, R. 1986. Import liberalization: The Chilean experience, 1973–1982. In *Military rule in Chile,* ed. J. S. Valenzuela and A. Valenzuela, pp. 51–84. Baltimore, MD: Johns Hopkins University Press.

Frühling, H. 1989. Nonprofit organizations as opposition to authoritarian rule: The case of human rights organizations in Chile. In *The nonprofit sector in international perspective: Studies in comparative culture and policy,* ed. E. James, pp. 358–377. New York: Oxford University Press.

Fuentes M. and A. G. Frank. 1989. Ten theses on social movements. *World Development* 17: 179–191.

Gaidzanwa, Rudo B. 1985. *Images of women in Zimbabwean literature.* Harare, Zimbabwe: The College Press.

Gashe, Marina. 1963. The village. In *Poems from black Africa,* ed. Langston Hughes. Bloomington: Indiana University Press.

Germain, Adrienne. 1987. Reproductive health and dignity: Choices by Third World women. Technical background paper prepared for the International Conference on Better Health for Women and Children Through Family Planning, Nairobi, Kenya, October. New York: The Population Council.

Ghai, D. and C. Hewitt de Alcantara. 1990. The crisis of the 1980s in Africa, Latin America and the Caribbean: Economic impact, social change and political implications. Discussion Paper, 7. Geneva: UNRISD.

Ghurye, G. S. 1950. *Caste and class in India.* Bombay: Popular Book Depot.

GISTI. 1990. Les batons dans les roues. *Plein Droit* 12: 11–14.

Gordon, Elizabeth. 1981. An analysis of the impact of labour migration on the lives of women in Lesotho. In *African women in the development process,* ed. Nici Nelson, pp. 59–76. London: Frank Cass.

Gore, M. S. 1968. *Urbanization and family change.* Bombay: Popular Prakashan.

Green, R. H. 1989. The broken pot: The social fabric, economic disaster and adjustment in Africa. In *The IMF, the World Bank and the African debt,* ed. B. Onimode, pp. 31–55. London: Zed Books.

Griffin, E. and L. Ford. 1980. A model of Latin American city structure. *Geographical Review* 37: 397–422.

Grown, Caren and Jennefer Sebstad. 1989. Introduction: Toward a wider perspective on women's employment. *World Development* 17: 937–952.

Guha, Ranajit. 1963. *A rule of property for Bengal: An essay on the idea of the permanent settlement.* Paris: Mouton.

Guzel, M. S. 1989. La grève de 15 et 16 juin 1970 à Istanbul. In *Urban crises and social movements in the Middle East,* ed. K. Brown et al. Paris: L'Harmattan.

Hale, Sondra. 1987. Women's culture/men's culture: Gender, separation, and space in Africa and North America. *American Behavioral Scientists* 31(1): 115–134.

Hammond, Jenny and Neil Druce. 1990. *Sweeter than honey. Ethiopian women and revolution: Testimonies of Tigrayan women.* Trenton, NJ: The Red Sea Press.

Hanmer, J. and M. Maynard, eds. 1987. *Women, violence and social control.* Atlantic Highlands, NJ: Humanities Press International.

Hanmer, J., J. Radford, and E. A. Stanko, eds. 1989. *Women, policing, and male violence: International perspective.* London: Routledge.

Hantrakul, S. 1983. The spirit of a fighter: Women and prostitution in Thailand. *Manushi* 18.

Hardy, C. 1987. *Organizarse para vivir.* Santiago, Chile: PET.

Hardy, C. and L. Razeto. 1984. Nuevos actores y practicas populares: Desafios a la concertacion. Documento de Trabajo No. 47, Santiago, Chile: CED.

Harper, E. 1968. Social consequences of an unsuccessful low caste movement. In *Social mobility in the caste system in India: An interdisciplinary symposium,* ed. James Silverberg, pp. 36–45. The Hague: Mouton.

Hartmann, Betsy and Hilary Standing. 1985. *Food, saris and sterilization.* London: Bangladesh International Action Group.

Haut Conseil à l'Intégration. 1991. *Pour un modèle français d'intégration.* Paris: La documentation Française.

Hay, M. J. and S. Stichter, eds. 1984. *African women south of the Sahara.* London: Longman.

Hay, M. J. and M. Wright. 1982. *African women and the law: Historical perspectives.* Boston: Boston University, African Studies Center.

Head, Bessie. 1974. *A question of power.* London: Heinemann.

Heise, L. 1989. Crimes of gender. *World Watch* (March–April): 12–21.

Hemmings-Gapihan, Grace S. 1982. International development and the evolution of women's economic roles: A case study from Northern Gulma, Upper Volta. In *Women and work in Africa,* ed. E. G. Bay, pp. 171–189. Boulder, CO: Westview.

Herz, Barbara and Anthony R. Measham. 1987. The safe motherhood initiative: Proposals for action. World Bank Discussion Papers, No. 9, Washington, DC: The World Bank.

Heyzer, Noeleen. 1986. *Working women in South-East Asia: Development, subordination and emancipation.* Philadelphia: Open University Press.

———. 1989. Asian women wage-earners: Their situation and possibilities for donor intervention. *World Development* 17: 1109–1123.

———, ed. 1988. *Daughters in industry: Work skills and consciousness of women workers in Asia.* Kuala Lumpur, Malaysia: Asian and Pacific Development Center.

Hill, M. Anne. 1983. Female labor force participation in developing and developed countries—Considerations of the informal sector. *The Review of Economics and Statistics* 65: 459–468.

Holden, Peter et al. 1983. *Tourism prostitution development: Documentation*. Bangkok: Ecumenical Coalition on Third World Tourism.

Hoodfar, Homa. 1988. Household budgeting and financial management in a lower-income Cairo neighborhood. In *A home divided: Women and income in the Third World*, ed. Daisy Dwyer and Judith Bruce, pp. 120–142. Stanford, CA: Stanford University Press.

Huaman, J. N.d. Comedores populares y estrategia de sobrevivencia. Mimeo. Lima: Pontificia Universidad Catolica del Peru.

Hull, Richard W. 1976. *African cities and towns before the European conquest*. New York: W. W. Norton and Co.

Humphrey, John. 1985. Gender, pay and skill: Manual workers in Brazilian industry. In *Women, work and ideology in the Third World*, ed. Haleh Afshar, pp. 214–231. London: Tavistock.

Ibbetson, D.C.J. 1883. *Report on the revision of the Panipat Tehsil and Karnal District, 1872–1880*. Allahabad, India: The Pioneer Press.

Ibrahim, Barbara. 1989. Policies affecting women's employment in the formal sector: Strategies for change. *World Development* 17: 1097–1107.

ILET (Instituto Latinamericano de Estudios Transnacionales). Mujer/Fempress, Santiago, Chile. December 1988, Especial "Contraviolencia"; November 1989, No. 97; February–March 1990, No. 100; June 1990, No. 104.

ILO. 1980. *Women in rural development: Critical issues*. Geneva: International Labour Office.

Ingraham, Larry. 1984. *The boys in the barracks: Observations on American military life*. Philadelphia: Institute for the Study of Human Issues.

ISIS International. 1990. Violencia en contra de la mujer en America Latina y el Caribe. Informacion y Politicas. Informe Final. Proyecto RLA/88/W0l. UNIFEM. Santiago, Chile: Isis Internacional.

Jaffe, P., S. Wilson, and D. A. Wolfe. 1986. Promoting changes in attitudes and understanding of conflict resolution among child witnesses of family violence. *Canadian Journal of Behavioral Science* 18: 356.

Jaquette, J. S., ed. 1989. *The women's movement in Latin America: Feminism and the transition to democracy*. Boston: Unwin Hyman.

Jayawardena, K. 1986. *Feminism and nationalism in the Third World*. London: Zed Books.

Jeffrey, Patricia, Roger Jeffrey, and Andrew Lyon. 1988. *Labour pains and labour power*. London: Zed Books.

Jelin, Elisabeth. 1977. Migration and labour force participation of Latin American women: The domestic servants in the cities. *Signs* 3: 129–141.

————, ed. 1990. *Women and social change in Latin America*. London and New Jersey: Zed Books and UNRISD.

Jenkins, C. L. and B. M. Henry. 1982. Government involvement in tourism in developing countries. *Annals of Tourism Research* 9: 499–521.

Jiggins, J. 1989. How poor women earn income in sub-Saharan Africa and what works against them. *World Development* 17: 953–963.

Joekes, Susan P. 1987. *Women in the world economy: An INSTRAW study*. United Nations International Research and Training Institute for the Advancement of Women. New York: Oxford University Press.

Jolly, R. and G. Cornia. 1984. *The impact of world recession on children.* Oxford: Pergamon Press.

Karnow, Stanley. 1983. *Vietnam: A history.* The first complete account of Vietnam at war. New York: Viking Press.

Karp-Toledo, Ed. 1983. Situacion alimentaria-nutricional en la sierra sud del Peru. AID-Lima/Sigma One Corporation, Raleigh, NC, October.

Karve, Irawati. 1961. *Hindu society: An interpretation.* Poona, India: Deccan College.

Keyes, C. 1984. Mother or mistress but never a monk: Buddhist notions of female gender in rural Thailand. *American Ethnologist* 11(2): 223–241.

Keysers, Loes. 1982. *Does family planning liberate women?* Master of Development Studies Thesis. The Hague: Institute of Social Studies.

Khan, M. R. 1986. Prospects and problems of integration of family planning with health services in Bangladesh. *The Bangladesh Development Studies* 14(2).

Kharas, Homi and Hisanobu Shishido. 1985. *Thailand: An assessemnt of alternative foreign borrowing strategies.* World Bank Working Papers, no. 781. Washington, DC: The World Bank.

Khoo, Siew-Ean, Peter Smith, and James T. Fawcett. 1984. Migration of women to cities: The Asian situation in comparative perspective. *International Migration Review* 18:1247–1263.

Killick, T. 1990. *A reaction too far: Economic theory and the role of the state in developing countries.* London: Overseas Development Institute.

Kim, Elaine. 1987. Sex tourism in Asia: A reflection of political and economic inequality. In *Korean women in transition: At home and abroad,* ed. Eui-Young Yu and Earl H. Phillips, pp. 127–144. Los Angeles: Center for Korean-American and Korean Studies, California State University.

Kim, Joo-Sook. 1985. Rural women and work. In *Korean women and work,* ed. Research Institute for Women in Korea. Seoul: Ewha Woman's University Press.

Kim, Tae-Dong. 1990. Soaring land prices: Reasons and countermeasures. *ECONOMIC JUSTICE, the first issue.* Seoul: Citizens Coaliton for Economic Justice.

Kim, Young Mo and Seok-jo Won. 1984. *A study on countermeasures of entertainment and prostitution.* Seoul: Research Institute for Contemporary Society.

Kirkwood, Julieta. 1983. Feminismo y participación política en Chile. In *Temas Socialisteas,* ed. Eduardo Ortiz. Santiago, Chile: Centro de Estudias Sociales y Econmicas.

Koenig, M. A., J. F. Phillips, R. S. Simmons, and M. A. Khan. 1987. Trends in family size preference and contraceptive use in Matlab, Bangladesh. *Studies in Family Planning* 18(3): 117–127.

———. 1988. Maternal mortality in Matlab, Bangladesh: 1976–85. *Studies in Family Planning* 19(2): 69–80.

Konie, Gwendoline. 1984. Feminist progress: More difficult than decolonization. In *Sisterhood is global,* ed. Robin Morgan, pp. 739–745. New York: Anchor/Doubleday.

Koop, C. E. 1989. Violence against women: A global problem. Address by the Surgeon General of the U.S. Public Health Service, at a Seminar of the Pan American Health Organization, Washington, DC: 22 May.

Korea. Economic Planning Board. 1960, 1986. *Annual report on the economically active population survey.* Seoul.

Korea. Ministry of Labor. 1987. *Women and employment.* Seoul.

Korea Church Women United. 1984. *Kisaeng tourism: A nation-wide survey report on conditions in four areas—Seoul, Pusan, Cheju, and Kyongju.* Research material No. 3. Seoul: Catholic Publishing House.

Korean Women's Association United. 1988. Statement. Mimeograph, Seoul, 14 December.

Korson, J. H. and M. Maskiell. 1985. Islamization and social policy in Pakistan. *Asian Survey* 25(6): 589–612.

Kothari, R. 1985. Peace and human rights. *END Journal.*

Kuzwayo, Ellen. 1985. *Call me woman.* San Francisco: Spinsters Ink Press.

Lafosse, V. S. 1984. Comedores comunales: La mujer frente a la crisis. Grupo de Trabajo, Servicios Urbanos y Mujeres de Bajos Ingresos. Lima, Peru.

Laureda, J., K. Parker, W. Rivera, and J. Scarpaci. 1988. *Human rights fact-finding mission to Santiago, Chile.* New York: Chile Center for Education and Development.

Lawson, Lesley, ed. 1985. *Working women. A portrait of South Africa's Black women workers.* Johannesburg: Sachad Press/Ravan, 1985.

Leacock, E., ed. 1979. Women, development and anthropological facts and fictions. In *Women in Latin America.* Riverside, CA: Latin American Perspectives.

Leacock, E. and H. Safa. 1986. *Women's work.* South Hadley, MA: Bergin & Garvey.

Leahy, M. 1986. *Development strategies and the status of women: A comparative study of United States, Mexico, Soviet Union, and Cuba.* Boulder, CO: Lynne Reinner.

Lele, Uma. 1986. Women and structural transformation. *Economic Development and Cultural Change* 34: 195–221.

LePoer, Barbara. 1989. *Thailand: A country study.* Washington, DC: Federal Research Division, Library of Congress.

Leslie, J. 1988. Women's work and child nutrition in the Third World. *World Development* 16: 1341–1362.

Leslie, J., M. Lycette, and M. Buvinić. 1986. *Weathering economic crises: The crucial role of women in health.* Washington, DC: Center for Research on Women.

Levinson, D. 1989. *Family violence in cross-cultural perspective.* Newbury Park, CA: Sage Publications.

Lewis, Barbara. 1984. The impact of development policies on women. In *African women south of the Sahara,* ed. M. J. Hay and S. Stichter, pp. 170–187. London: Longman.

Liauzu, C. 1989. Crises urbaines, crise de l'Etat, mouvements sociaux. In *Urban crises and social movements in the Middle East/Etat, ville et mouvements sociaux au Maghreb et au Moyen-Orient,* ed. K. Brown et al., pp. 23–41. Paris: L'Harmattan Villes et Entreprises.

Lihamba, Amandina. 1986. Culture and political struggle: Theatre and cultural development. Paper presented at the Conference of the Review of African Political Economy, University of Liverpool, 26–28 September. Mimeo.

Lim, Linda Y. C. 1991. Women's work in export factories: The politics of a cause. In *Persistent inequalities: Women and world development,* ed. Irene Tinker, pp. 101–119. New York: Oxford University Press.

Loewenson, René. 1991. Harvests of disease: Women at work on Zimbabwean plantations. In *Women and health in Africa,* ed. Meredeth Turshen, pp. 35–49. Trenton, NJ: Africa World Press.

Lomnitz, L. 1978. Mechanisms of articulation between shantytown settlers and the urban center. *Urban Anthropology* 7: 185–205.

Lopez, A. D. and L. T. Rudicka, eds. 1983. *Sex differentials in mortality: Trends, determinants, and consequences.* Canberra: Australian National University Press.

Loutfi, Martha F. 1980. *Rural women: Unequal partners in development.* Geneva: International Labour Organisation.

———. 1987. Development with women: Action, not alibis. *International Labour Review* 126(1): 111–124.

Loveman, B. 1988. *Chile: The legacy of Hispanic capitalism.* New York: Oxford.

Mack, Beverly. 1986. Songs from silence: Hausa women's poetry. In *Ngambika: Studies of women in African literature,* ed. Carole Boyce Davies and Anne Adams Graves, pp. 181–190. Trenton, NJ: Africa World Press.

MacLeod, L. 1980. *Wife battering in Canada: The vicious circle.* Quebec: Government Publishing Center.

———. 1990. The city for women: No safe place. *Women and Environments* 12(1): 6–7.

Marshall, J. 1990. Structural adjustment and social policy in Mozambique. *Review of African Political Economy* 47: 28–43.

Marshall, S.L.A. 1964. *Men against fire.* New York: Morrow.

Marshall, Susan E. 1985. Development, dependence, and gender inequality in the Third World. *International Studies Quarterly* 29: 217–240.

Mason, T. 1981. The workers' opposition in Nazi Germany. *History Workshop* 11: 120–137.

Massiah, J. 1989. Women's lives and livelihoods: A view from the Commonwealth Caribbean. *World Development* 17: 965–977.

Matsui, Yayori. 1987. Women's Asia. London: Zed Books.

Matthews, Harry. 1978. *International tourism: A political and social analysis.* Cambridge: Schenkman Publishing Company.

McGlen, Nancy E. 1985. Book reviews. *The Journal of Politics* 47: 1305–1308.

McIntosh, Mary. 1978. The state and the oppression of women. In *Feminism and materialism: Women and modes of production,* ed. A. Kuhn and A.-M. Wolpe, pp. 254–289. London: Routledge & Kegan Paul.

McKinnon, Catherine. 1987. *Feminism: Unmodified discourse on life and law.* Cambridge, MA: Harvard University Press.

Merrick, Thomas and Marianne Schmink. 1983. Households headed by women and urban poverty in Brazil. In *Women and poverty in the Third World,* ed. Mayra Buvinić, Margaret A. Lycette, and William Paul McGreevey, pp. 244–271. Baltimore, MD: Johns Hopkins University Press.

Mhlope, Gcina. 1988. The toilet. In *Somehow tenderness survives,* selected by Hazel Rochman, pp. 77–86. New York: Harper & Row Publishers.

Michel, A., A. Fatoumata-Diarra, and H. Agbessi-Dos Santos, eds. 1981. *Femmes et multinationales.* Paris: Editions Karthala.

Mies, Maria. 1984. Capitalism and subsistence: Rural women in India. *Development: Seeds of Change* 4: 18–25.

———. 1986. *Patriarchy and accumulation on a world scale: Women in the international division of labour.* London: Zed Books.

Mies, Maria, Veronika Bennholdt-Thomsen, and Claudia von Werlhof. 1988. *Women: The last colony.* London: Zed Books.

Miller, Barbara D. 1981. *The endangered sex: Neglect of female children in rural North India*. Ithaca, NY: Cornell University Press.

Miyan, M. Alimullah. 1984. The management of population assistance programmes in Bangladesh. In *The management of population assistance programmes: Examples of public management of population projects in Bangladesh and Indonesia*, ed. M. A. Miyan and the Yayasan Indonesia Sejahtera. Paris: OECD.

Molyneux, Maxine. 1984. Mobilisation without emancipation? Women's interests, state and revolution in Nicaragua. *Critical Social Policy* 10(7): 59–75.

———. 1986. Mobilisation without emancipation? Women's interests, state and revolution in Nicaragua. In *Transition and development: Problems of Third World socialism*, ed. Richard Fagan et al., pp. 280–302. New York: Monthly Review Press.

Momsen, Janet H. and Janet Townsend, eds. 1987. *Geography of gender in the Third World*. London: Hutchinson, and Albany: State University of New York Press.

Morell, D. and S. Chai-anan. 1981. *Political conflict in Thailand: Reform, reaction, revolution*. Cambridge, MA: Delegeschlager, Gunn and Hain, Inc.

Morley, David, Jon Rohde, and Glen Williams. 1983. *Practicing health for all*. Oxford: Oxford University Press.

Morrow, Lance. 1986. Women in sub-Saharan Africa. In *The cross-cultural study of women*, ed. Margot I. Duley and Mary I. Edwards, pp. 290–375. New York: The Feminist Press.

Moser, Caroline O. N. 1987. Women, human settlements, and housing: A conceptual framework for analysis and policy-making. In *Women, human settlements, and housing*, ed. Caroline O. N. Moser and Linda Peake, pp. 12–32. London: Tavistock.

———. 1988. The impact of recession and structural adjustment policies at the micro-level: Low-income women and their households in Guyaquil, Ecuador. Paper prepared for UNICEF, New York.

———. 1989. Gender planning in the Third World: Meeting practical and strategic gender needs. *World Development* 17: 1799–1825.

Moser, Caroline O. N. and Caren Levy. 1986. *A theory and methodology of gender and planning*. London: Gender and Planning Working Paper No. 11, Development Planning Unit, University College.

Moser, Caroline O. N. and Linda Peake, eds. 1987. *Women, human settlements, and housing*. London: Tavistock.

Muecke, Marjorie. 1990. The AIDS prevention dilemma in Thailand. *Asian and Pacific Population Forum* 4(4): 2–27.

Munachonga, Monica. 1988. Income allocation and marriage options in urban Zambia. In *A home divided: Women and income in the Third World*, ed. Daisy Dwyer and Judith Bruce, pp. 173–194. Stanford, CA: Stanford University Press.

———. 1989. Women and development in Zambia. in *Women and development in Africa: Comparative perspectives*, ed. Jane L. Parpart, pp. 279–311. Lanham, MD: University Press of America.

Muntemba, D. 1989. The impact of IMF-World Bank programmes on women and children in Zambia. In *The IMF, the World Bank and the African debt*, ed. B. Onimode, pp. 111–124. London: Zed Books.

Mutiso, G.C.M. 1974. *Socio-political thought in African literature*. London: Macmillan.

Nash, June and Helen Safa, eds. 1985. *Women and change in Latin America.* South Hadley, MA: Bergin & Garvey.

National Center for Women and Family Law. 1988. *Information package on battered women.* No. 47. New York: National Center for Women and Family Law.

Nelson, J. 1985. *Short-run public reactions to food subsidy cuts in selected Sub-Saharan and North African countries.* Report to the office of Long-range Assessments and Research, U.S. Department of State and the Agency for International Development, February.

New Internationalist. 1983. Interview with Halfdan Mahler, Director-General, WHO, September, p. 127.

Ngcobo, Lauretta. 1981. *Cross of gold.* London: Longman.

Njau, Rebeka. 1975. *Ripples in the pool.* London: Heinemann.

Noiriel, G. 1988. *Le creuset français. Histoire de l'immigration XIXe–XXe siècles.* Paris: Editions du Seuil.

Noponen, H. 1989. Grassroots women's worker organizations: Rhetoric and reality. Unpublished essay.

Nwapa, Flora. 1966. *Efuru.* London: Heinemann.

———. 1981. *One is enough.* Nigeria: Tana Press.

Obbo, Christine. 1980. *African women: Their struggle for economic independence.* London: Zed Books.

Ogundipe-Leslie, Omolara. 1984. African women, culture and another development. *The Journal of African Marxists* 5: 77–92.

———. 1990. African women and the politics of development. Paper presented at the Decentering Discourses Conference, SUNY-Binghamton, New York.

O'Hanlon, R. 1988. Recovering the subject: Subaltern studies and histories of resistance in colonial South Asia. *Modern Asian Studies* 22: 189–224.

Okoye, Ifeoma. 1984. *Men without ears.* London: Longman.

Omvedt, Gail. 1986. *Women in popular movements: India and Thailand during the decade of women.* UNRISD Participation Programme, Report no. 86.9. Geneva: UNRISD.

———. 1990. *Violence against women: New movements and new theories in India.* New Delhi: Kali for Women.

Onimode, B., ed. 1989. *The IMF, the World Bank and the African debt: The social and political impact.* London: Zed Books.

Orlansky, Dora and Silvia Dubrovsky. 1978. *The effects of rural-urban migration on women's role and status in Latin America.* Paris: UNESCO.

Osborne, Christine. 1990. *Essential Thailand: The essential travel guide series.* Toronto: Brown and Company.

Pahl, Ray. 1984. *Divisions of labour.* Oxford: Basil Blackwell.

Panigrahi, Lalita. 1972. *British social policy and female infanticide in India.* New Delhi: Munshiram Manoharlal.

Papanek, Hanna. 1976. Women in cities: Problems and perspectives. In *Women and world development,* ed. I. Tinker and M. B. Bramsen, pp. 54–69. Washington, DC: Overseas Development Council.

———. 1979. The differential impact of programs and policies on women in development. Prepared by I. Tinker. In *Women and development: Final report of a workshop*. Washington, DC: American Association for the Advancement of Science.

Parfitt, T. 1990. Lies, damned lies and statistics: The World Bank/ECA structural adjustment controversy. *Review of African Political Economy* 47: 128–141.

Park, Se-Il. 1982. An analysis of male-female wage differentials in Korea. *Korea Development Review* 4(2): 59–89.

Parpart, Jane L. 1988. Sexuality and power on the Zambian copperbelt: 1926–1964. In *Patriarchy and class: African women in the home and the workforce*, ed. S. B. Stichter and J. L. Parpart, pp. 115–138. Boulder, CO: Westview Press.

———, ed. 1989. *Women and development in Africa: Comparative perspectives*. Lanham, MD: University Press of America.

Paul, J. 1984. States of emergency: The riots in Tunisia and Morocco. *MERIP Reports* 127(14): 3–6.

Perlez, J. 1990. Toll of AIDS on Uganda's women put their roles and rights in question. *New York Times*, 28 October, p. A16.

———. 1991. Uganda's women: Children, drudgery, and pain. *New York Times*, 24 February, p. A10.

Pessar, Patricia R. 1988. The constraints on and release of female labor power: Dominican migration to the United States. In *A home divided: Women and income in the Third World*, ed. D. Dwyer and J. Bruce, pp. 195–215. Stanford, CA: Stanford University Press.

Pheterson, Gail, ed. 1989. *A vindication of the rights of whores*. Seattle: The Seal Press.

Phillips, J. F., R. Simmons, J. Chakraborty, and A. I. Chowdhury. 1984. Integrating health services into an MCH-FP program: Lessons from Matlab, Bangladesh. *Studies in Family Planning* 15(4): 153–161.

Phongpaichit, Pasuk. 1980. *Rural women of Thailand: From peasant girls to Bangkok masseuses*. World Employment Programme Research Working Paper, November. Geneva: ILO.

———. 1982. *From peasant girls to Bangkok masseuses*. Geneva: International Labour Office.

———. 1988. Two roads to the factory: Industrialisation strategies and women's employment in South-East Asia. In *Structures of patriarchy: State, community and household in modernising Asia*, ed. Bina Agarwal, pp. 151–163. London: Zed Books.

Pickvance, C. 1989. Social movements in the Middle East. In *Urban crises and social movements in the Middle East*, ed. K. Brown et al. Paris: L'Harmattan.

Pinstrup-Andersen, Per. 1987. The impact of macro-economic adjustment on nutrition. Paper prepared for the conference on The Design and Impact of Adjustment Programmes on Agriculture and Agricultural Institutions. London: Overseas Development Institute (ODI).

Pion-Berlin, D. 1989. *The ideology of state terror: Economic doctrine and political repression in Argentina and Peru*. London and Boulder, CO: Lynne Reinner.

Piven, F. F. and R. A. Cloward. 1977. *Regulating the poor: The functions of public welfare*. New York: Vintage Books.

PREALC. 1985a. *Household behaviour and economic crisis: Costa Rica 1979–1982*. Santiago, Chile: Program Regional de Empleo en America Latina y el Caribe.

———. 1985b. *Mas alla de la crisis: trabajos presentados a la IV conferencia del*

PREALC. Santiago, Chile: Program Regional de Empleo en America Latina y el Caribe.

Pryer, J. 1987. Production and reproduction of malnutrition in an urban slum in Khulna, Bangladesh. In *Geography of gender in the Third World*, ed. J. H. Momsen and J. Townsend, pp. 131–149. Albany: State University of New York Press and Hutchinson.

Raczynski, D. 1989. Social policy, poverty, and vulnerable groups: Children in Chile. In *Adjustment with a human face: Ten country case studies*, vol. 2, ed. G. Cornia, R. Jolly, and F. Stewart, pp. 57–92. Oxford: Clarendon Press.

Raczynski, D. and C. Serrano. 1985. *Vivir la pobreza: Testimonio de mujeres*. Santiago, Chile: Corporacion Investigaciones Economicas Latino America (PISPAL-CIEPLAN).

Rahal-Sidhoum, Saïda Marie. 1988. Des femmes de France. In *Le féminisme et ses enjeux: Vingt-sept femmes parlent*, pp. 353–368. Paris: Center fédéral FEN.

Ramazanoglu, C. 1989. *Feminism and the contradictions of oppression*. London and New York: Routledge.

Ramos, S. 1985. *Maternidad de Buenos Aires: La experiencia popular*. Buenos Aires. CEDES.

Responses to wife abuse in four Western countries. 1985. *Response* (Spring): 15–18.

Reynolds, L. 1984. Rape: A social perspective. *Journal of Offender Counseling, Services, and Rehabilitation* (Fall-Winter): 149–160.

Richter, Linda. 1989. *The politics of tourism in Asia*. Honolulu: University of Hawaii Press.

Rios, A. R. 1984. The invisible economy of poverty: The case of Brazil. *La pauvrété, mondes en développement* 12(45): 1–191.

Robertson, Claire and Iris Berger, eds. 1986. *Women and class in Africa*. New York: Africana Publishing Co.

Rodney, Walter. 1974. *How Europe underdeveloped Africa*. Washington, DC: Howard University Press.

Rogers, Barbara. 1980. *The domestication of women: Discrimination in developing societies*. London: Tavistock.

Rogombe, Rose Francine. 1985. Equal partners in Africa's development. *Africa Report* (March–April): 17–20.

Roldan, Martha. 1988. Renegotiating the marital contract: Intrahousehold patterns of money allocations and women's subordination among domestic outworkers in Mexico City. In *A home divided: Women and income in the Third World*, ed. Daisy Dwyer and Judith Bruce, pp. 229–247. Stanford, CA: Stanford University Press.

Roy, M. 1982. *The abusive partner*. New York: Van Nostrand Reinhold.

Russell, D.E.H. 1984. *Sexual exploitation, rape, child sexual abuse and workplace harassment*. Newbury Park, CA: Sage Publications.

Russell, D.E.H. and N. Van de Ven. 1976. *The proceedings of the international tribunal on crime agaisnt women*. East Palo Alto, CA: Frog in the Well.

Sae Gae Times. 1989. Ministry of health and social affairs raided 150 corrupt barbershops in southern Seoul, 22% of female employees found with STD. New York edition, 18 February, p. 2.

Safa, H. and E. Leacock. 1976. *Sex and class in Latin America*. New York: Praeger.

Sager, Mike and Michael Nichols. 1984. Americans in Thailand. *Rolling Stone*, 10 May, pp. 27–28.

Salhoz, Eloise. 1990. Women under assault. *Newsweek* 116(3): 23–24.

Sassen-Koob, Saskia. 1983. Labor migration and the new industrial division of labor. In *Women, men and the international division of labor*, ed. J. Nash and M. P. Fernandez Kelly, pp. 175–204. Albany: State University of New York Press.

Scarpaci, J. 1987. HMO promotion and privatization in Chile. *Journal of Health Politics, Policy and Law* 12:551–567.

———. 1989. Dismantling public health programs in authoritarian Chile. In *Health services privatization in industrial societies*, ed. J. L. Scarpaci, pp. 219–244. New Brunswick, NJ: Rutgers University Press.

———. 1990. Medical care, welfare state and deindustrialization in the Southern Cone. *Environment and Planning D: Society and Space* 8: 191–209.

———. 1991. Primary-care decentralization in the Southern Cone: Shantytown health care as urban social movement. *Annals of the Association of American Geographers* 81: 103–126.

Scarpaci, J., A. Gaete, and R. Infante., 1988. Planning residential segregation: The case of Santiago, Chile. *Urban Geography* 9: 19–36.

Schmink, Marianne. 1985. Women and urban industrial development in Brazil. In *Women and Change in Latin America*, ed. June Nash and Helen Safa, pp. 136–164. South Hadley, MA: Bergin & Garvey.

Scholnick, M. and B. Teitelboim. 1988. *Pobreza y desempleo en poblaciones: La otra cara del modelo neoliberal*. Santiago, Chile: PET, Coleccion Temas Sociales 2.

Schuler, Margaret, ed. 1986. *Empowerment and the law: Strategies of Third World women*. Washington, DC: OEF International.

Scott, Alison MacEwan. 1986. Women and industrialisation: Examining the "female marginalisation" thesis. *Journal of Development Studies* 22(4): 649–680.

Scott, J. C. 1985. *Weapons of the weak: Everyday forms of peasant resistance*. New York and London: Yale University Press.

Seager, Joni and Olson, Ann. 1986. *Women in the world: An international atlas*. London: Pan, New York: Simon and Schuster.

Seddon, D. 1989. Riot and rebellion in north Africa: Political responses to economic crisis in Tunisia, Morocco and Sudan. In *Power and stability in the Middle East*, ed. B. Berberoglu, pp. 114–135. London: Zed Books.

———. 1990. The politics of "adjustment" in Morocco. In *Structural adjustment in Africa*, ed. B. Campbell and J. Loxley, pp. 234–265. London: Macmillan.

Sen, Amartya. 1990a. More than 100 million women are missing. *New York Review of Books*, December, pp. 37, 20, 61–66.

Sen, A. K. 1990b. Gender and cooperative conflicts. In *Persistent inequalities: Women and world development*, ed. Irene Tinker, pp. 123–149. New York: Oxford University Press.

Sen, Gita and Caren Grown. 1987. *Development, crises, and alternative visions: Third World women's perspectives*. New York: Monthly Review Press.

Senkoro, F.E.M.K. 1982. *The prostitute in African literature*. Dar es Salaam, Tanzania: University Press.

Seoul YMCA. 1989a. *The realities of the entertainment culture and countermeasures*. Report 10, Citizen's Self-Help Movement Series. Seoul: Seoul YMCA.

————. 1989b. *The entertainment industry and overconsumption.* Report 13, Citizen's Self-Help Movement Series. Seoul: Seoul YMCA.

————. 1989c. *A survey report of white collar workers' usage of the entertainment establishments.* Report 20, Citizen's Self-Help Movement Series. Seoul: Seoul YMCA.

Sereewat, Sudarat. 1985. Prostitution: Thai-European connections. *Thai Development Newsletter* 2(3).

Serrano, C. 1989. Integracion social: Desde la perspectiva de las mujeres (mimeo). Forthcoming in *David y Goliath*, ed. Programa de Economia de Trabajo (PET). Santiago, Chile: CLACSO.

Shin, In-Ryong. 1985. The organized workers and women in Korea. In *Korean women and work*, ed. Research Institute on Women in Korea. Seoul: Ewha Womans University Press.

Shivji, I. 1984. Reawakening of politics in Africa? Lecture given at the Institute of International Relations, University of California, Berkeley, September.

Siddiqui, Musab U., and Earl Y. Reeves. 1987. Mate selection practices of Indians in India and Indian nationals in the United States. *Man in India* (December): 306–331.

Sidel, Ruth. 1986. *Women and children last.* New York: Viking.

Sigmund, P. 1977. *The overthrow of Allende and the politics of Chile.* Pittsburgh, PA: University of Pittsburgh Press.

Silberman, R. 1990. Quelle politique pour quelles families. *Plein Droit* 12: 4–10.

Simmons, Ruth, Marjorie A. Koblinsky, and James F. Phillips. 1986. Client relations in South Asia: Programmatic and societal determinants. *Studies in Family Planning* 17: 263.

Singer, P. 1982. Neighbourhood movements in Sao Paulo. In *Towards a political economy of urbanization in Third World countries*, ed. Helen I. Safa, pp. 283–303. New Delhi: Oxford University Press.

Sivard, R. L. 1985. *Women . . . A world survey.* Washington, DC: World Priorities.

Skrobanek, Siriporn. 1983a. The transnational sex-exploitation of Thai women. Master's dissertation. The Hague: Institute of Social Studies.

————. 1983b. Strategies against prostitution in Thailand. In *Third World, second sex*, comp. M. Davies, pp. 211–217. London: Zed Books.

————. 1990. Child prostitution in Thailand. *Voices of Thai Women*, 4 December, p. 10.

Smith, B. 1989. Nonprofit organizations and socioeconomic development in Latin America. Paper presented at the conference The Voluntary Sector Abroad, Center for Philanthropy, 26 April, New York, Graduate Center.

Sow Fall, Aminata. 1981. *The beggars' strike.* London: Longman.

Standing, Guy. 1989. Global feminization through flexible labor. *World Development* 17: 1077–1095.

Stark, E. and A. Flitcraft. 1979. Domestic violence and female suicide attempts. Paper presented at the 107th annual meeting of the American Public Health Association. New York, November.

Steady, Filomina. 1981. *The Black woman cross-culturally.* Cambridge: Schenkman.

Stokland, T., M. Vajrathon, and D. Nicol, eds. 1982. *Creative women in changing societies: A quest for alternatives.* Dobbs Ferry, NY: Transnational Publishers.

Straus, N. A., R. Gelles, and S. K. Steinmetz. 1981. *Behind closed doors: Violence in the American family.* New York: Doubleday.

Sudarkasa, Niara. 1977. Women and migration in contemporary West Africa. *Signs* 3: 178–189.

Sutherland, Efua. 1983. New life at Kyrefaso. In *Unwinding threads,* selected and ed. Charlotte H. Bruner, pp. 17–23. London: Heinemann.

Tauzin, Aline and Marie Virolle-Souibès. 1990. *Femmes, famille, société au Maghreb et en émigration: Répertoire.* Paris: Editions Karthala.

Taylor, I. 1983. *Structuralist macroeconomics: Applicable models for the Third World.* New York: Basic Books.

Thadani, V. N. 1978–79. Women in Nairobi: The paradox of urban progress. *African Urban Studies* (Winter): 67–84.

Thitsa, Khin. 1980. *Providence and prostitution: Image and reality for women in Buddhist Thailand.* London: Change International Reports.

Thompson, E. P. 1971. The moral economy of the English crowd in the eighteenth century. *Past and Present* 50 (February): 76–136.

Thorbek, Susanne. 1987. *Voices from the city: Women of Bangkok.* London: Zed Books.

Tiano, Susan. 1986. Women and industrial development in Latin America. *Latin America Research Review* 21(3): 157–170.

Tinker, Irene. 1991. The making of a field: Advocates, practitioners, and scholars. In *Persistent inequalities: Women and world development,* ed. Irene Tinker, pp. 27–53. New York: Oxford University Press.

Tinker, Irene and Jane Jaquette. 1987. UN Decade for Women: its impact and legacy. *World Development* 15: 419–427.

Tlali, Miriam. 1979. *Muriel at Metropolitan.* London: Longman Drumbeat.

Tokman, Victor E. 1989. Policies for a heterogeneous informal sector in Latin America. *World Development* 17: 1067–1076.

Trager, Lillian. 1988. *The city connection: Migration and family interdependence in the Philippines.* Ann Arbor: University of Michigan Press.

Tripp, A. M. 1989. Informal economy, labor and the state in Tanzania. Paper presented to the Midwest Political Science Association Annual Meeting, Chicago, April.

Truong, Thanh-Dam. 1990. *Sex, money and morality: Prostitution and tourism in Southeast Asia.* London: Zed Books.

Tucker, Karen and Diva Sanjur. 1988. Maternal employment and child nutrition in Panama. *Social Science and Medicine* 26: 605–612.

Tupper, C. L. 1881. *Punjab customary law.* 3 vols. Calcutta: Superintendent of Government Printing.

Turton, A. 1984. Limits of ideological domination and the formation of social consciousness. In *History and peasant consciousness in South East Asia,* ed. A. Turton and S. Tanabe, pp. 19–73. Senri Ethnological Studies, no. 13. Osaka: National Museum of Ethnology.

Turton, A. and S. Tanabe, eds. 1984. *History and peasant consciousness in South East Asia.* Senri Ethnological Studies, no. 13. Osaka: National Museum of Ethnology.

UNICEF. 1989. *The state of the world's children, 1989.* New York: Oxford University Press.

UNICEF-Peru. 1985. Comedores multifamiliares. Mimeo. Lima, Peru: UNICEF.

United Nations. 1985. *The Nairobi forward-looking strategies for the advancement of women.* Adopted by the World Conference to Review and Appraise the Achievements of the United Nations Decade for Women: Equality, Development and Peace. Nairobi, Kenya, 15–26 July. New York: United Nations.

———. 1989. *Violence against women in the family.* Center for Social Development and Humanitarian Affairs. Division for the Advancement of Women. Prepared by J. F. Connors. New York: United Nations.

———. 1990. *Human development report 1990.* United Nations Development Program. New York: Oxford University Press.

———. 1991. *The world's women 1970–1990: Trends and statistics.* New York: United Nations.

Valdes, T. 1988. *Venid, benditas de mi padres: Las pobladoras, sus rutinas y sus suenos.* Santiago, Chile: FLACSO.

Van der Linde, M. 1984. Sistematizacion de la experiencia de los comedores familiares y/o populares al nivel de Lima Metropolitana. Mimeo. Lima, Peru.

van Praag, Eric. 1988. *Midterm review of the Third World Bank Co-Financers Population and Family Health Project, 1986–1991, Bangladesh.* Amsterdam: Government of the Netherlands.

Vargas, Virginia. 1990. The women's social movement in Peru: Rebellion into action. Paper presented to the Social Movements Seminar, Institute of Social Studies, The Hague.

Vasquez, R. y G. Tamayo. 1989. *Violencia y legalidad.* Lima, Peru: Concytec.

Velez-Ibanez, C. 1983. *Rituals of marginality.* Berkeley and Los Angeles: University of California Press.

von Freyhold, M. 1987. Labour movements or popular struggles in Africa. *Review of African Political Economy* 39: 23–32.

Walker, H. 1986. *Transformation of practices in grass roots organizations: A case study in Chile.* Ph.D. dissertation, University of Toronto (microfiche, ISBN 0–315–31491–5).

Walker, L.E.A. 1989. Psychology and violence against women. *American Psychologist* (April): 695–701.

Walton, J. 1987. Urban protest and the global political economy. In *The capitalist city,* ed. M. P. Smith and J. R. Feagin. London: Basil Blackwell.

———. 1989. Labor and popular protest: Latin American responses to structural adjustment. Paper prepared for the International Conference on the Impact of the Foreign Debt on Latin American Unions, Center for Labor Research and Studies, Florida International University, Miami, December.

White, Luise. 1988. Domestic labor in a colonial city: Prostitution in Nairobi, 1900–1952. In *Patriarchy and class: African women in the home and the workforce,* ed. S. B. Stichter and J. L. Parpart, pp. 139–160. Boulder, CO: Westview Press.

Whiteford, M. B. 1978. Women, migration and social change: A Colombian case study. *International Migration Review* 12: 236–247.

White House Task Force on Infant Mortality Report. 1990. Cited in *New York Times,* 12 August.

Wicomb, Zoe. 1987. *You can't get lost in Capetown.* New York: Pantheon.

Wilkinson, Clive. 1987. Women, migration and work in Lesotho. In *Geography of gender in the Third World,* ed. Janet H. Momsen and Janet Townsend, pp. 225–239. Albany: State University of New York Press.

Winikoff, Beverly. 1988. Women's health: An alternative perspective for choosing interventions. *Studies in Family Planning* 19(4): 197–214.

Winikoff, Beverly and Maureen Sullivan. 1987. Assessing the role of family planning in reducing maternal mortality. *Studies in Family Planning* 18(3): 128–143.

Wisner, Ben. 1988. GOBI versus PHC? Some dangers in selective primary health care. *Social Science and Medicine* 26(9): 963–970.

Women's Global Network on Reproductive Rights and Latin American and Caribbean Women's Health Network/ISIS International. 1988. *Maternal mortality: A call to women for action.* Amsterdam/Santiago, Chile.

Won, Seok-jo. 1985. An empirical study on female employees of entertainment. *Korean Journal of Social Policy* 7: 5–59.

———. 1988. Urban culture and the entertainment culture. *Contemporary Society* 29: 228–246.

World Bank. 1985. Bangladesh, staff appraisal report. Third Population and Family Health Project. Washington, DC: Population, Health and Nutrition Department, February.

———. 1987a. *Bangladesh: Promoting higher growth and human development.* Washington, DC: World Bank.

———. 1987b. Briefing note of IDA-Cofinanciers' mission for Third Population and Family Health Project. Dhaka, Bangladesh, 11 February.

———. 1988. *World development report, 1988.* Washington, DC: World Bank.

———. 1990. *Report on world development.* Washington, DC: World Bank.

World Development. 1989. Beyond survival: Expanding income-earning opportunities for women in developing countries. *World Development* (Special Issue) 17(7).

Yllo, K. and M. Bograd, eds. 1988. *Feminist perspectives on wife abuse.* Newbury Park, CA: Sage Publications.

Young, J. D. 1985. *Women and popular struggles: A history of British working-class women, 1560–1984.* Edinburgh: Mainstream Publishing.

Young, Kate. 1982. The creation of a relative surplus population: A case study from Mexico. In *Women and development: The sexual division of labor in rural societies,* ed. Lourdes Beneria, pp. 149–178. New York: Praeger.

———, ed. 1988. *Women and economic development: Local, regional and national planning strategies.* Oxford: Berg/UNESCO.

Yudelman, S. 1987. *Hopeful openings: A study of five women's development organizations in Latin America and the Caribbean.* West Hartford, CT: Kumarian Press.

Youssef, Nadia H., Mayra Buvinić, and A. Kudat. 1979. *Women in migration: A Third World focus.* Washington, DC: International Center for Research on Women.

Zalaquett, José. 1981. *The human rights issue and the human rights movement.* Geneva: World Council of Churches.

Zghal, A. 1989. "The bread riot" and the crisis of the one party system (in Tunisia). Paper presented to the Conference on Social Movements, Social Transformation and Democracy in Africa, organized by the Council for the Development of Economic and Social Research in Africa (CODESRIA), Algiers, July.

Zinn, Howard. 1967. *Vietnam: The logic of withdrawal.* Boston: Beacon Press.

Zwi, A. and A. Ugalde. 1989. Towards an epidemiology of political violence in the Third World. *Social Science and Medicine* 28: 633–642.

Index

Adjustment strategies, 2, 7, 11; international organizations, 4–5; poverty, 4; women and, 5–8
Africa, 9, 12; migration from, 83–96; women's literature of, 171–81
AIDS, 110, 142
Algerian women, 90, 91, 92, 93
Allende Gossens, Salvatore, 35, 36, 37, 46
All India Women's Conference (AIWC), 25
Alma Ata conference, 72
Arpilleras, 38, 39, 40, 46
Arranged marriages: castes, 161–62; harassment of women, 161; mother-in-laws, 161; preference for, 160, 161, 167–68; relocation of the bride, 163
Asia, 9, 102
Asia and Pacific Women Law and Development Network, 100
Asia Women's Research and Action Network (AWRAN), 102
Association for the Development and Integration of Women (ADIM) (Lima, Peru), 109
Association for the Promotion of the Status of Women (Thailand), 141
Association Novelle Génération Immigré(e)s (France), 96
Association Soleil d'Afrique (France), 87, 96

Austerity: household strategies for coping, 15–16; survival under, 11–15; women as victims of, 5
Australian Committee on Violence, 108
Autonomy of women, 164
Aylwin, Patricio, 46, 47

Bangladesh, 13, 70, 72; discussed, 69–82; health care, 69, 72–82
Bangladesh Institute for Development Studies, 78
Bengal, 152, 153, 154
Bolivia, 102
Brazil, 19, 23–24, 62, 65
Bread riots, 27–28
Bride burnings, 145–46, 165, 166
Briscoe, John, 74

Canada, 100, 101, 107
Caribbean, 11, 12, 13, 16
Caste-cluster, 160
Caste dispersal, 162–64
Castes, 25, 159, 160, 161–62; terminology, 151, 154–55, 157
Checchi Report, 136
Chile, 12, 13, 16, 17–18; arpilleras, 38, 39, 40, 46; Atacama Desert, 34; Catholic church, 40, 44, 48; health care, 47, 49; human rights, 38, 46; job training, 49; literacy campaigns, 39,

About the Editors and Contributors

CAROLE BOYCE DAVIES has an ongoing commitment to feminist criticism of African, Caribbean, and African-American literatures and feminist literary theory for women of color. She has published widely in these fields and has edited two volumes of criticism: *Ngambika, Studies of Women in African Literature* (1986) and *Out of the Kumbla, Caribbean Women and Literature* (1990). She is Associate Professor with joint appointments in English, Afro-American, and African Studies and Comparative Literature at the State University of New York at Binghamton.

HÉLÈNE BRETIN holds a doctorate in sociology from the University of Paris. She does research on social inequalities and health at INSERM, the National Institute for Health and Medical Research, in Paris. She is the author of *Contraception: quel choix pour quelle vie? Histoires de femmes, paroles de médecins* (1992).

CHARLOTTE BUNCH, feminist author and organizer for over two decades, was a founder of D.C. Women's Liberation and of *Quest: A Feminist Quarterly*. She has edited seven anthologies and her latest book is *Passionate Politics: Feminist Theory in Action* (1987). Having worked on global feminism and the UN Decade for Women with a variety of organizations, Bunch is currently Director of the Rutgers University Center for Women's Global Leadership and Professor in the Faculty of Planning at Rutgers University.

ROXANNA CARRILLO, a Peruvian feminist who has been active in the development of the women's movement in her country, currently works at the United Nations Development Fund for Women (UNIFEM). She is a doctoral student in political science at Rutgers University, where she wrote chapter 6 while on the staff of the Center for Women's Global Leadership.

VICTORIA DAINES is legal sociologist specializing in employment law. She runs training courses on discrimination law and represents women in sex discrimination and equal pay cases in the United Kingdom.

BETSY HARTMANN is Director of the Population and Development Program at Hampshire College. She is author of *Reproductive Rights and Wrongs: The Global Politics of Population Control and Contraceptive Choice* (1987) and coauthor of A *Quiet Violence: View from a Bangladesh Village* (1983).

CATHERINE HILL is a Ph.D. candidate at Rutgers University in Urban Planning and Policy Development. She has a masters degree in regional planning and a bachelors in anthropology from Cornell University. She recently published two papers on converting the military economy in the United States. She is currently writing her dissertation on military bases in the United States and is working toward a graduate certificate in women's studies.

BRIAVEL HOLCOMB is Chair and Associate Professor in the Department of Urban Studies and Community Health at Rutgers University. She is the coauthor of *Revitalizing Cities* (1981) and *The United States: A Contemporary Human Geography* (1988). She recently taught a course on women and development while circumnavigating the world on Semester at Sea, visiting Asia, Africa, and Latin America.

UMA NARAYAN is Assistant Professor of Philosophy at Vassar College. She grew up in India. She obtained a B.A. in philosophy from Bombay University, an M.A. in philosophy from Poona University, and a Ph.D. from Rutgers University.

VEENA TALWAR OLDENBURG, an Indian feminist, is Associate Professor of History at Baruch College of the City University of New York. Her contribution to this volume, chapter 9, is part of an ongoing project based on extensive archival research on the political economy of dowry in India.

TAMAR Y. ROTHENBERG is a doctoral student in the Department of Geography at Rutgers University.

JOSEPH L. SCARPACI is Associate Professor at the College of Architecture and Urban Studies of Virginia Polytechnic Institute and State University. He is the author of *Primary Medical Care in Chile: Accessibility Under Military Rule* (1988) and editor of *Health Care Privatization in Industrial Societies* (1989). He has spent over two years in Chile with Fulbright and National Science Foundation funding. He recently coedited (with Connie Weil) *Health and Health Care in Latin America During the "Lost Decade": Insights for the 1990s.*

DAVID SEDDON is Professor of Development Studies at the University of East Anglia and has written extensively on popular struggles in the Third World and on the politics of structural adjustment. He is currently working on a book (with John Walton) on urban popular protest in the 1980s, *Free Markets and Food Riots: The Politics of Global Adjustment.*

HEISOO SHIN holds a doctorate in sociology. She teaches women's studies at Ewha Women's University in Seoul, South Korea and is actively engaged in three areas: writing new laws on sexual violence, in the issue of the "comfort women," drafted by the Japanese during World War II, and the movement for battered women.

ANNIE THÉBAUD-MONY holds a state doctorate in sociology from the University of Paris. She is a senior research associate at INSERM, the National Institute for Health and Medical Research, in Paris, and author of *L'envers des sociétés industrielles* (1990) and *La reconnaissance des maladies professionelles* (1991).

MEREDETH TURSHEN is Associate Professor in the Department of Urban Studies and Community Health at Rutgers University. She worked for twelve years in the United Nations system with UNICEF and WHO. She is author of two books, *The Political Economy of Disease in Tanzania* (1984) and *The Politics of Public Health* (1989), and is editor of *Women and Health in Africa* (1991).